I0810051

IMAGES
of America

HUMBLE

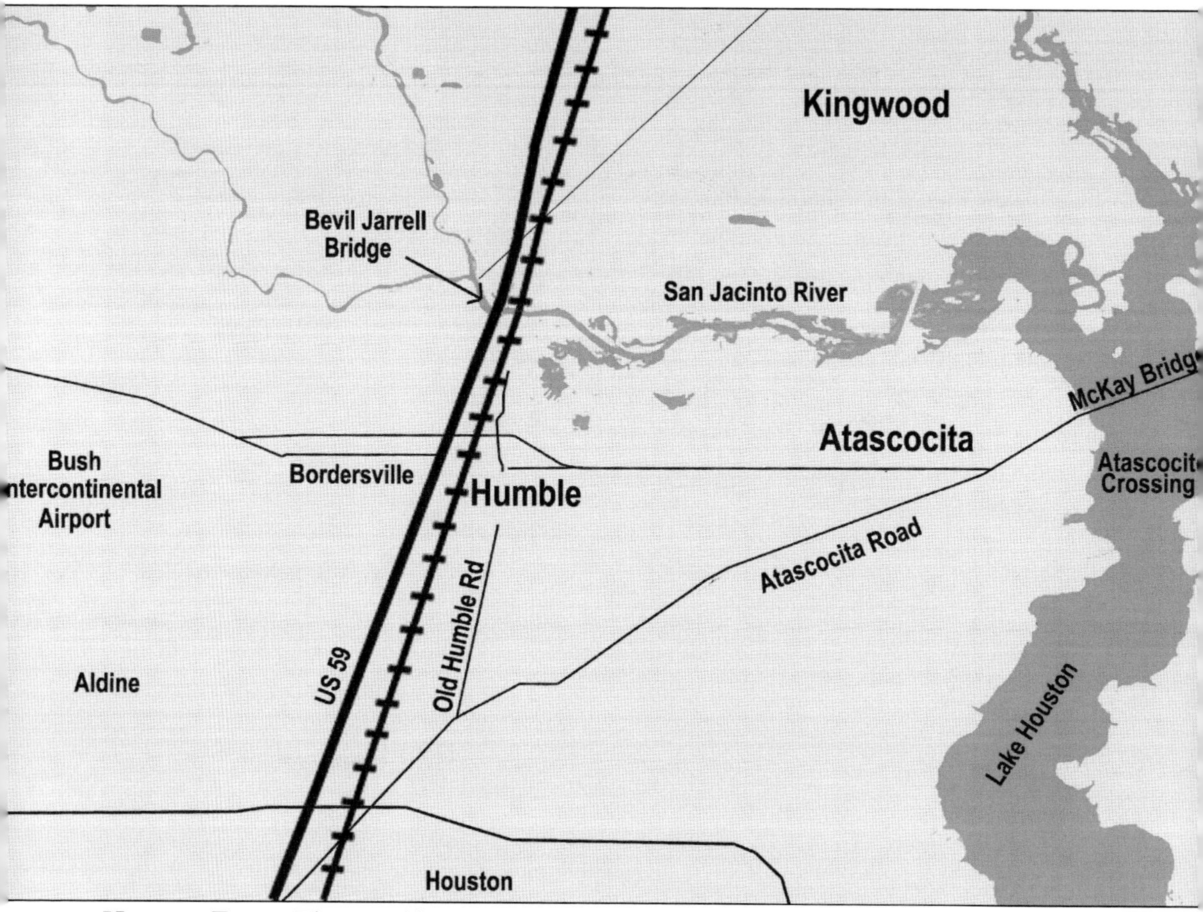

Humble, Texas. The Humble area is comprised of the City of Humble, the Atascocita area, and Kingwood (a master-planned community). Humble is bordered by the San Jacinto River to the north, Aldine and Bordersville to the west, Houston to the south, and Lake Houston to the east. The Old Humble Road, originally called the Houston-Humble Road, was the first major thoroughfare built between Houston and Humble.

On the Cover: During the early years of the Humble oil boom, it was common to see mule teams pulling oil tanks through fields. In 1904, when oil was first discovered in Humble, heavy equipment was difficult to move because of the primitive dirt roads in the area. It was not until 1918 that the road from Humble to Moonshine Hill became one of the first concrete roads in Harris County.

IMAGES
of America

HUMBLE

Dr. Robert Meaux and the Humble Museum

ARCADIA
PUBLISHING

ISBN 978-1-4671-3100-1

Published by Arcadia Publishing
Charleston, South Carolina

Printed in the United States of America

Library of Congress Control Number: 2013945599

For all general information, please contact Arcadia Publishing:
Telephone 843-853-2070
Fax 843-853-0044
E-mail sales@arcadiapublishing.com
For customer service and orders:
Toll-Free 1-888-313-2665

Visit us on the Internet at www.arcadiapublishing.com

To my parents, George Joseph Meaux and Deffie Lee Brock Meaux, for nurturing my love of history.

CONTENTS

Acknowledgments

Since the Humble Museum opened in 1976, many families and individuals have donated photographs, stories, and artifacts in order to preserve the history of Humble. Although they are too numerous to name here, without these contributors' generous donations, this book would not have been possible.

We wish to thank the following persons and organizations for their assistance: Houston Metropolitan Research Center, Sarah Canby Jackson at the Harris County Archives, Texas State Library Archives, Curtis Davis and Connie Robertson at the Harris County Department of Education, James Tull Chapter of the Daughters of the American Revolution, Margaret Byron, Mark Martin, Sue Baker, A.W. Jones, Jim McCary of the Humble Camera Center, Ken Burke for logo work and image processing, and Scott Meaux for photography consultation. We would especially like to thank the City of Humble for its continuous support of the museum.

Assistance from the Humble Independent School District was provided by Supt. Dr. Guy Sconzo, Peggy Young, Vickie Rosier, Tiffany Large, Joanne Bailey Monic, Deborah Yocham, Karen Collier, Jamie Mount, Allan Griffin Jr., Penny Mixon, J.C. Evans, and Sandie Coleman. We appreciate the continuous support of the Humble Alumni Association.

Several people paved the way for this book through their research and writings of local history. The history of Humble would have been lost to time without the diligent work of the following: James Tull Chapter of the Daughters of the American Revolution, Charles Goodwin, Jerry Moore, Peggy Huffman, Bevil Jarrell, and Estelle Woodyard.

Nancy Coker, Jerri Christian, and Bertie Hammonds of the Humble Museum provided historical insights. We wish to thank Katie Meaux, Kathleen Scott, and Dr. Jamie Bryson for reviewing the material for grammatical accuracy. We are also thankful for the guidance of Laura Bruns, our acquisitions editor at Arcadia Publishing.

We have attempted to present an accurate history of Humble. While it is impossible to include all aspects of that history in a book of this type, the reader will gain a better understanding of the forces that helped shape this portion of Harris County. Unless noted, all images are provided courtesy of the Humble Museum.

Introduction

Humble is located in the northeast part of Harris County, Texas, where the forests of the Big Thicket merge with the coastal plains bordering the Gulf of Mexico. It was this combination of timberland, farmland, and abundance of wild game that first attracted settlers to the area. In 1824, David Harris, a member of Stephen F. Austin's colony, received the first land grant in this part of Harris County. Another early settler, Joseph Dunman, was the rider who carried Col. William Travis's letter (a plea for reinforcements) from the Alamo to Liberty in early 1836. After Texas gained independence from Mexico, Dunman and other settlers received land grants in this area in the 1840s.

By 1869, a Civil War veteran named Pleasant Smith Humble migrated to the area and purchased land along the south side of the San Jacinto River, where a ferry had been in operation since the 1850s. Humble took over the ferry and ran a grocery store. A civic-minded person, Pleasant Humble was elected as a Harris County commissioner, serving from 1876 to 1878.

In 1875, Paul Bremond began work on a railway that would traverse the timberlands of East Texas. By April 1877, 28 miles of track for his Houston East & West Texas (HE&WT) Railway had been completed, from Houston to New Caney. As the railway neared completion, and to generate funds, Bremond ran daily entertainment excursions for the citizens of Houston. In 1878, one popular excursion ran 19 miles from Houston to San Jacinto Spring, located on the north side of the San Jacinto River, near present-day Hamblen Road.

As the railway opened up access through the East Texas forests, Bremond sold land on the train's right-of-way to sawmill companies. In 1882, the sawmill town of Lord was the first town to develop in this part of Harris County, roughly two miles north of present-day Humble along the HE&WT Railway. The town evolved around the San Jacinto Spring Station and consisted of four sawmills, a US post office, and livestock businesses. By 1884, the town listed a population of 150.

The area farther south of the river, near the Atascocito Road (pronounced "A-tusk-a-see-toe"), was known as Dunman's Prairie. Joe Dunman, son of early settler Joseph Dunman, owned land here and opened a school in 1873. Joe Dunman's Schoolhouse became the local polling place for county elections. In 1884, Texas passed the Common School Law, which provided for a system of county schools to be established across the state. Joe Dunman's Schoolhouse became the first official school for Harris County Common School District No. 28.

Lord was not able to survive as a town. In February 1886, the post office was closed, and the name of the station was changed to San Jacinto Park Station. Pleasant Humble took over responsibility for the local mail, most likely out of his store or home. Local legend states that mail carriers from other towns were instructed to "deliver to Humble," meaning Pleasant Humble. Through continued use of this phrase, "Humble" eventually became the name of the town. Whether this story is true or not, when the application was made to have a US post office established in his town in August 1886, the official name on the application was listed as "Humble, Texas." Pleasant Humble became the town's first postmaster in 1886 and was elected as the local Harris County justice of the peace in May 1887. The pronunciation of the town name was based on the way Pleasant Humble spoke his last name, with a silent "H," so the town's name was pronounced "Umble."

Joe Dunman's Schoolhouse was located in the center of the school district, which was a long way from downtown Humble. In 1888, desiring to build a school closer to town, and to gain total control of the school board, the citizens petitioned to have the district split in two. The northern portion remained as District No. 28 (Humble), and the southern portion became District No. 35 (Dunman).

In 1889, Charles Bender purchased one of the bankrupt Lord sawmills and moved it to the south side of the San Jacinto River. The purchase included hundreds of acres of timberland as well as land occupied by the town of Humble. He built housing for his employees and filed an official street plan for the town of Humble in 1904. With the addition of the Bender sawmill, Humble continued to thrive as a sawmill town.

The fortunes of the town improved dramatically on November 7, 1904, when the Moonshine Company struck oil in Humble. Humble became an oil boomtown overnight. Land that had been selling the previous week for $10 an acre was now selling for $20,000 an acre! The first true "gusher" occurred in Humble the following January. The population increased from a few hundred residents to several thousand, as Texans descended upon Humble to make their fortunes in the oil field. At that time, the Humble oil field was the largest producing oil field in Texas.

Early oil strikes were in an area known as the Echols Ridge. By 1907, this area was called Moonshine Hill, most likely after the company that made the first strike. Moonshine Hill was the primary location for oil production in Humble, but oil wells were located all over the Humble area. The oil boom died quickly, and some of the oil companies moved on to other boomtowns. However, the Humble field yielded two more production booms, one in 1914, and the other in 1929.

The success of the oil field resulted in more buildings, homes, and schools as the population increased. The first brick schoolhouse was built in 1909 on Higgins Street. The first brick business building was the Humble State Bank, owned by Ross Sterling. However, a fire in Humble on February 14, 1912, destroyed two and a half blocks of the downtown area, including the original Humble State Bank building.

In the summer of 1918, the two school districts were consolidated back into one, now called District No. 50. A few months later, the Texas Legislature transformed District No. 50 into the Humble Independent School District, thereby removing it from under the management of the Harris County Department of Education. Today, the Humble ISD educates over 37,000 students at 43 campuses.

Humble residents survived hard times in the first half of the 20th century, including hurricanes, fires, and the Great Depression. Many men from Humble served during both World War I and World War II. Sadly, a large number of those men never made it back to their homes. Humble was incorporated as a city in 1933. In the 1950s, the area's population grew, as people moved to Humble to escape life in the city of Houston. In 1969, Houston's largest airport, now called George Bush Intercontinental Airport, was built on the west side of Humble. The 1970s saw the development of Kingwood, Atascocita, and other residential communities around Humble. Today, the Humble area continues to thrive as a commercial, economic, and social hub for northeast Harris County.

One

Early Years

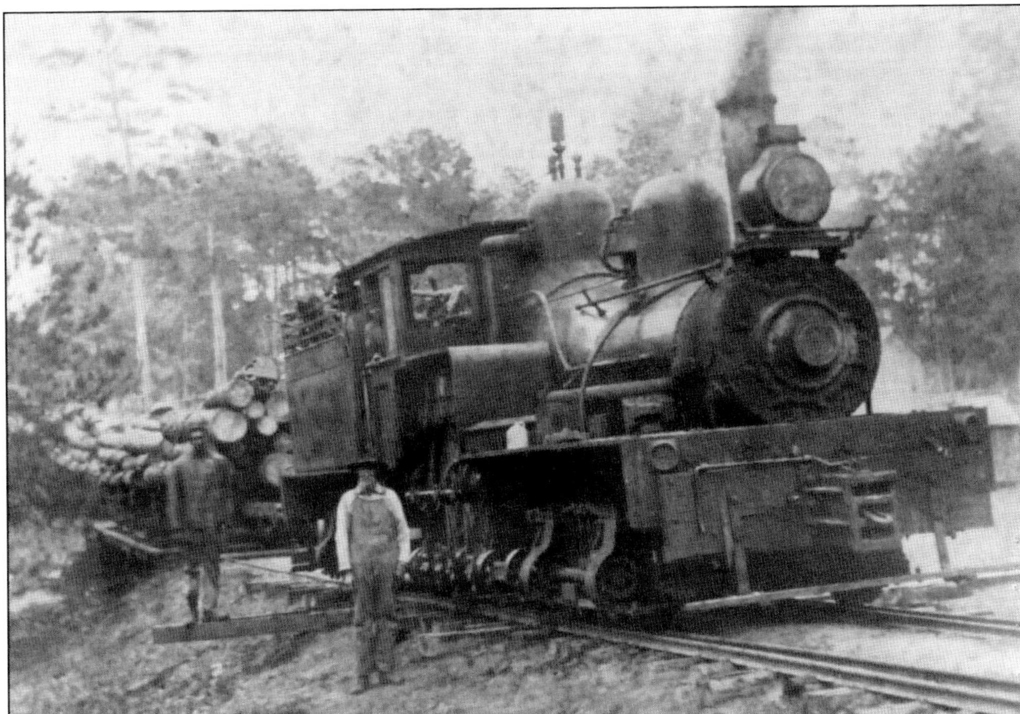

Bender Company Logging Train. The Humble area was known as Dunman's Prairie when Paul Bremond started the Houston East & West Texas (HE&WT) Railway in 1877. The railway opened up the timberlands of East Texas to the world. Many sawmills and lumber towns developed along the railroad's right-of-way. Savvy sawmill owners laid their own tracks and purchased logging trains to move lumber to their mills.

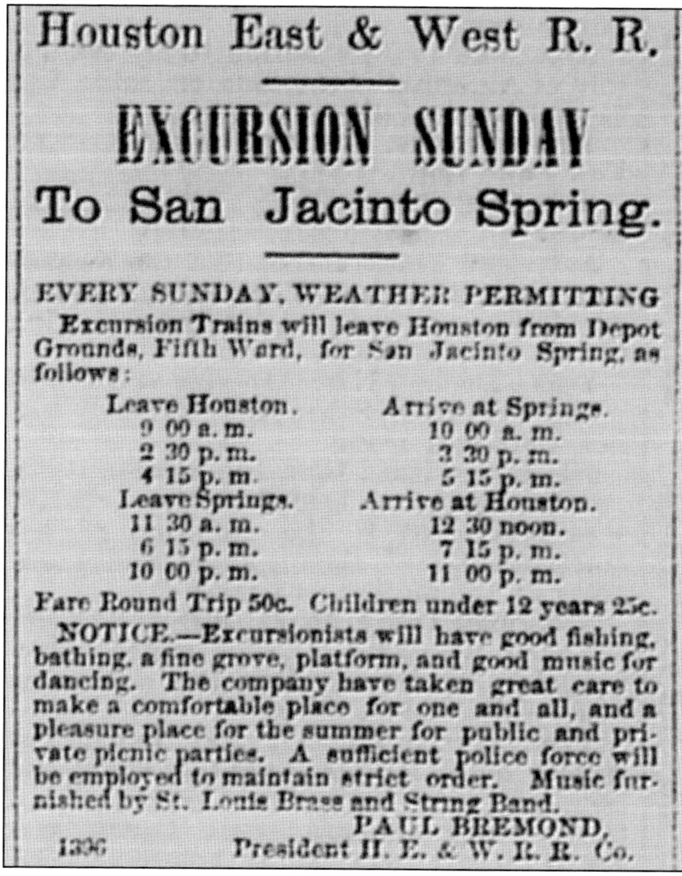

Houston East & West R. R.

EXCURSION SUNDAY

To San Jacinto Spring.

EVERY SUNDAY, WEATHER PERMITTING

Excursion Trains will leave Houston from Depot Grounds, Fifth Ward, for San Jacinto Spring, as follows:

Leave Houston.	Arrive at Springs.
9 00 a. m.	10 00 a. m.
2 30 p. m.	3 30 p. m.
4 15 p. m.	5 15 p. m.
Leave Springs.	Arrive at Houston.
11 30 a. m.	12 30 noon.
6 15 p. m.	7 15 p. m.
10 00 p. m.	11 00 p. m.

Fare Round Trip 50c. Children under 12 years 25c.

NOTICE.—Excursionists will have good fishing, bathing, a fine grove, platform, and good music for dancing. The company have taken great care to make a comfortable place for one and all, and a pleasure place for the summer for public and private picnic parties. A sufficient police force will be employed to maintain strict order. Music furnished by St. Louis Brass and String Band.

PAUL BREMOND,
President H. E. & W. R. R. Co.

1306

San Jacinto Spring. To generate needed funds, in 1878, Paul Bremond sold seats on the HE&WT Railway to San Jacinto Spring. Located just north of Humble, where Hamblen Road crosses the railroad tracks today, Bremond's company provided dancing, fishing, and swimming. All of these activities, plus the train ride, cost adults 50¢ each. These excursions introduced Houston residents to the natural beauty of this part of Harris County.

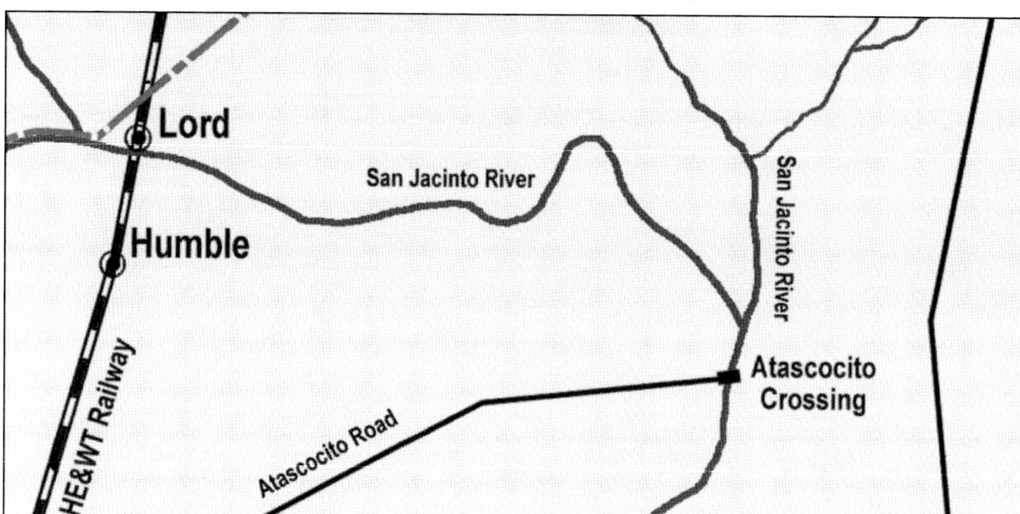

Lord, Texas. By 1883, the sawmill community of Lord had developed along the HE&WT railway at the location of the San Jacinto Spring Depot. Named for sawmill owner I.C. Lord, the town consisted of four sawmills, a US post office, and livestock businesses. The town also shipped lumber and country produce. In 1884, Lord had a population of 150. I.C. Lord served as mayor of Houston in 1875–1876.

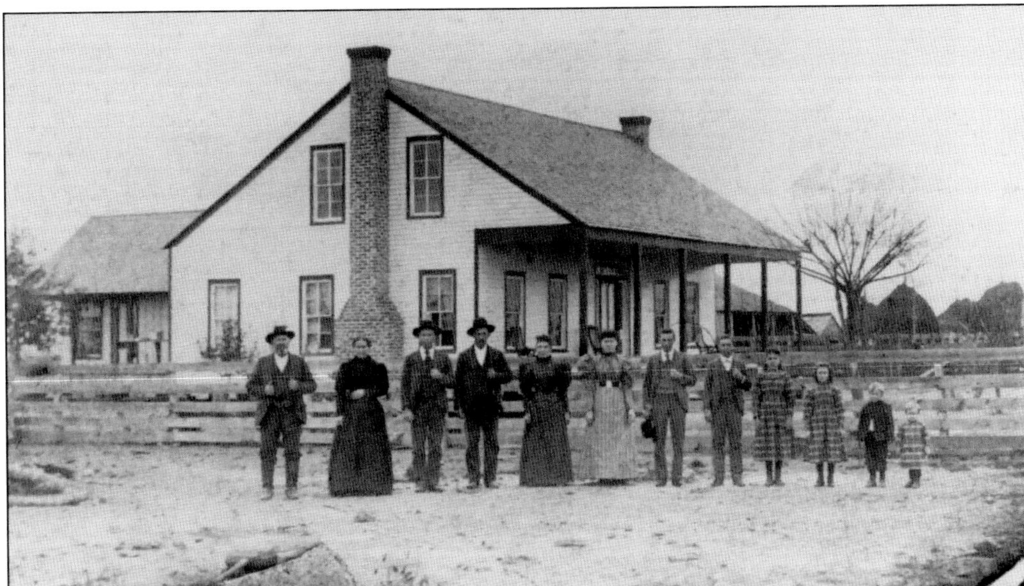

Reed Singleton Farmhouse, c. 1898. Reed Singleton and his family pose in front of their home. Located south of Humble, the house was built in the 1880s. It burned down around 1916. Folklore states that John Wesley Hardin, a notorious Texas outlaw, stayed at the house as a guest of the Singletons. Pictured from left to right are Reed Singleton, his wife Margaret Hufman Singleton, and their children Henry, Jim, Maggie, Ada, Joe, Reed Jr., Martha, Cinda, Allen, and Jeff. (Courtesy of the Houston Metropolitan Research Center.)

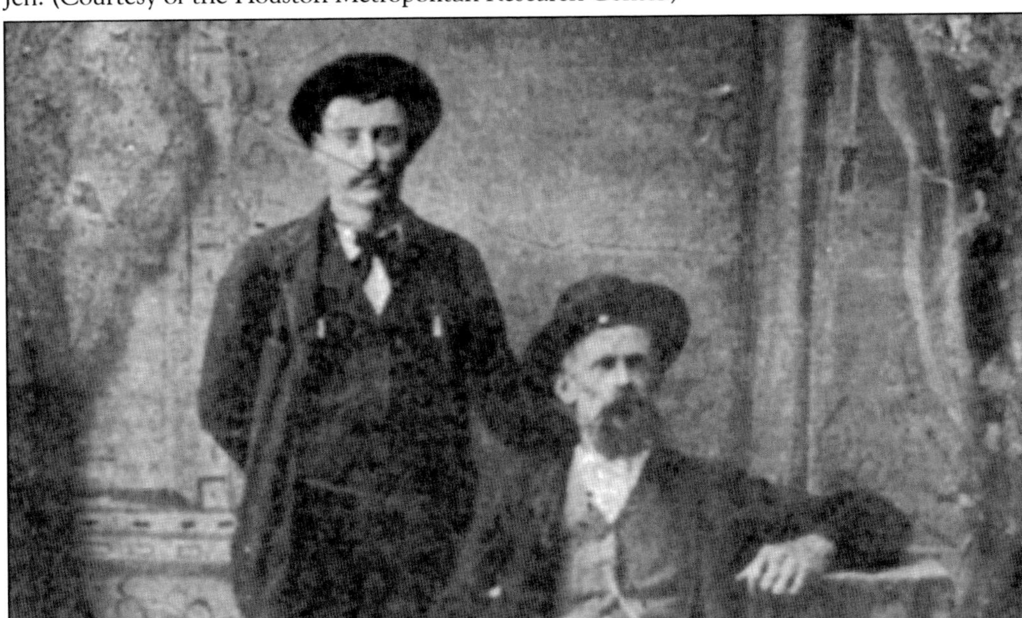

William and Pleasant Humble. William Humble (left) served as the postmaster for Lord in 1885 and as the constable for Harris County Precinct 4 in 1887 and again from 1903 to 1906. The town of Humble was named for his father, Pleasant Humble (right), a Harris County commissioner (1876–1878), the first postmaster for Humble (1886–1894), and elected as Justice of the Peace for Harris County Precinct No. 4 (1887–1895).

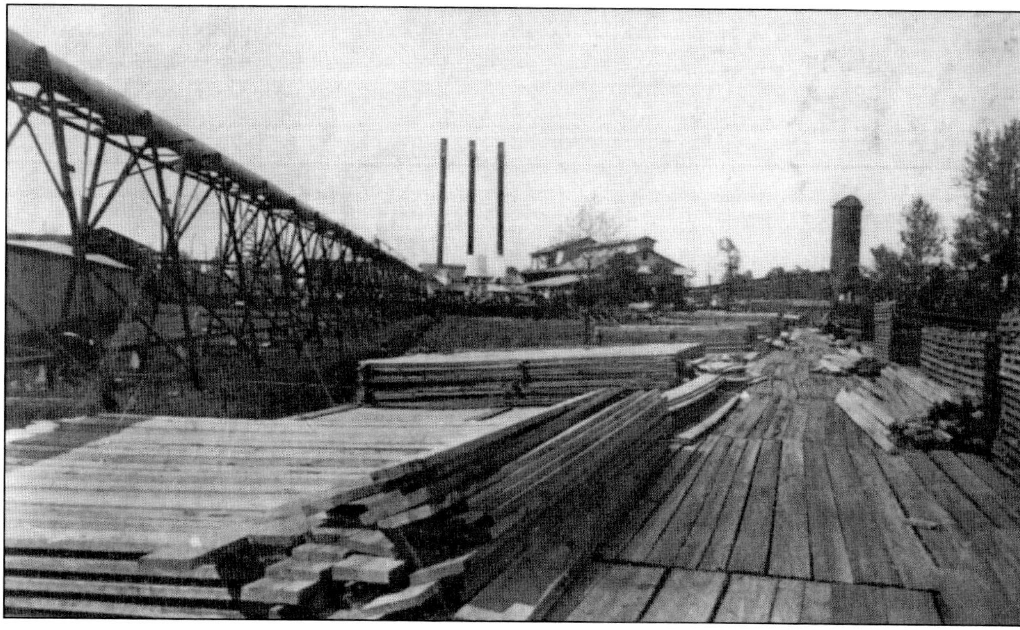

BENDER SAWMILL. George L. Milledge and T.T. Calhoun operated a sawmill on the north side of the river at San Jacinto Park Station., Forced into bankruptcy, Milledge and Calhoun sold their sawmill to C. Bender and Co. on November 9, 1889. The sale of the sawmill to Bender included 17 mules, 2 horses, 73 head of oxen, log tramcars, log wagons, mill machinery, and tools. It also included 3,600 acres of timberland south of the San Jacinto River. Bender moved the sawmill to the south side of the river, on the opposite side of the tracks from the town of Humble. By 1912, the Bender operation had a daily capacity of 75,000 feet of longleaf and shortleaf yellow pine. Lumber was shipped to all parts of the country, including destinations in Canada.

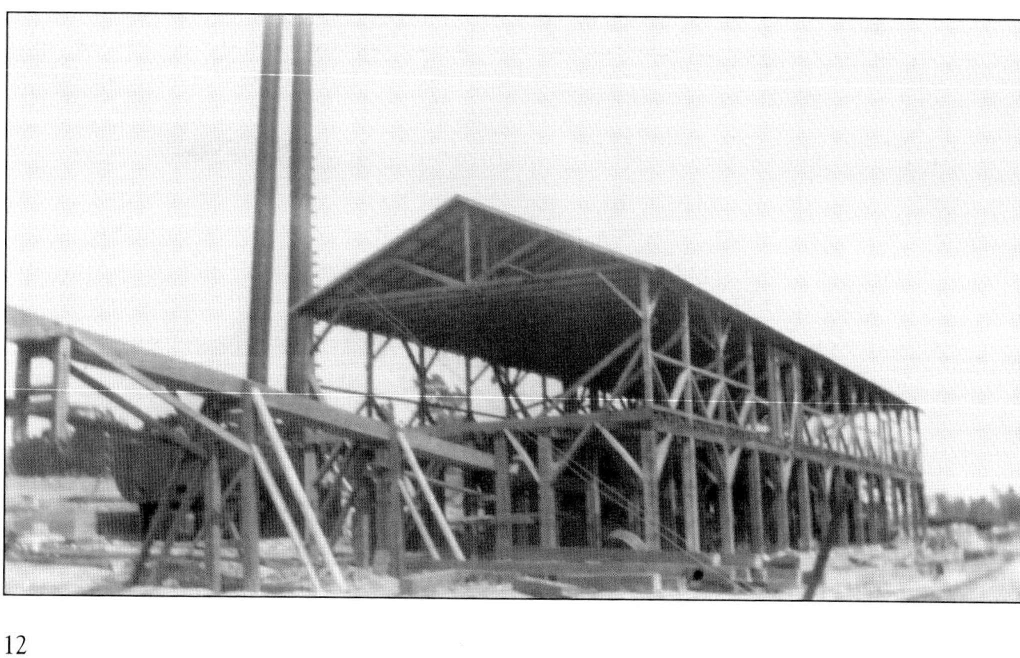

CHARLES BENDER SR. (1829–1906). German native Charles Bender operated a sawmill at Spring Station, Texas. His purchase and relocation of the Milledge and Calhoun sawmill gave a boost to the town of Humble's existence. Bender provided for his employees and for the Humble residents. His name lives on in Aldine-Bender Road, Bender Avenue, and Charles Bender High School. After his death, the business was continued by his sons.

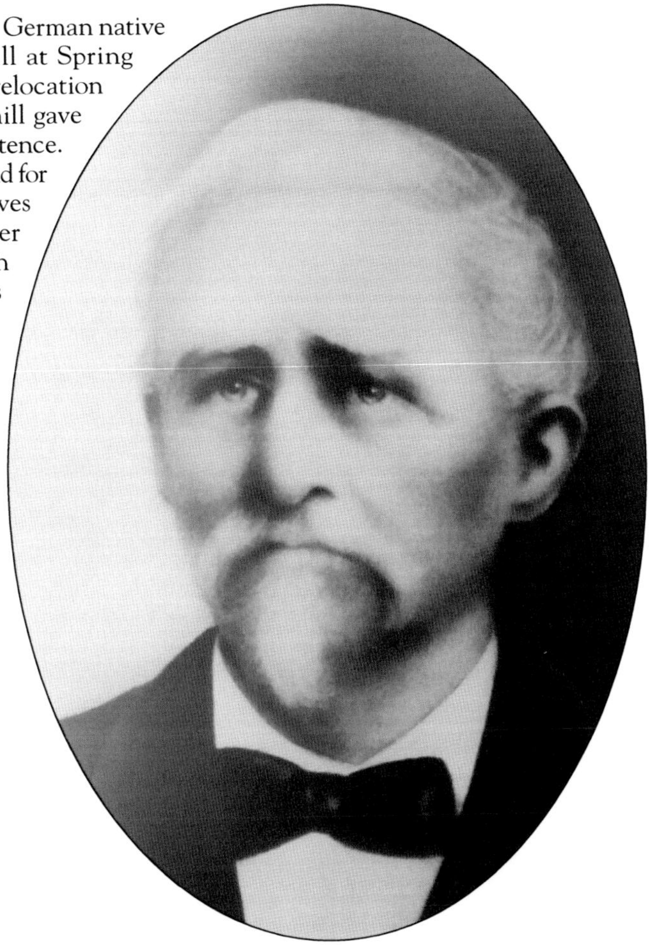

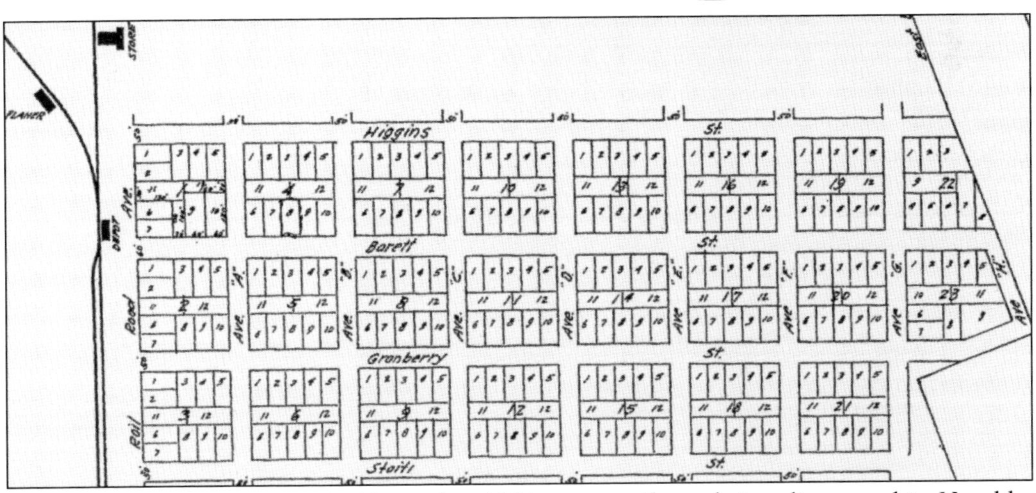

HUMBLE TOWN MAP, 1904. In November 1904, just as oil was being discovered in Humble, Charles Bender laid out a plat for the town that is still in use today. He named the four main streets through the town after the four oil pioneers drilling in Humble: Patillo Higgins, Charles E. Barrett, Prentiss Granberry, and Henry Staiti. Barrett Street was later renamed Main Street.

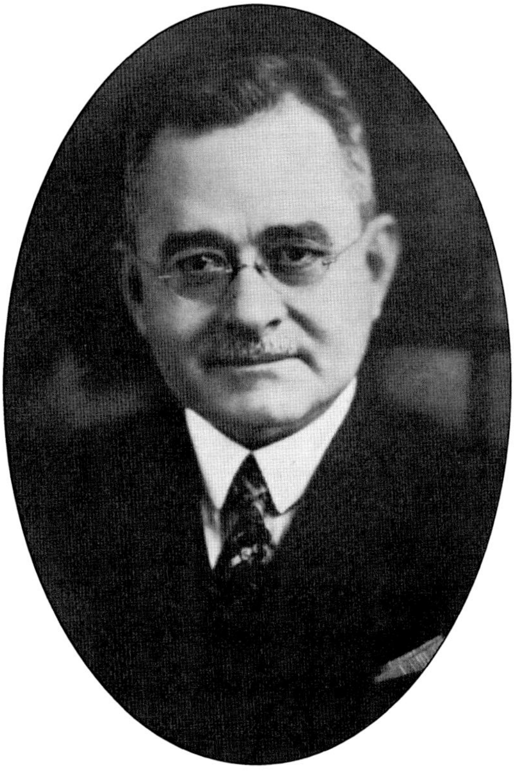

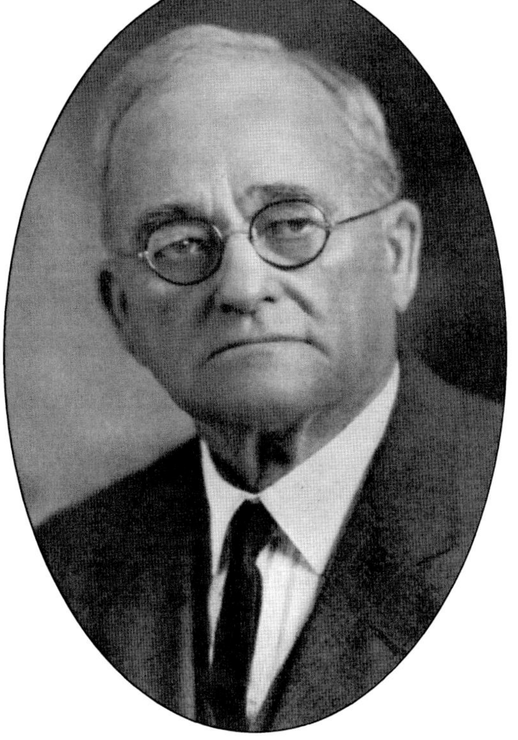

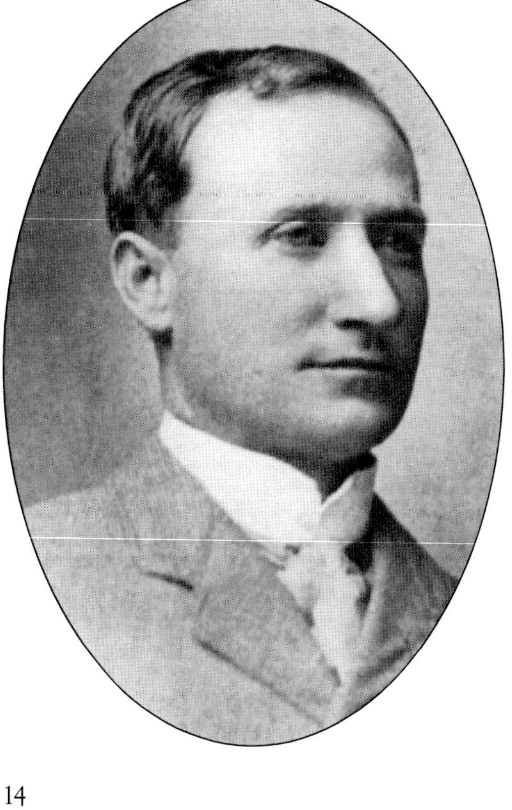

Humble Oil Men. The first oil well in Humble was brought in by the Moonshine Company in November 1904. Three other oil pioneers also struck oil in Humble in 1904. Charles Bender named the streets of Humble after these men. Staiti Street was named for Henry Staiti (top left), owner of the Texas Exploration Company. Granberry Street was named for Prentiss Granberry (top right). Both Granberry and Staiti worked together on the Staiti-Granberry well in Humble. Higgins Street was named for Pattillo Higgins (bottom left), known as the prophet of Spindletop. Barrett Street was named for Charles Barrett.

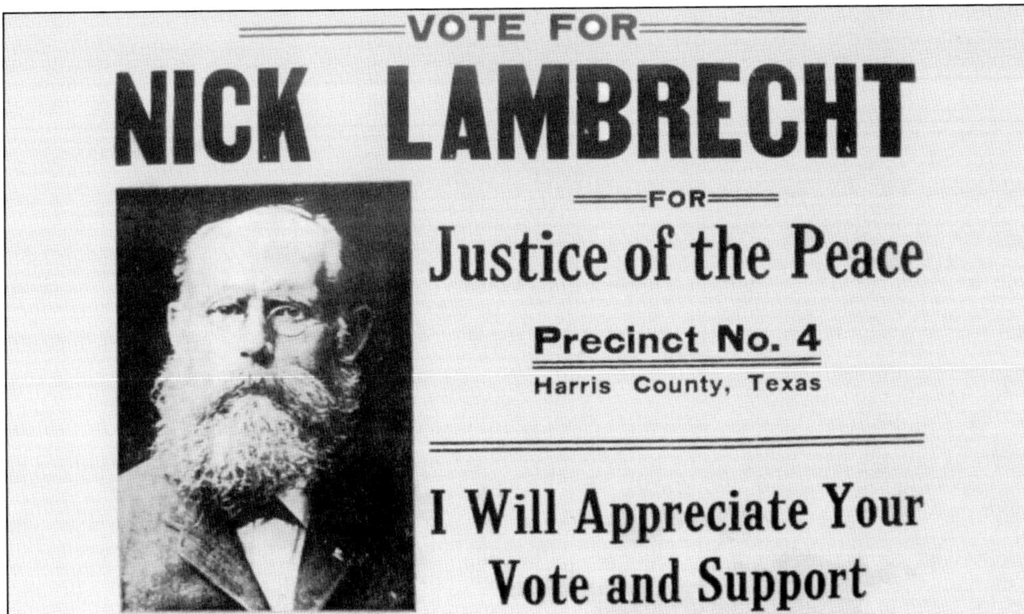

NICHOLAS LAMBRECHT. First elected to office in 1904, Nick Lambrecht served as justice of the peace for Harris County Precinct No. 4 for five years. He was defeated for reelection by F.K. Wise in 1910. Lambrecht also ran the Humble Water Works, the main water supplier for the town. A story about Lambrecht appeared in the *Houston Chronicle* on April 7, 1917, immediately after the United States declared war on Germany. Humble had many German natives that were torn over the declaration of war on their homeland. German native Lambrecht refused to allow two local men to hoist an American flag to the top of the water tower. After a mob of passionate citizens showed up to support the two men, Lambrecht relented and allowed the flag to be raised. The below photograph shows Lambrecht's justice of the peace office.

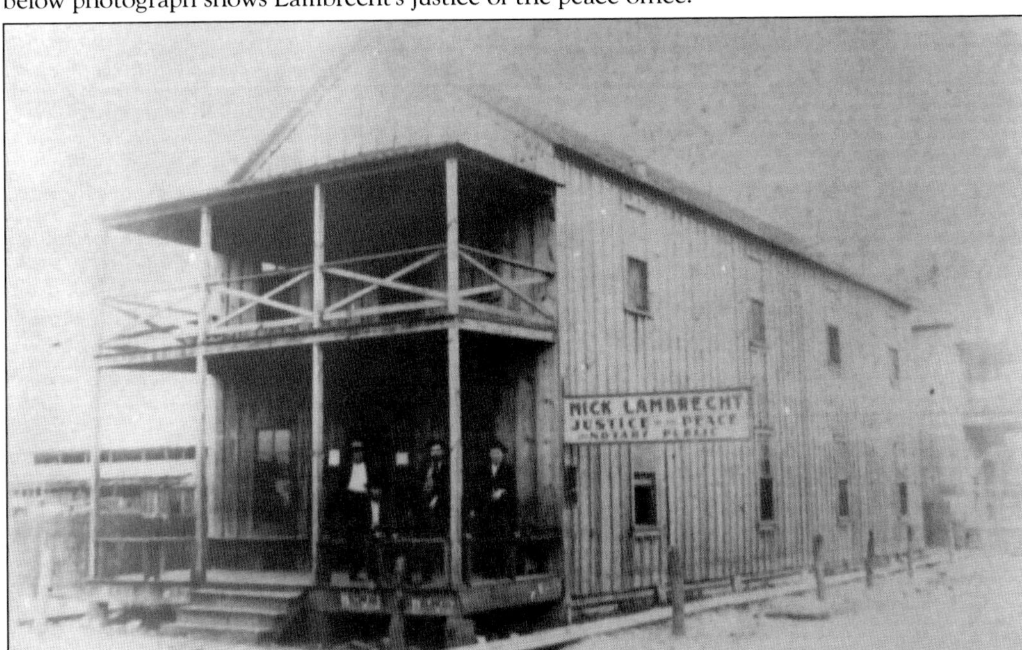

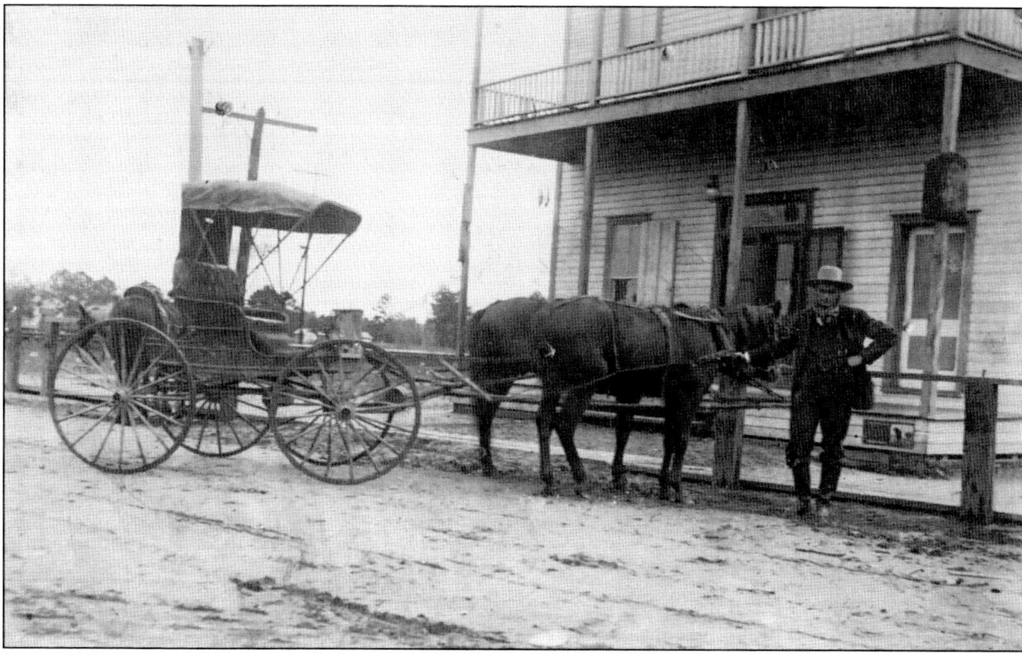

EARLY HUMBLE, 1905. As the oil boom brought more people to Humble, a string of new businesses opened downtown. Opera houses, hotels, pharmacies, restaurants, and saloons were established to accommodate the increasing number of businesspeople passing through town. Wooden sidewalks were installed to keep residents out of the dirt streets, which were frequently muddied by rain. A lack of stock laws allowed goats and pigs to roam the streets. The town had many saloons, and fights among oil-field workers were common when they came to town to drink. In the below photograph, note the tree in the middle of Barrett Street (Main Street) in 1908.

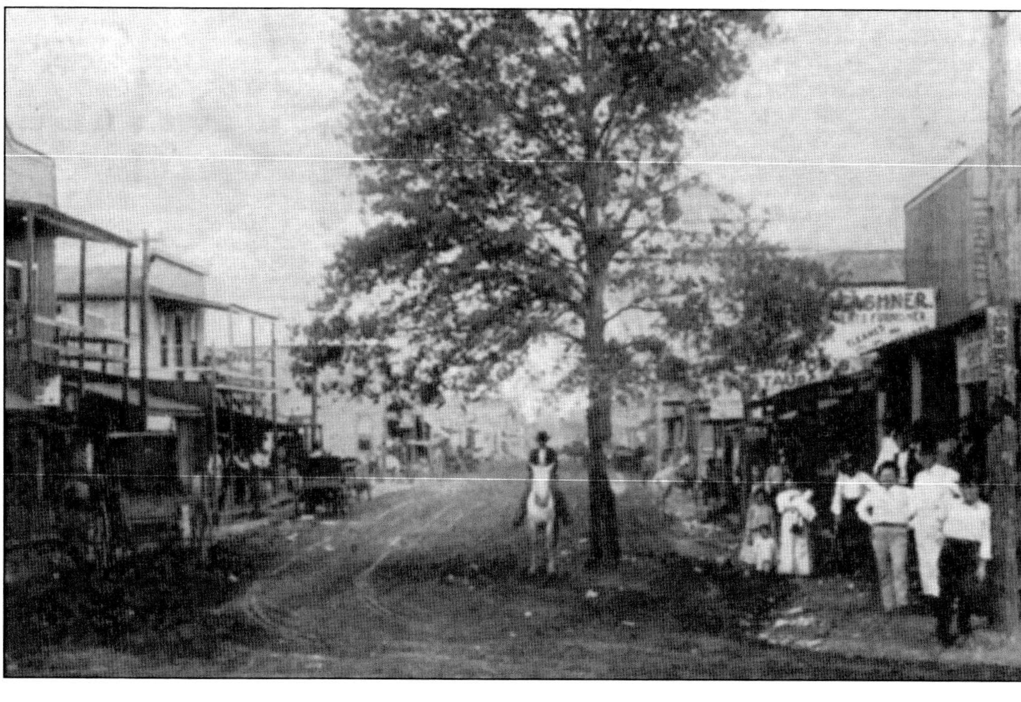

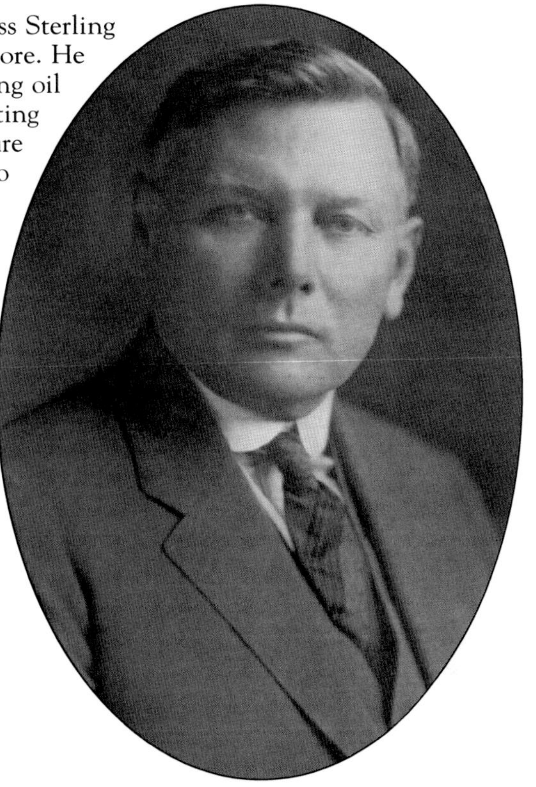

Ross Sterling. Innovative businessman Ross Sterling arrived in Humble in 1904 to open a feed store. He later went into banking, and began purchasing oil wells. He joined other oil-well owners in creating the Humble Oil Company in 1911. This venture made Sterling very wealthy, and he went on to become governor of Texas from 1931 to 1933. Ross Sterling Middle School in Humble ISD is named in his honor.

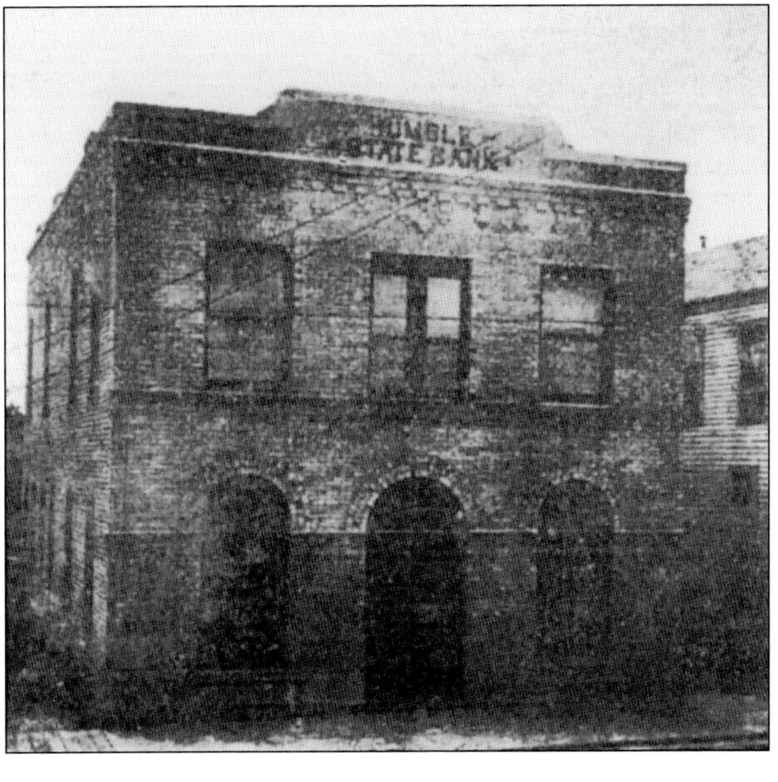

Humble State Bank Building, 1911. During the panic of 1907, Ross Sterling purchased four privately owned banks and converted them to state banks. Constructed in 1908, the Humble State Bank building was the first business structure made of brick in Humble. Sterling built the second floor of the bank to accommodate the Humble Masonic Lodge. This building was destroyed in the downtown Humble fire of February 1912.

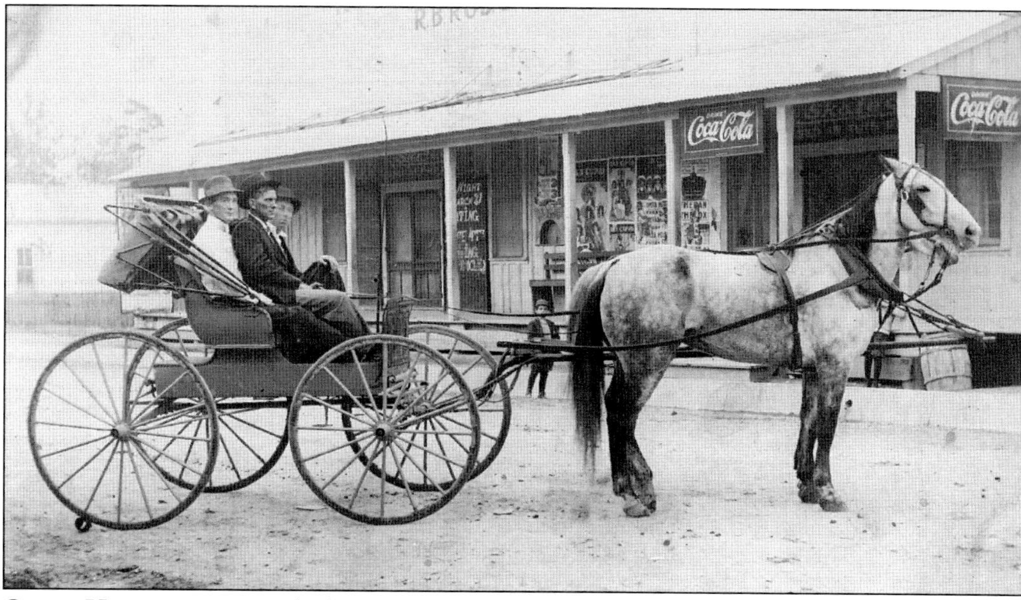

OPERA HOUSE, 1908. With the proliferation of railroads across the country, traveling shows were able to bring culture and entertainment to small towns throughout Texas. Built in 1908, Rodger's Dixie Theatre and Skating Rink (known as the Opera House) provided patrons with the opportunity to see Broadway productions and vaudeville acts. Beginning in the 1910s, with the introduction of motion pictures, opera houses were converted into movie theaters.

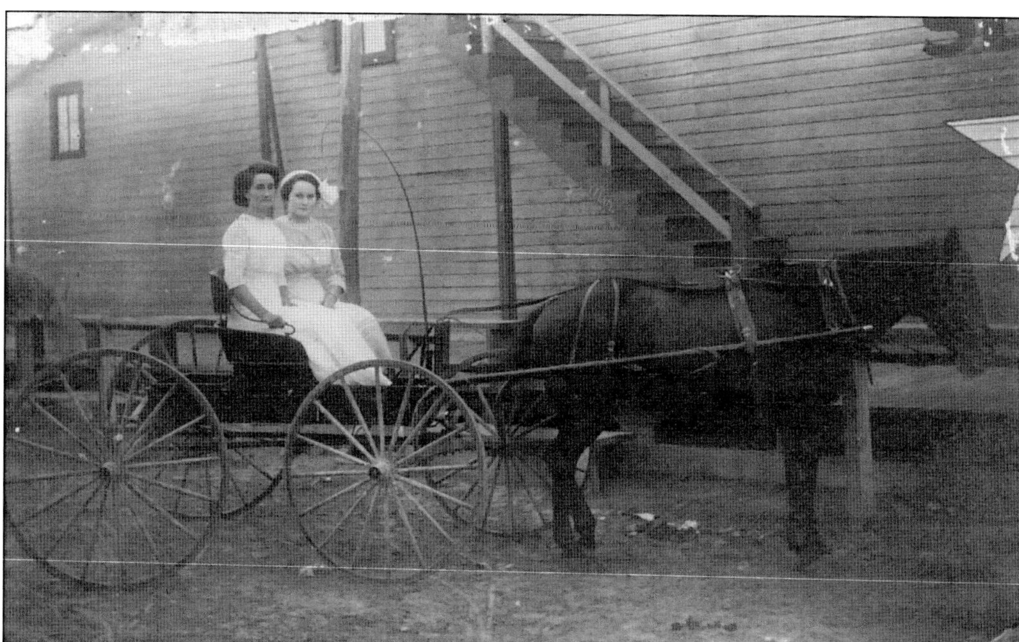

LETITIA AND IMA LEE, 1910. The Lee family moved to the Humble area in 1859. They lived at Neal's Prairie, southwest of Humble, near the present-day location of George Bush Intercontinental Airport. By 1916, the Lee family had become respected cattle ranchers. Lee Road is named after Needham Lee, the father of Letitia (left) and Ima.

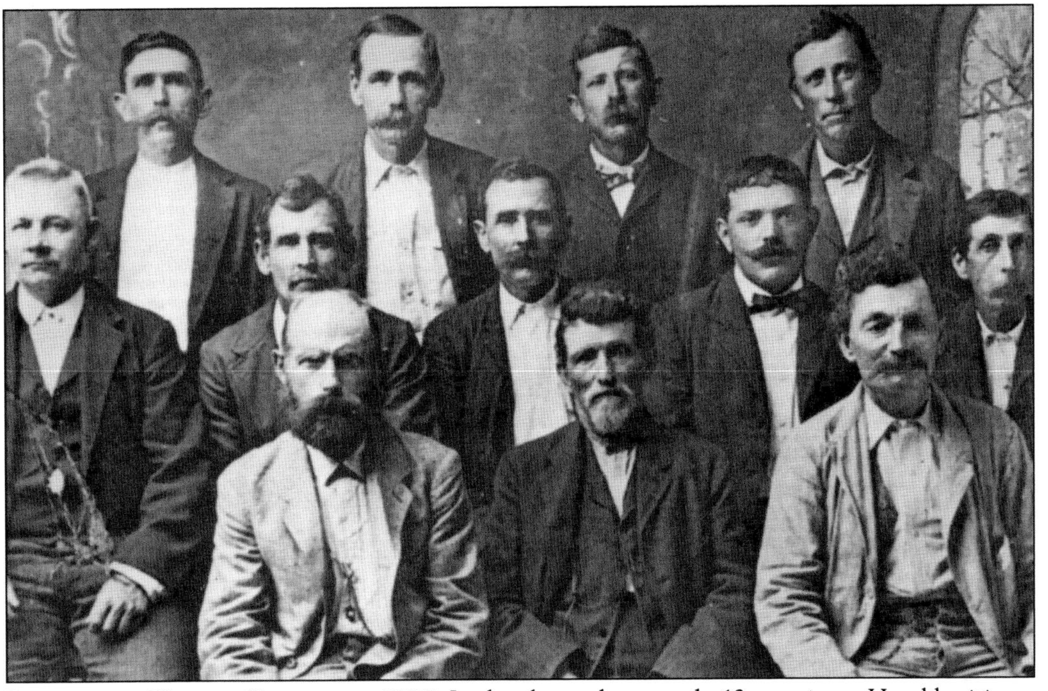

INFLUENTIAL HUMBLE CITIZENS, C. 1908. In the above photograph, 12 prominent Humble citizens gathered around 1908. From left to right are (first row) justice of the peace Nick Lambrecht, former justice of the peace Pleasant Humble, and J.H. Slaughter; (second row) Needham Lee, Wiley Ferrell, J. Ferrell, H.L. Koinm, and Jim Fulgham; (third row) Zeke Durdin, Asa Lee, J.H. Koinm, and Bill Koinm. In the below photograph, the same 12 gentlemen stand outside of the Heaton & Polk Bank and Drug Company. The medical practices of Dr. James W. Sandlin and Dr. John DuBose shared an office at the top of the stairway.

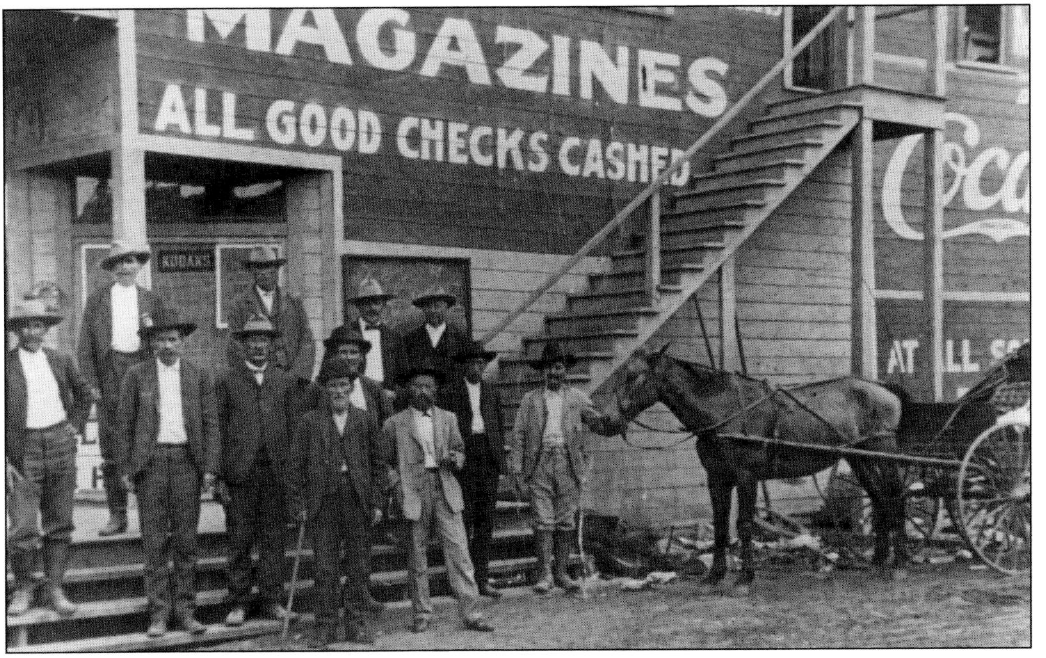

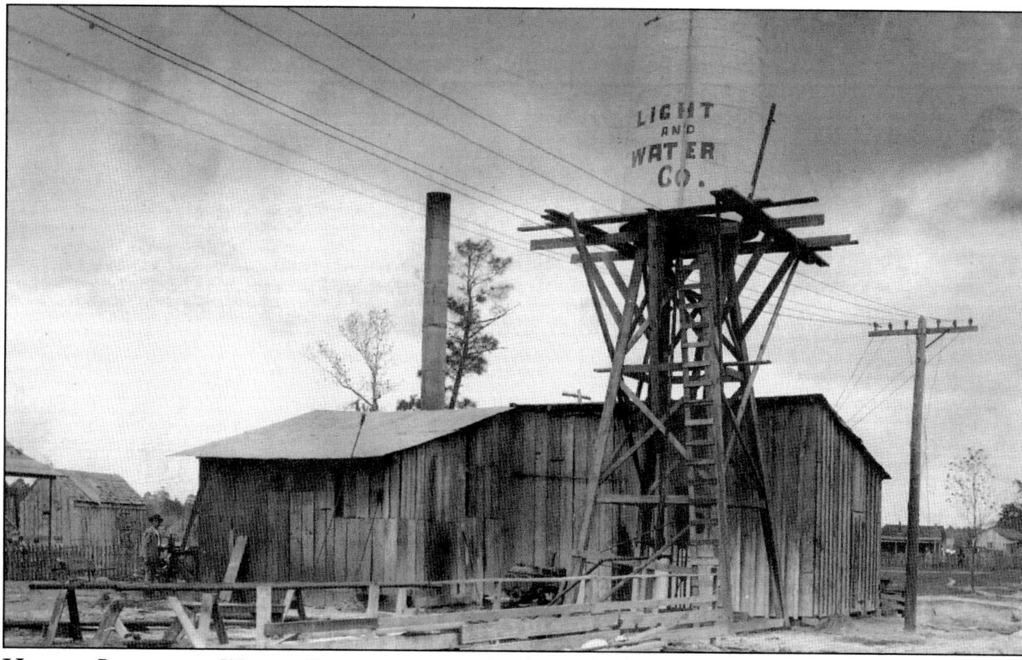

Humble Light and Water Company, 1907. In the early days of Humble, utility companies were owned and operated by individuals. Frank A. Peters was an inspector for the Houston Light and Power Company from 1897 to 1906. In 1906, he moved to Humble and established the Humble Light and Water Company. This building burned down in 1907, but it was later rebuilt.

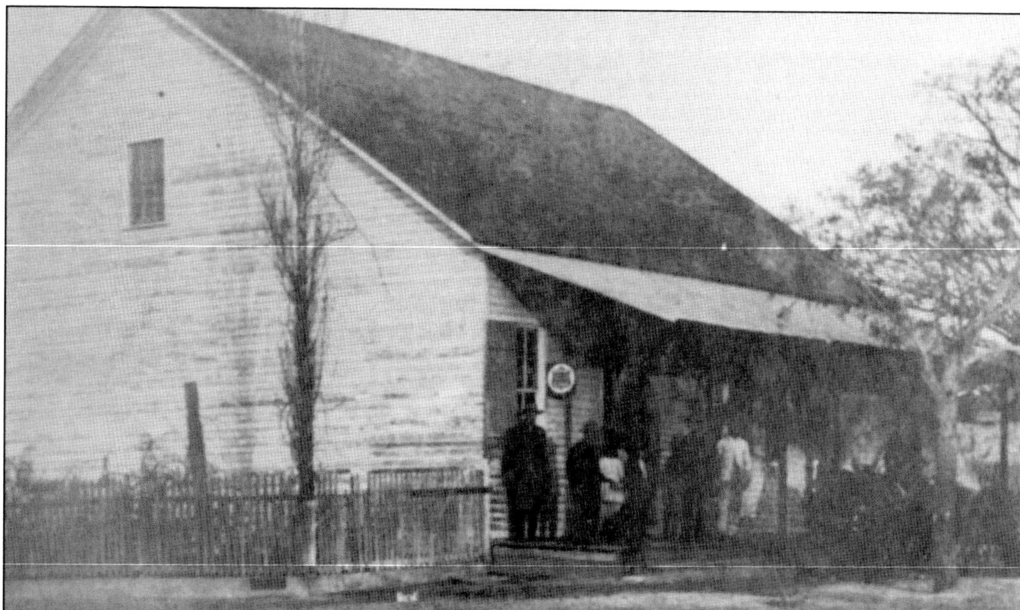

Mutual Telephone Company, 1910. The Mutual Telephone Company was established in Humble in 1904 by Mr. Clinton. It was originally located at 203 Barrett Street, at the corner of Avenue A. In 1911, it was sold and became the Home Telephone Company. The phone company building burned down during the downtown Humble fire of 1912. (Courtesy of the James Tull Chapter of the Daughters of the American Revolution.)

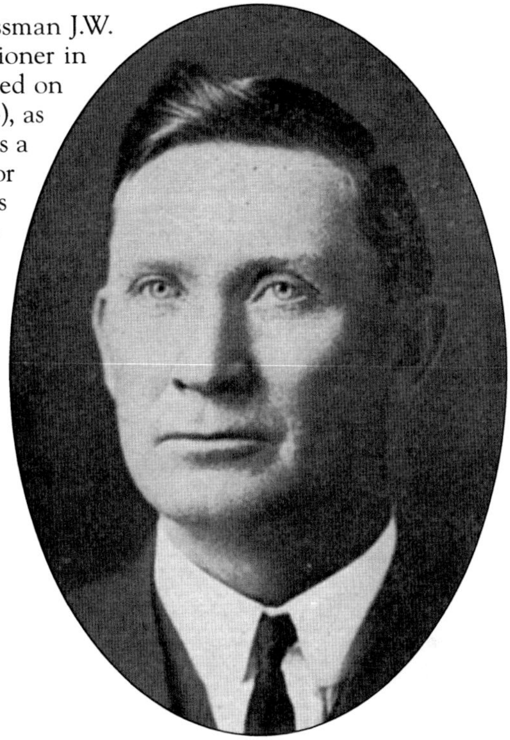

James William Hall, 1912. Humble businessman J.W. Hall was elected as a Harris County commissioner in 1908. Ever a diligent public servant, Hall served on the school board for District No. 28 (1909–1913), as a state representative (1919–1922, 1925–1926), as a state senator (1927–1928), and as the tax assessor and collector for Harris County (1935). He was responsible for the construction of the Houston-Humble Road (Old Humble Road).

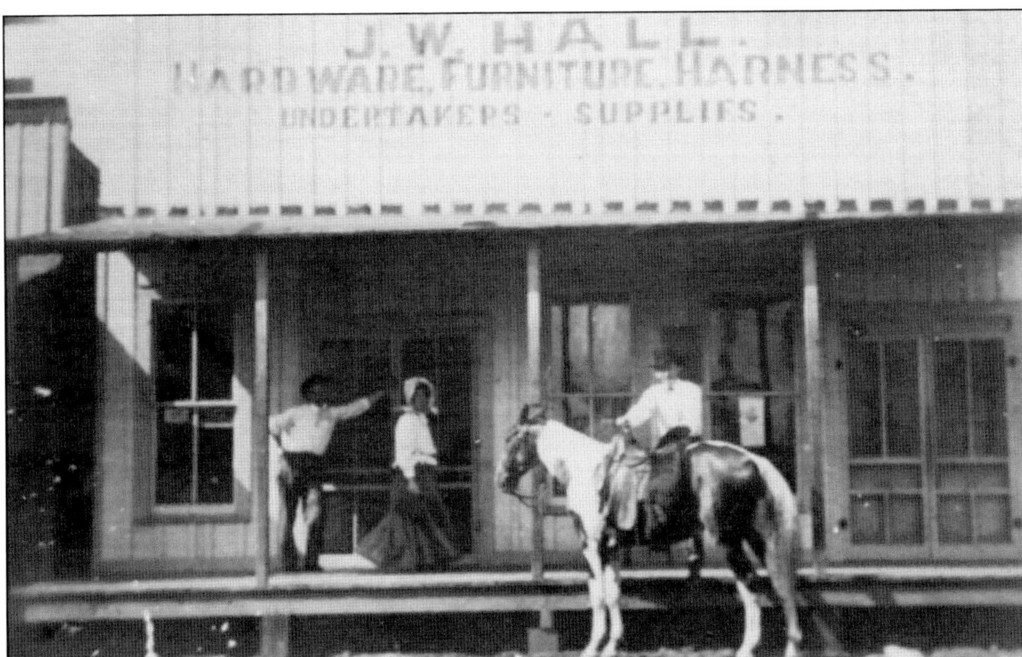

J.W. Hall Hardware Store, 1912. The J.W. Hall Hardware store was located in downtown Humble, in the 200 block of Barrett Street. The wooden building was destroyed in the Humble town fire of February 1912. A brick building was built in its place. It eventually became the Harvey Hardware Store.

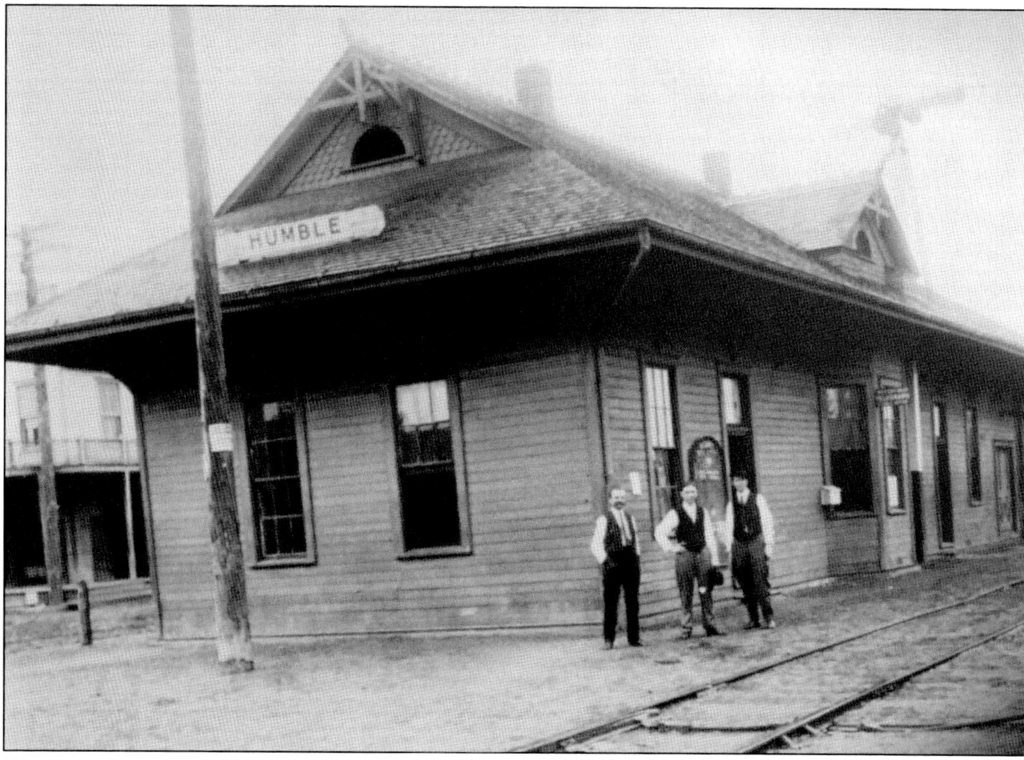

HUMBLE TRAIN DEPOT. Built for the Houston East & West Texas Railway, this depot was vital for people coming into Humble. The depot was located next to the railway tracks, in the center of Barrett Street (Main Street). In the 1940s, the depot was moved a few hundred feet southward to allow Main Street to continue west across the tracks.

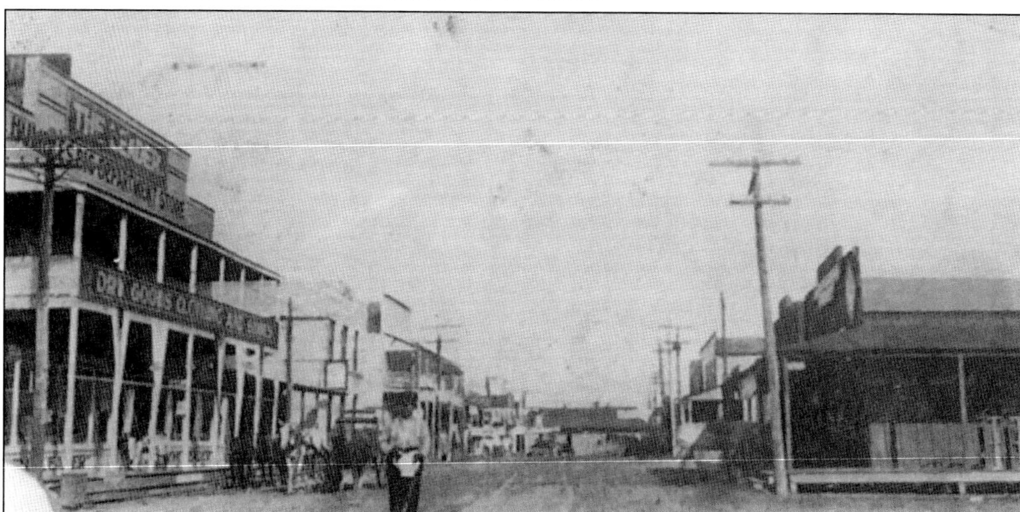

HUMBLE TOWN FIRE, 1912. The above photograph shows downtown Humble just prior to a fire that consumed 2.5 blocks on February 14, 1912. With no fire department, and flames fanned by a strong wind, the wooden buildings succumbed quickly. Among the first buildings to be consumed was the Humble State Bank Building, the only brick structure downtown. The fire was brought under control by the Houston Fire Department. Losses for the destruction exceeded $200,000.

Two

MOONSHINE HILL AND OIL

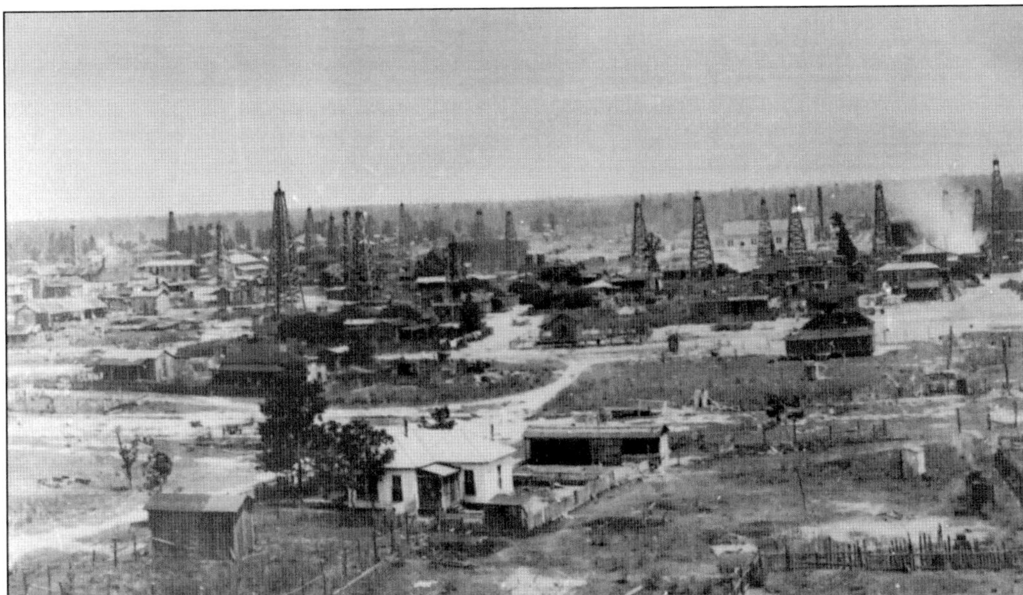

MOONSHINE HILL. Moonshine Hill is a low-elevation hill, barely more than 20 feet above the surrounding prairie. It sits on top of a salt dome. It was in this area that James H. Slaughter first noticed gas bubbles seeping to the surface of the San Jacinto River, which later led to the discovery of oil in Humble. The area was known as the Echols Ridge until around 1907.

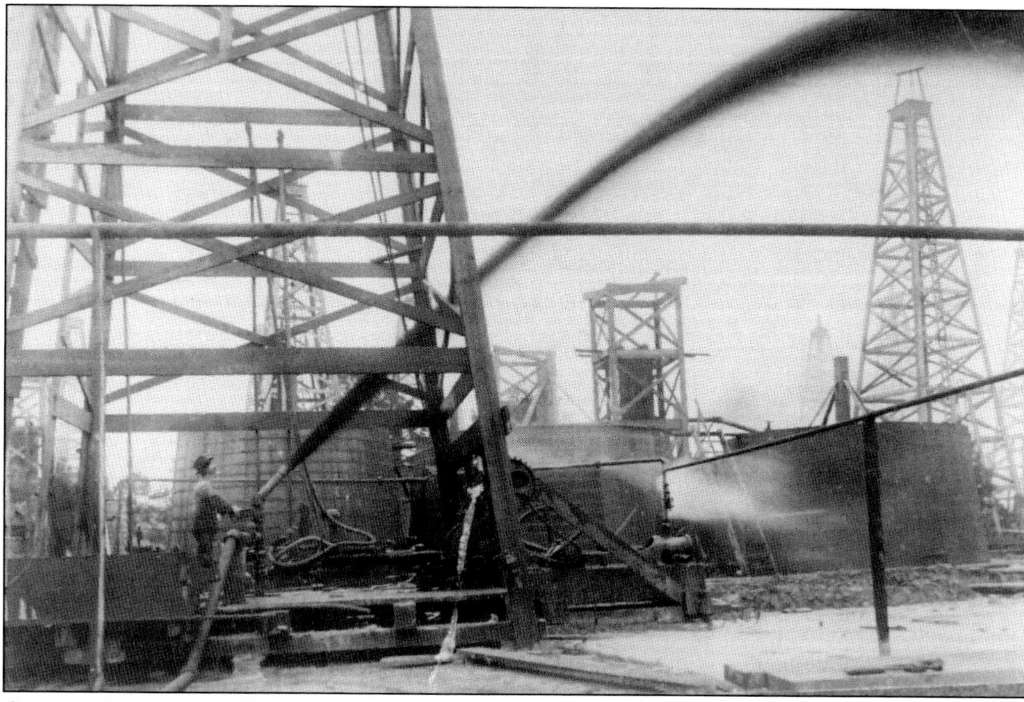

Gusher. Prior to Spindletop, oil was "scooped" out of oil wells. The well at Spindletop was drilled into a salt dome, where the oil was under high pressure, causing the oil to shoot out of the top of the derrick. The Humble oil field was also a salt dome field, resulting in several "gushers." The man in the photograph is demonstrating the pressure coming up from the well.

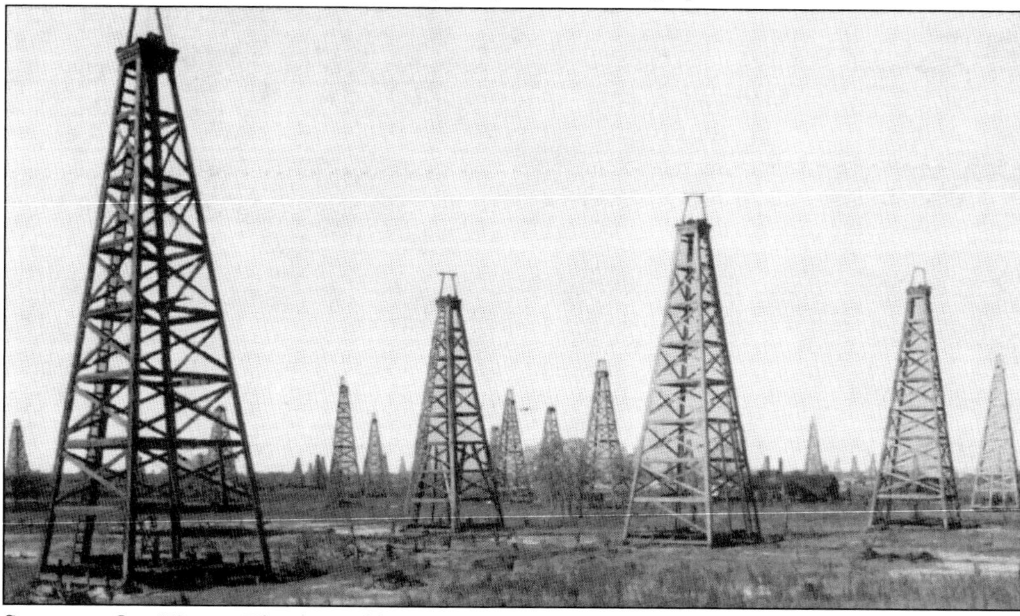

Shallow Oil Wells. The first oil boom in Humble was made up of shallow wells. These wells were drilled no deeper than about 1,000 feet. The derricks, made of wood, were littered across the landscape in Humble. The second and third Humble oil booms were the result of deeper drilling techniques. (Courtesy of Margaret Byron.)

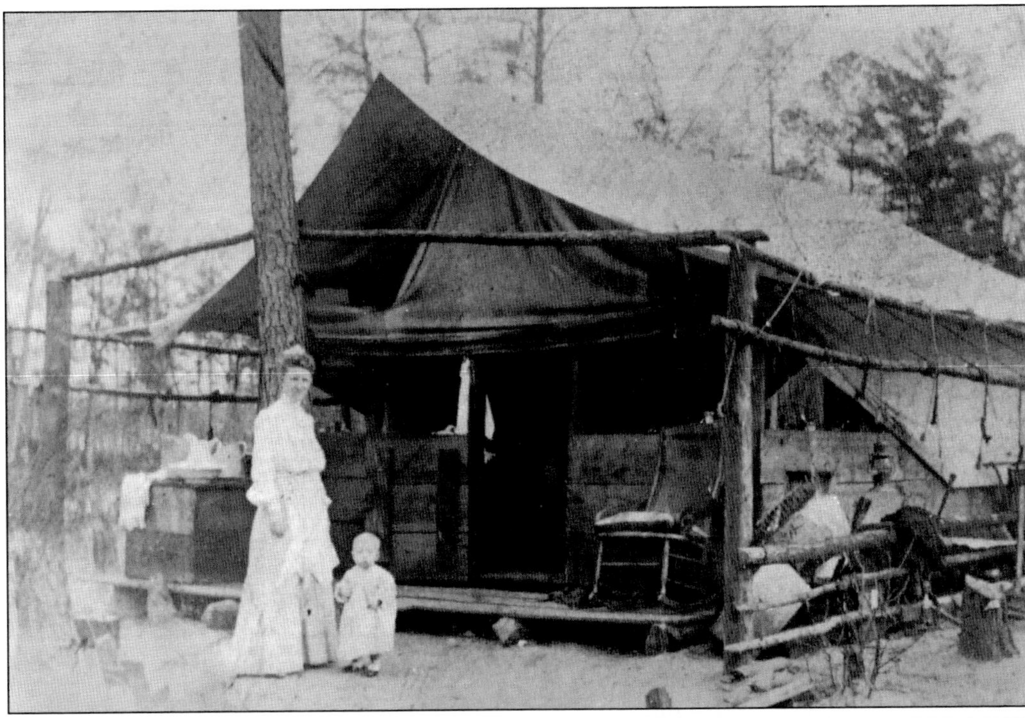

Tent City. When the oil boom began in Humble, a large influx of men came into town to work in the fields. Boardinghouses and hotels were quickly filled to capacity. The few homes that were available sold quickly. Unfortunately, there was a shortage of building materials, and not enough living places to accommodate everyone. To solve the housing problem, oil companies allowed workers to build tents on their oil leases. The workers built wooden frames and hung tents over the frames. Eventually, the workers' families came to Humble and lived in the tents with them. (Right photograph courtesy of Margaret Byron.)

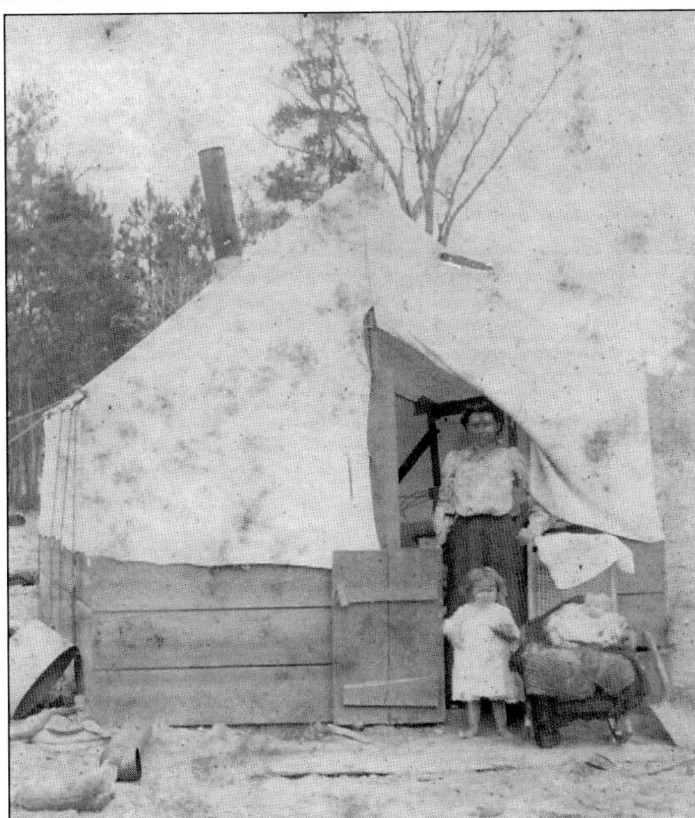

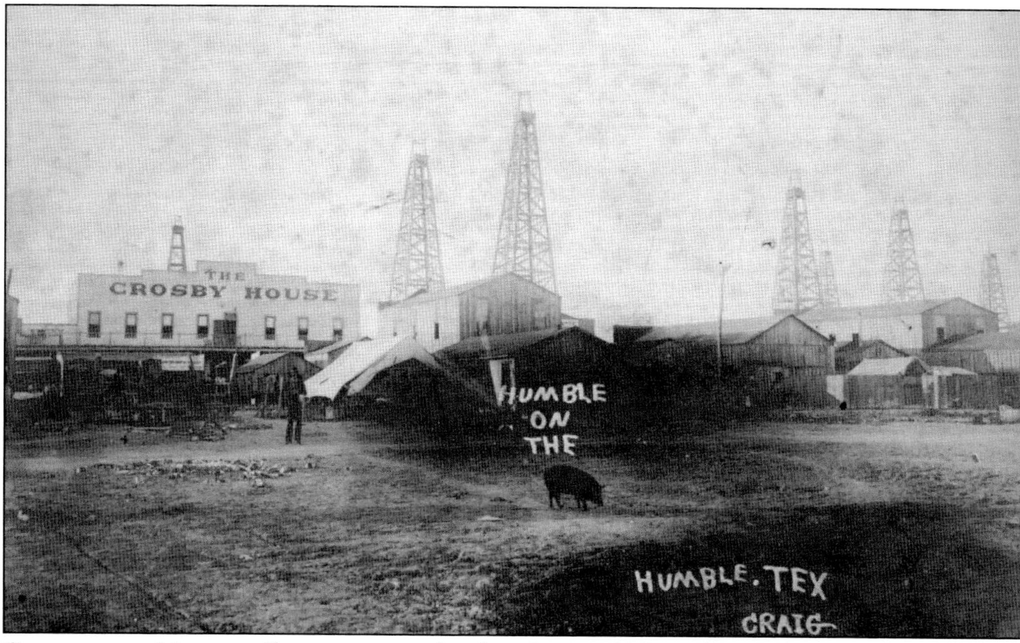

CROSBYTOWN. Many small communities developed around Moonshine Hill, including Sand Hill, Baby Hill, Middletown, and Crosbytown, the latter of which was a community that developed between Humble and Moonshine Hill. Crosbytown was more a collection of saloons and boardinghouses than an actual town. The center of the community was a boardinghouse called the Crosby House (shown here).

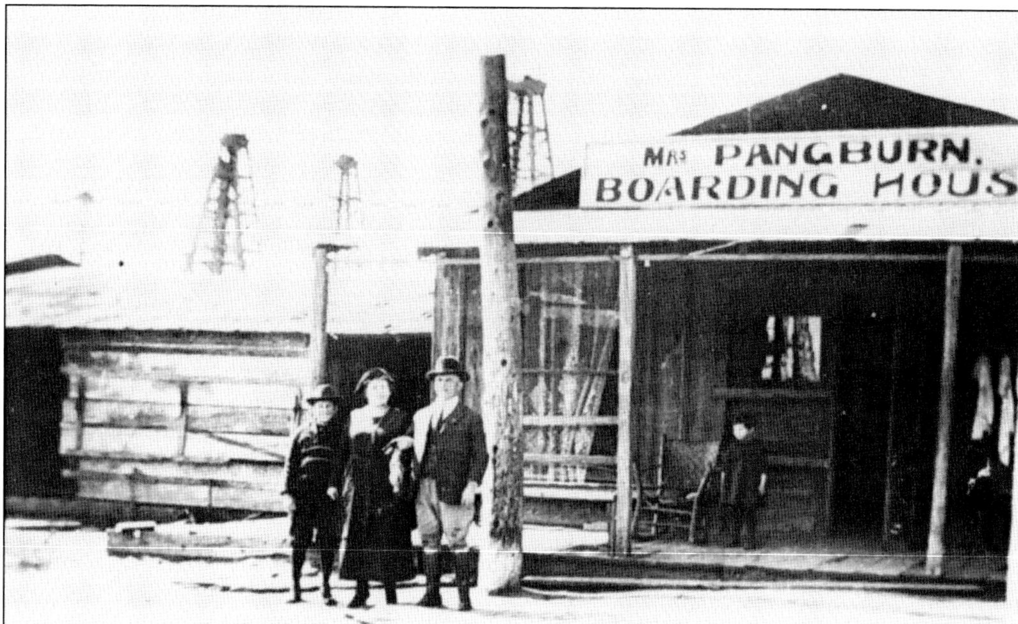

MRS. PANGBURN'S BOARDING HOUSE. Erected in 1905 by Bill and Nancy "Granny" Pangburn, Mrs. Pangburn's Boarding House was a landmark at Moonshine Hill, and many oil millionaires dined at her table. Room and board was $1 per day. A single meal was 35¢. Granny Pangburn continued to run the boardinghouse until her death in 1933.

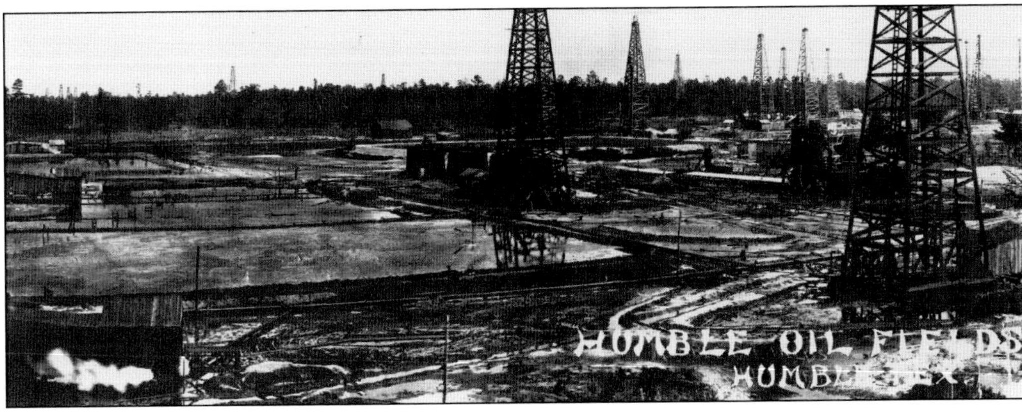

Earthen Oil Tanks. In the early days of the Humble oil boom, there were no tanks to hold the oil as it was brought up from the ground. Oil from a gusher would simply pool around the derrick. These pools of oil would flow everywhere, causing safety problems with other oil wells and flowing into tents where families lived. To solve this problem, the oil companies constructed giant dikes, built of dirt, to contain the oil. Over time, the number of these dikes grew, until the derricks were surrounded by lakes of oil. (Photographs courtesy of the Houston Metropolitan Research Center.)

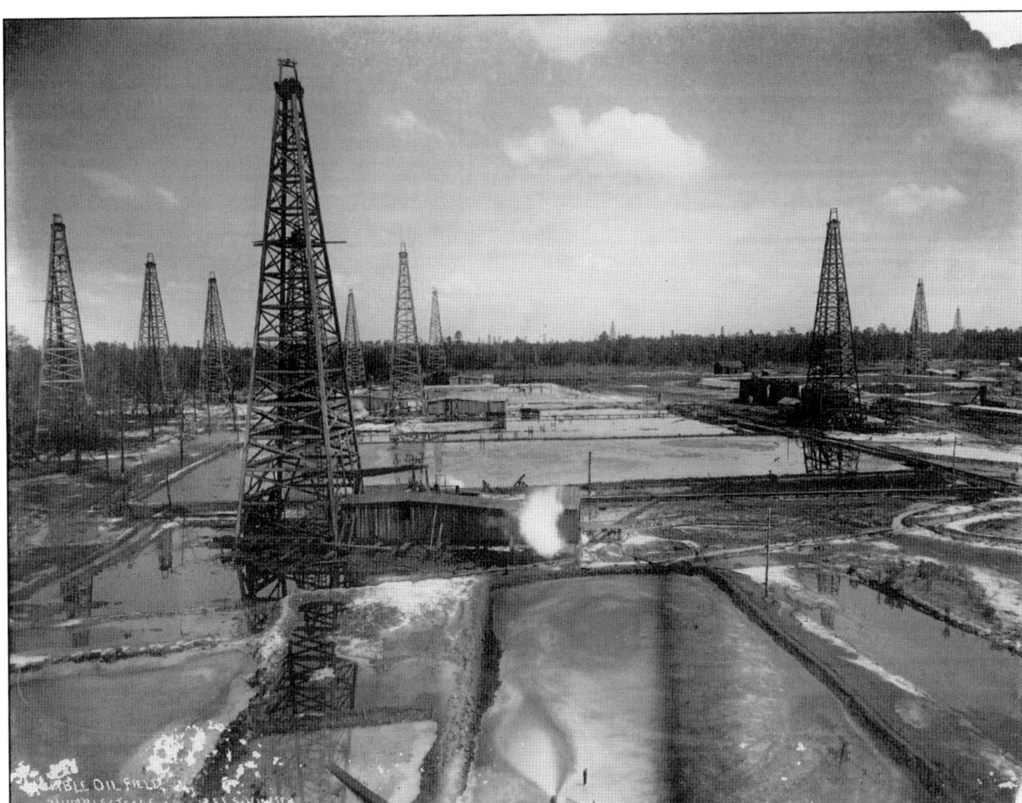

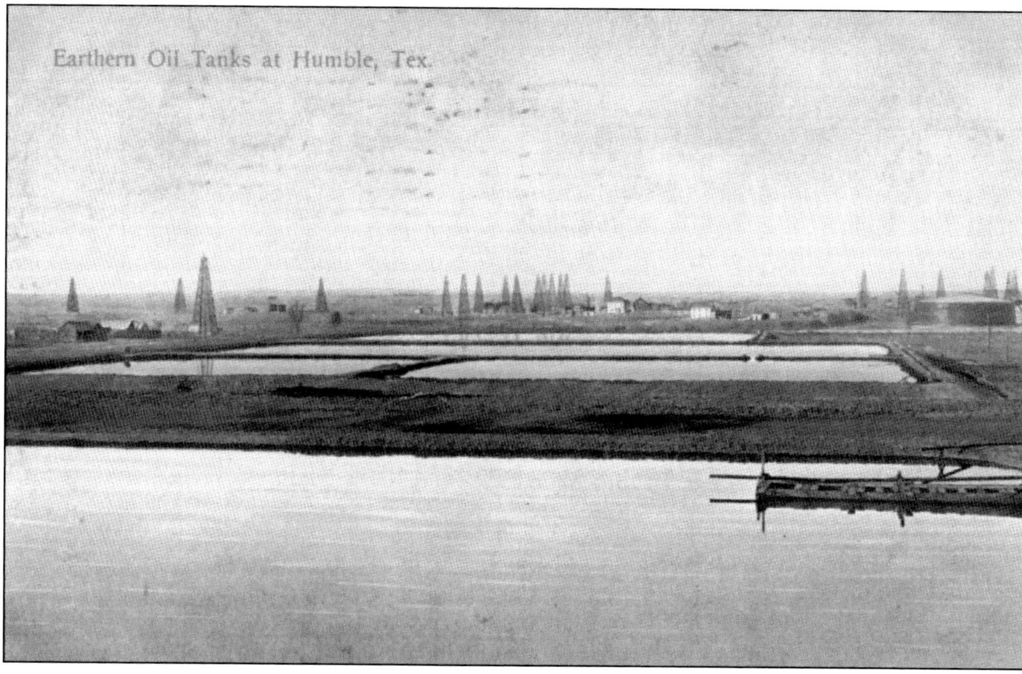

LAKES OF OIL. The simple solution for storing oil, and to prevent it from spreading from derrick to derrick, was to store the oil in open earthen dikes. While simple, this solution was also problematic. The open tanks were a safety hazard for workers, who could fall into the tanks. The real danger became evident when a bolt of lightning set an earthen tank on fire. Such fires spread quickly from tank to tank, causing a massive loss of oil and much damage to the surrounding oil rigs. In the below photograph, four men can be seen standing on a pier inspecting a lake of oil.

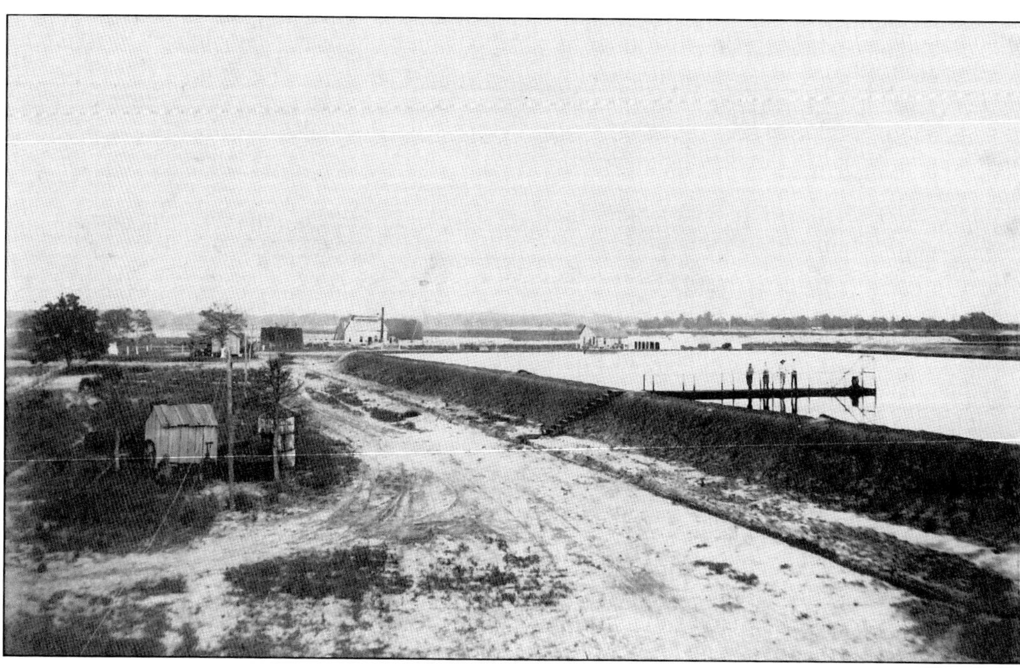

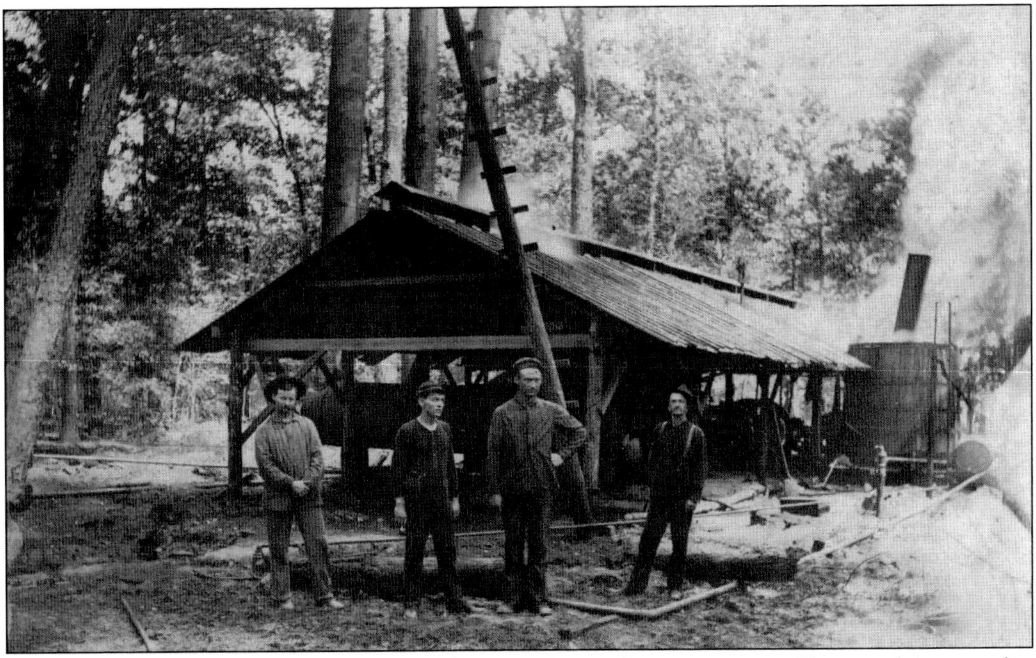

Get Rich Quick. The Humble oil field was a place where a man could get rich overnight. However, few local residents made money from the fields. Experienced "oilmen" came to Humble and purchased land (frequently way below value), set up derricks, got rich on the oil, and moved to Houston or other fields.

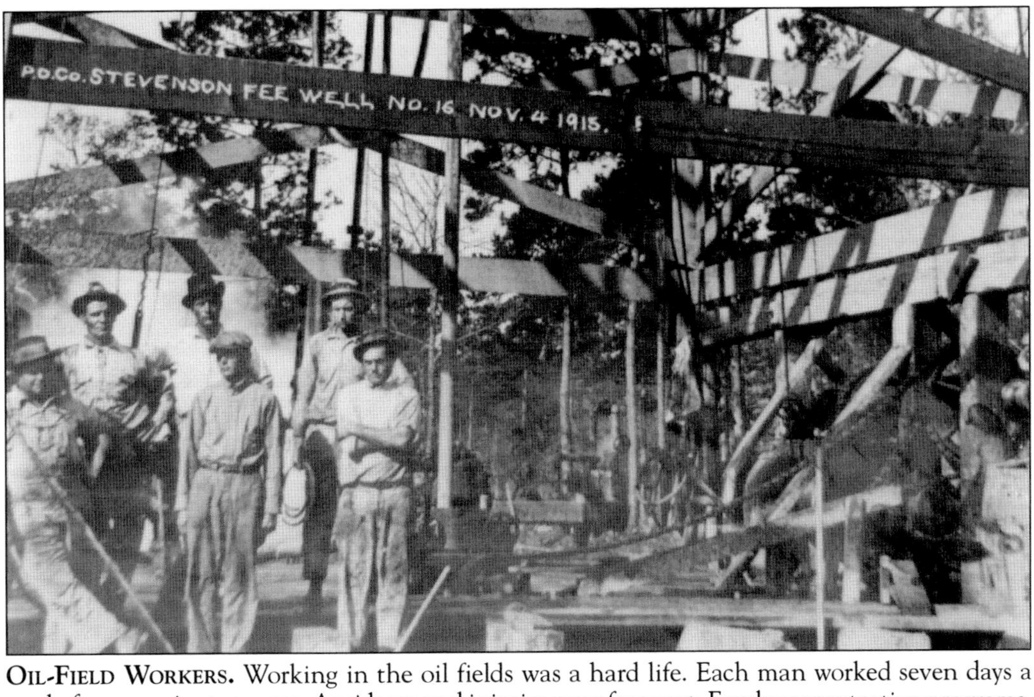

Oil-Field Workers. Working in the oil fields was a hard life. Each man worked seven days a week, from sunrise to sunset. Accidents and injuries were frequent. Employee protection programs, such as workers' compensation, did not exist. An injured man who could no longer perform his job was dismissed.

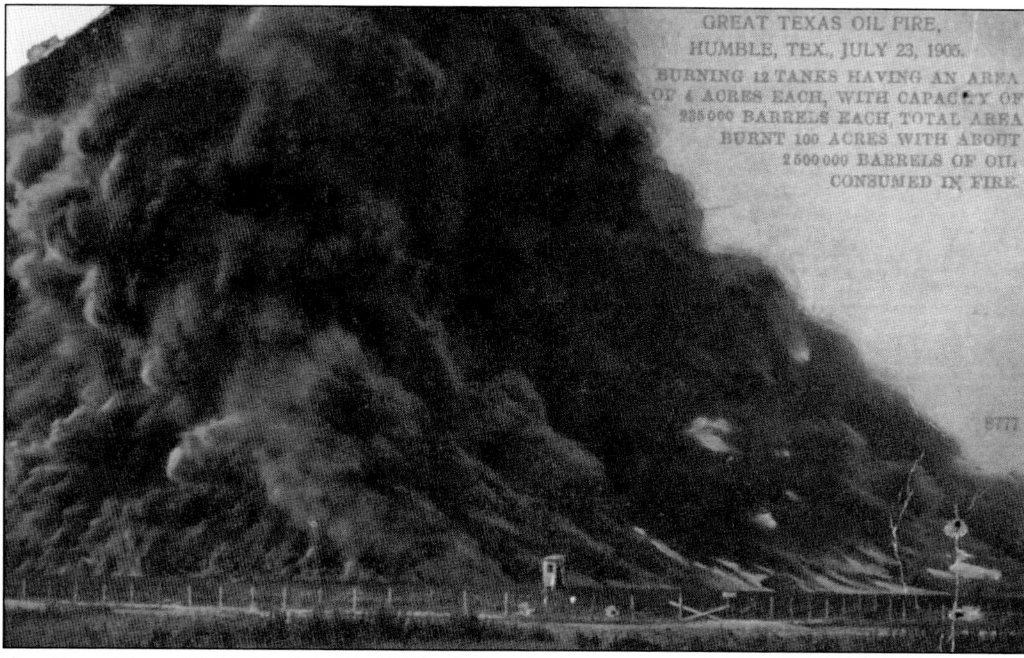

Oil Tank Fire, 1905. On July 23, 1905, a bolt of lightning ignited oil in one of the large storage tanks. The fire spread from one tank to the next and quickly became a raging inferno. The heat from the fire was intense. The blaze consumed over 100 acres, and two million barrels of oil were lost. At least 40 men and 160 mules were incinerated in the fire.

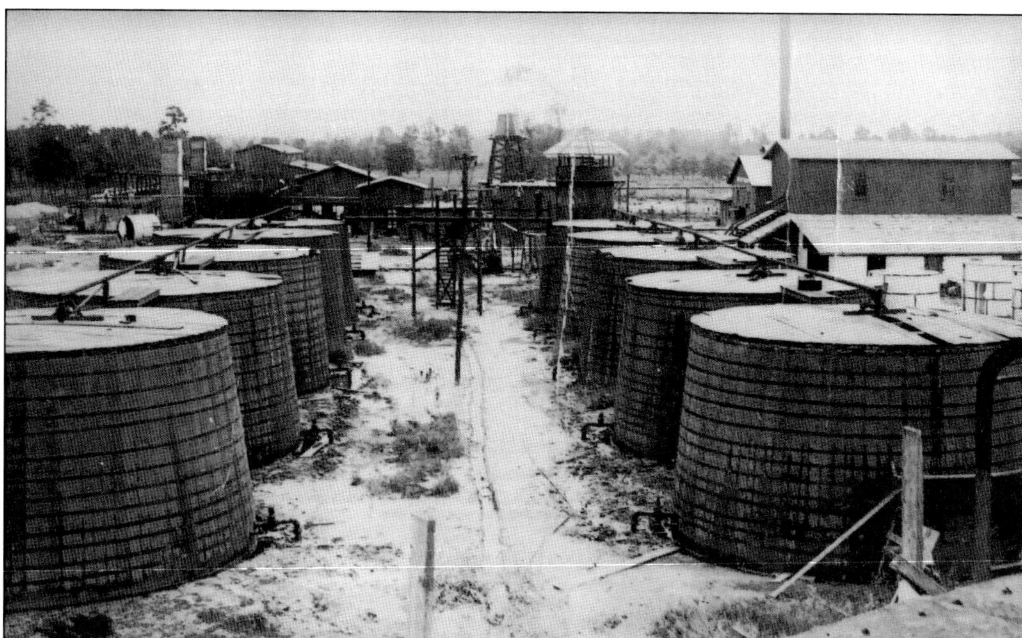

Wooden Oil Tanks. Following a disastrous fire in the earthen oil tanks, the oil companies started constructing storage tanks out of wood. They were still built close together, but these tanks had tops on them that could be closed to help prevent fires caused by lightning strikes. This also helped slow the spread of fire when a tank was set ablaze.

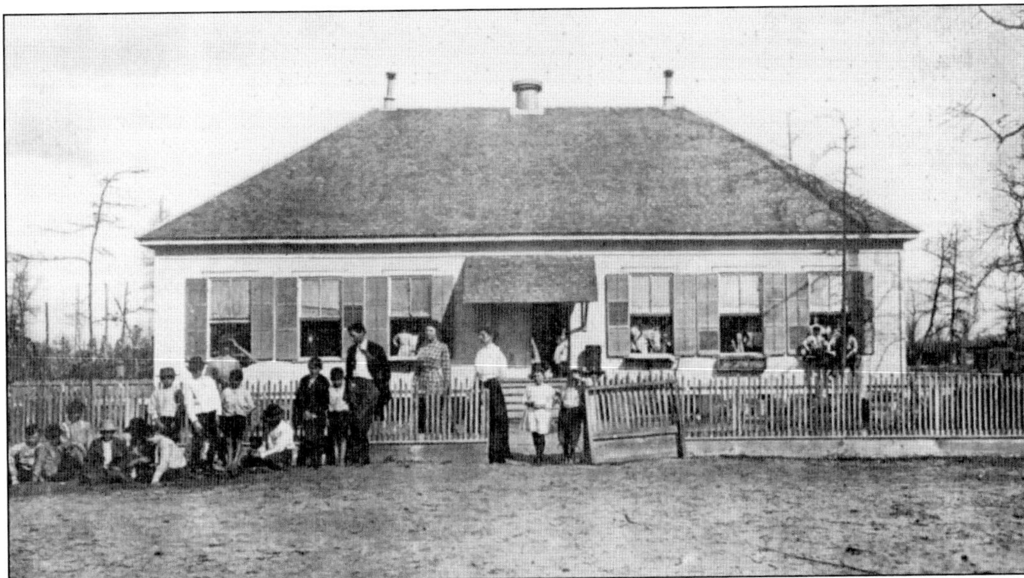

THE WOODWARD SCHOOL, 1910. The Woodward School was built at Moonshine Hill by District No. 35 in 1910. W.B. Sharp and the Producers Oil Company donated land in the Moonshine Heights neighborhood for construction of the school. The Woodward School was an intermediate school, housing grades one through seven. (Courtesy of the Houston Metropolitan Research Center.)

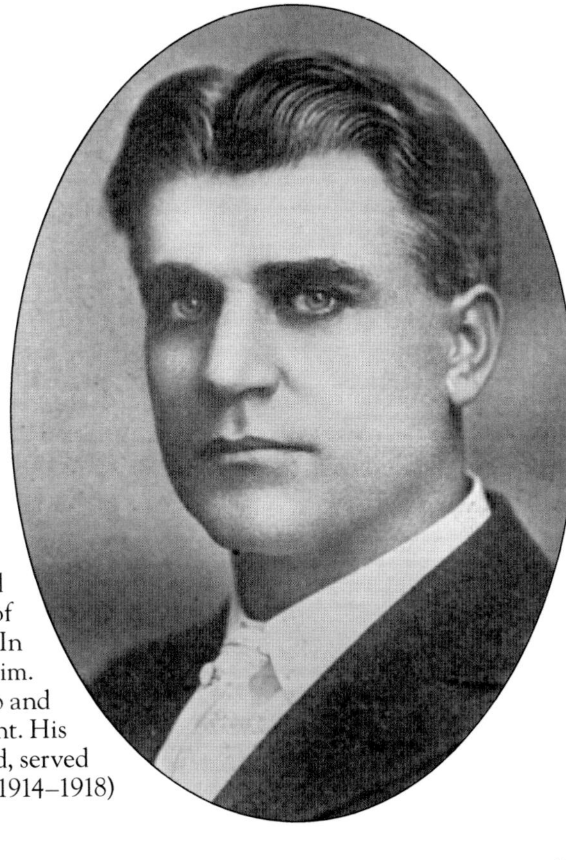

EMERSON FRANCIS WOODWARD. Assistant superintendent of the Producers Oil Company's southern division, Woodward (1879–1943) approved the donation of land for the school at Moonshine Hill. In appreciation, the school was named for him. He was founder of the Houston Gun Club and was once listed as Houston's richest resident. His younger brother, William Zane Woodward, served on the school board for District No. 28 (1914–1918) and District No. 50 (1918–1919).

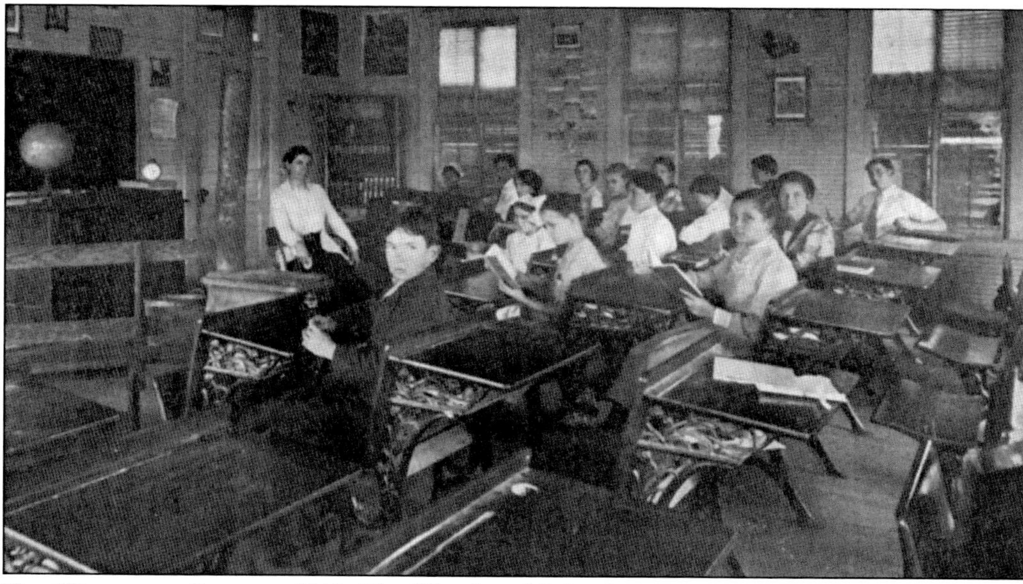

The Woodward School, 1912. The Woodward School, a two-room schoolhouse, was built at Moonshine Hill in 1910 by District No. 35. The Harris County Commissioner's Court determined that District No. 35 had mistakenly built the school on land within District No. 28's boundary. As a result, control of the Woodward School was given to District No. 28 in 1915. (Courtesy of the Houston Metropolitan Research Center.)

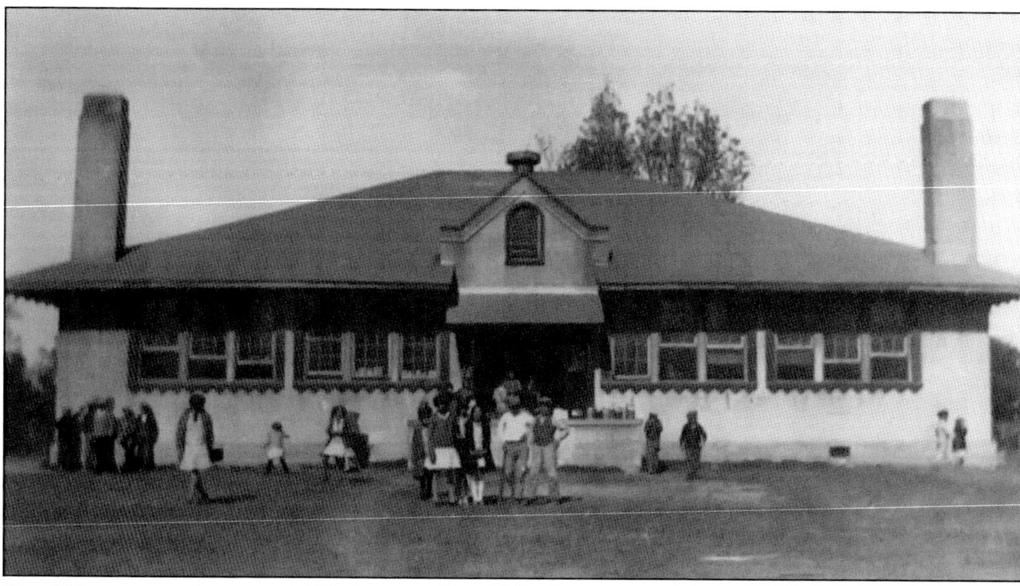

The Woodward School, 1918. District No. 28 built a masonry structure to replace the wooden schoolhouse at Moonshine Hill in 1917. While still officially known as the Woodward School, this school was frequently referred to as the Moonshine Hill School, or simply as the Hill School. The old wooden building was moved across the railroad tracks and used as one of the buildings for the Colored School.

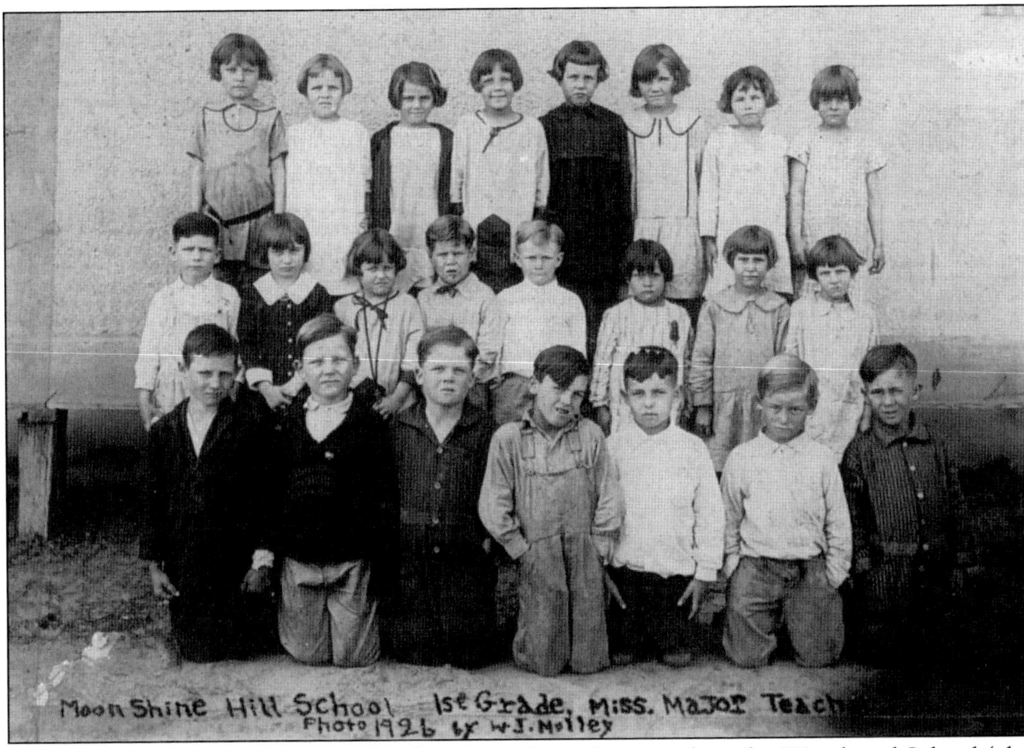

THE WOODWARD SCHOOL, 1926. Students pose for a photograph at the Woodward School (also known as the Moonshine Hill School) in 1926. As the oil boom subsided, enrollment at the school slowly declined. Humble ISD closed the school in 1931, but reopened it after parents protested. The school was permanently closed in 1932 due to low enrollment.

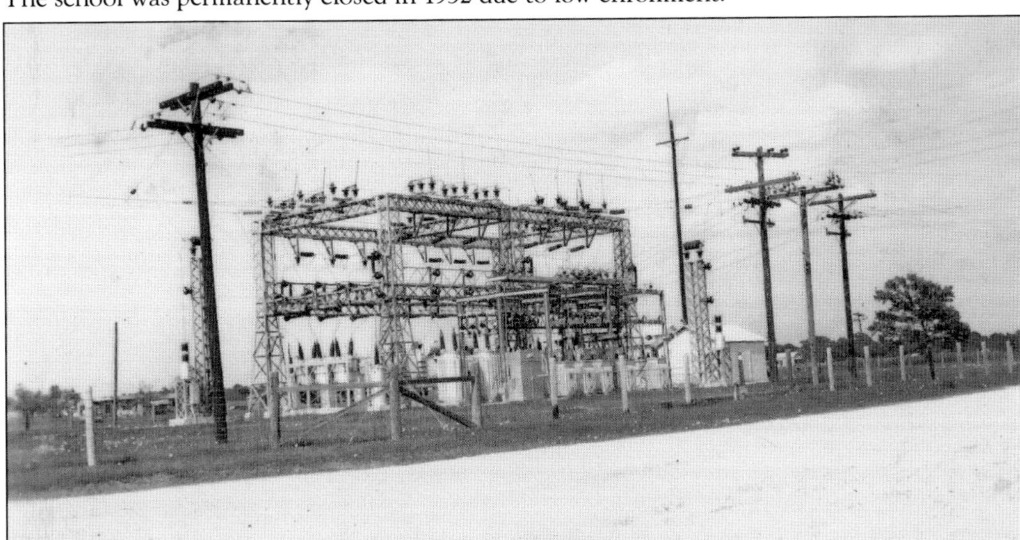

MOONSHINE HILL POWER STATION, 1950s. Shortly after company founder Frank A. Peters died in 1924, the Humble Light and Water Company was sold to the Louisiana-Texas Utility Co. It was eventually sold to Houston Lighting and Power (HL&P), which installed an electrical substation at Moonshine Hill, on FM1960, in the 1950s.

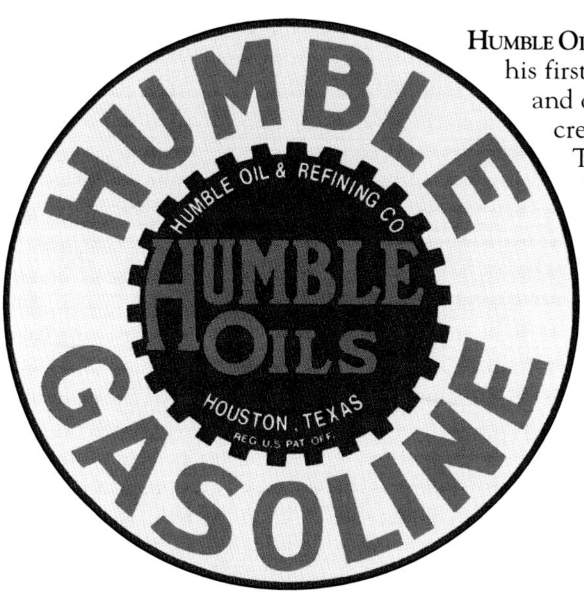

HUMBLE OIL COMPANY. In 1910, Ross Sterling purchased his first two oil wells. As he purchased more, he and other well owners pooled their assets and created the Humble Oil Company in 1911. The company merged with Standard Oil of New Jersey in 1959, although Sterling had sold his shares by that time. Subsequent mergers transformed the company into Exxon in 1972.

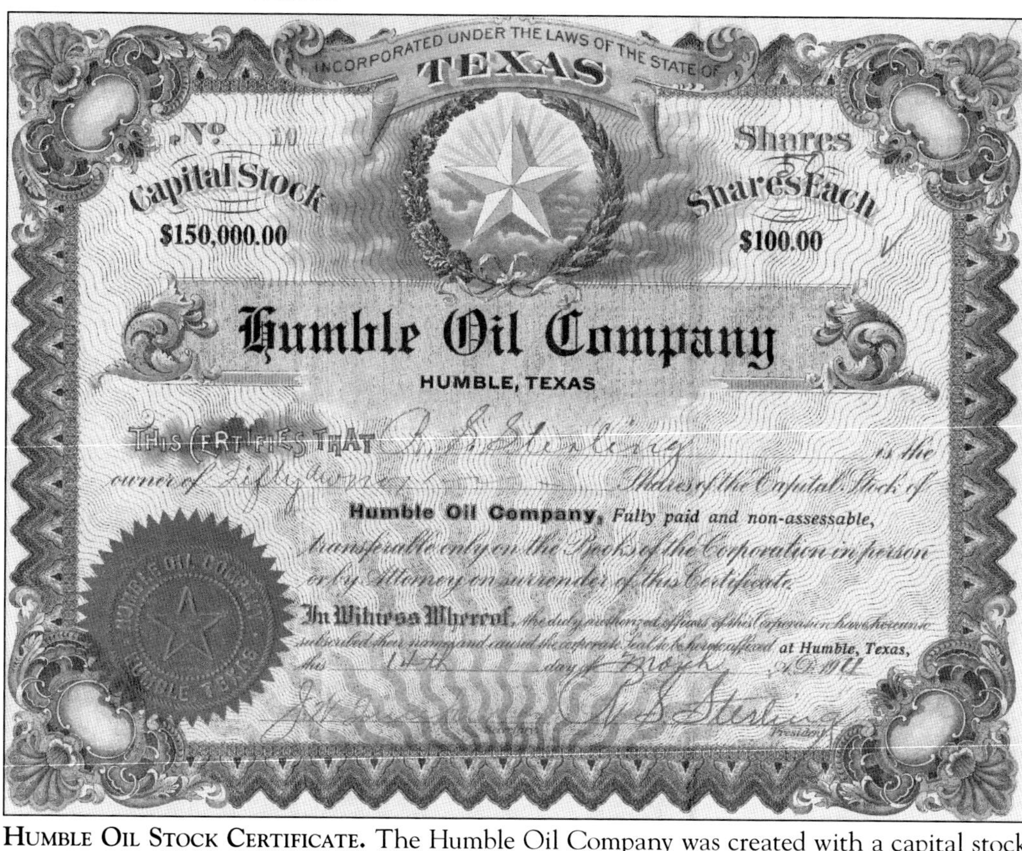

INCORPORATED UNDER THE LAWS OF THE STATE OF TEXAS

No. 10 — Shares 50

Capital Stock $150,000.00 — Shares Each $100.00

Humble Oil Company

HUMBLE, TEXAS

This Certifies That R. S. Sterling is the owner of Fifty ... Shares of the Capital Stock of Humble Oil Company, Fully paid and non-assessable, transferable only on the Books of the Corporation in person or by Attorney on surrender of this Certificate.

In Witness Whereof, the duly authorized officers of this Corporation have hereunto subscribed their names and caused the corporate Seal to be hereto affixed at Humble, Texas, this 14th day of March A.D. 1911

R. S. Sterling, President

HUMBLE OIL COMPANY — HUMBLE, TEXAS

HUMBLE OIL STOCK CERTIFICATE. The Humble Oil Company was created with a capital stock of $150,000, one-third of which belonged to Ross Sterling. Afraid of losing money, the other stockholders started selling their shares soon after the company was formed. The certificate shown here represents 50 shares of stock ($5,000) purchased by Sterling on March 14, 1911. He signed the certificate as president of the company.

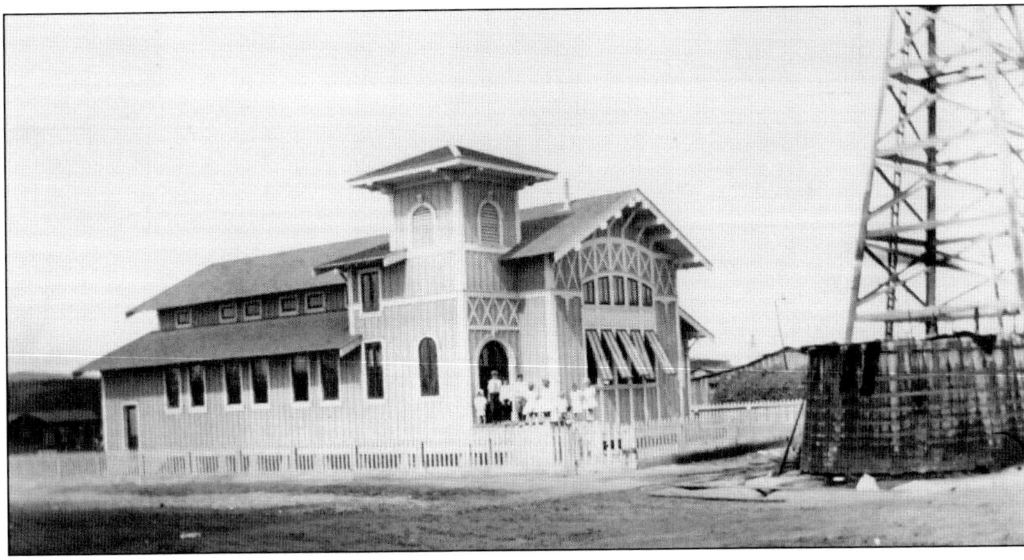

UNION CHURCH AT MOONSHINE HILL. Church services, and Sunday school services for children, at Moonshine Hill had previously been held in the Woodward School building. An increasing church membership, and a Sunday school enrollment of 150 pupils, created a need for a separate church building. The Producers Oil Company donated the land, and prominent oil companies and citizens contributed funds to build the Moonshine Hill Union Church in 1916. The church bell was provided by the firm of Girten and Bowman. The church did not have a regular pastor. Instead, ministers from different denominations occupied the pulpit every Sunday. This allowed for a service at which everyone, regardless of faith, could worship.

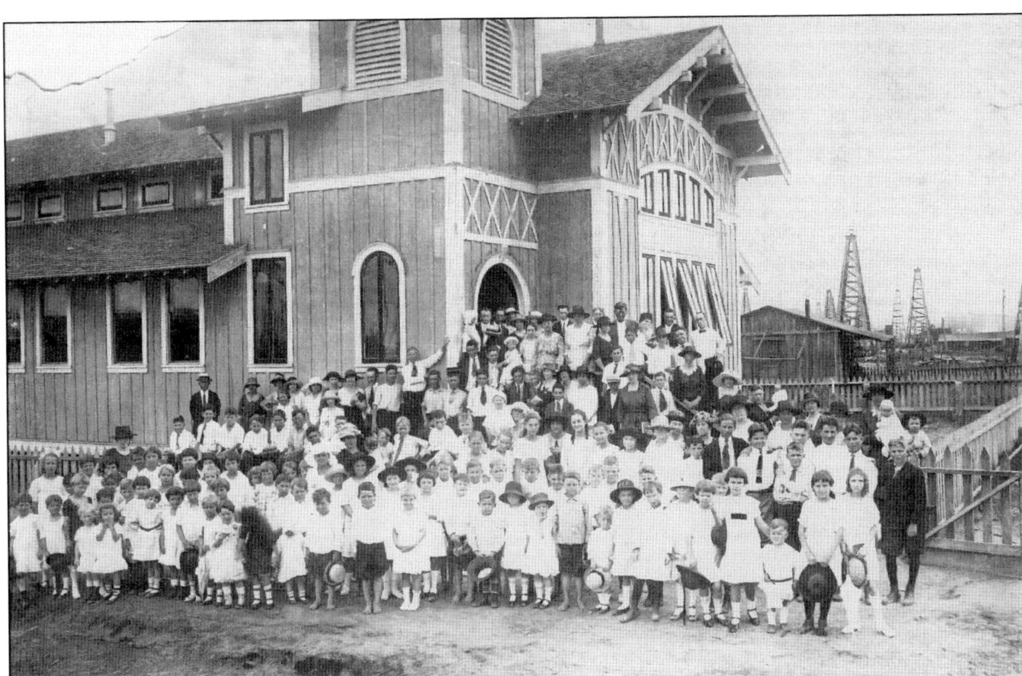

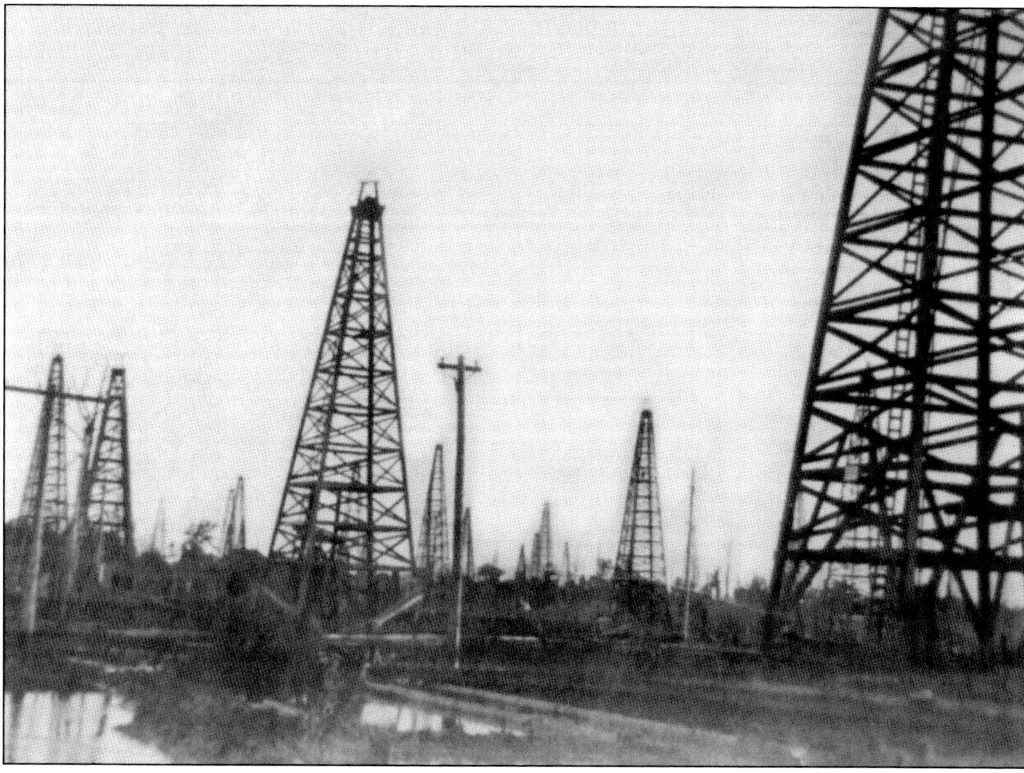

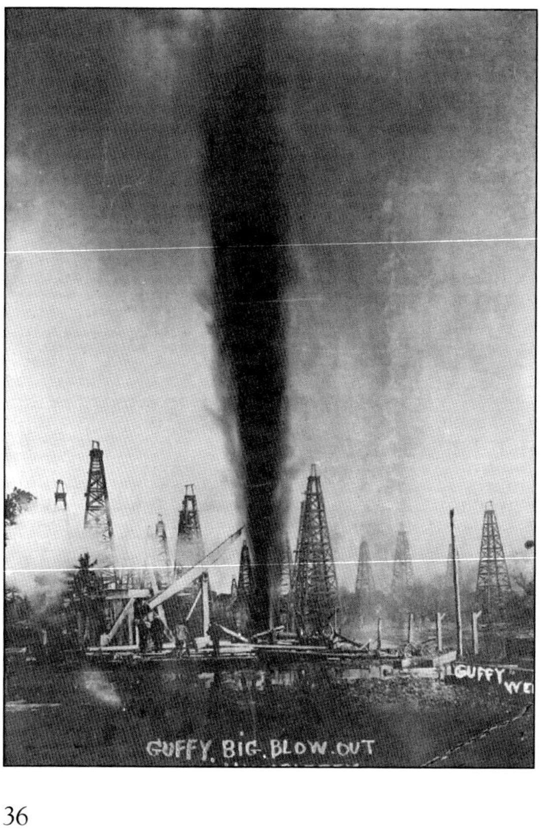

A Plethora of Derricks. During the height of the Humble oil boom, small tracts of land, called "carpet tracts," were sold to oilmen. These lots were just large enough to contain a derrick. This resulted in derricks so close together that a man could walk from one to another without ever touching the ground.

Oil Well Blowout. Oil well blowouts were common in the Humble oil field. When a well blew out, the drill bit was usually shot through the top of the derrick by the high pressure of the oil in the well. In the process, the derrick was totally destroyed. Shown here is the blowout of an oil well owned by the J.M. Guffey Company (later the Gulf Oil Company).

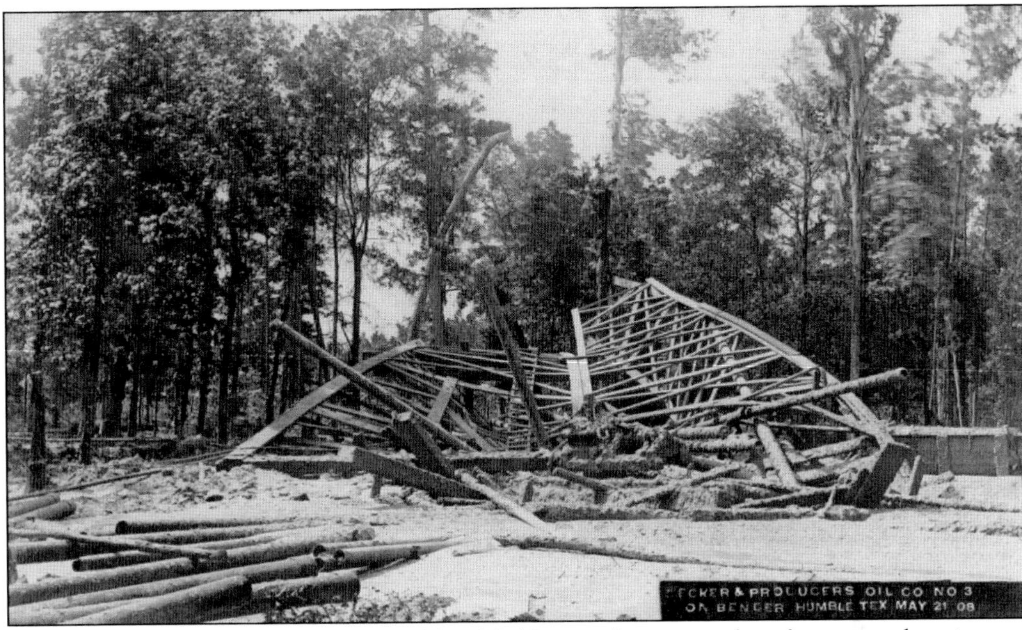

DESTROYED DERRICK, 1908. The Humble oil field was a dangerous place for men and equipment. An oil derrick could be destroyed by a blowout or through a series of unfortunate mishaps. Blowouts were typically caused by either oil being struck while under high pressure, or by a vein of natural gas being tapped. This derrick was destroyed by a high-pressure gas explosion during drilling operations.

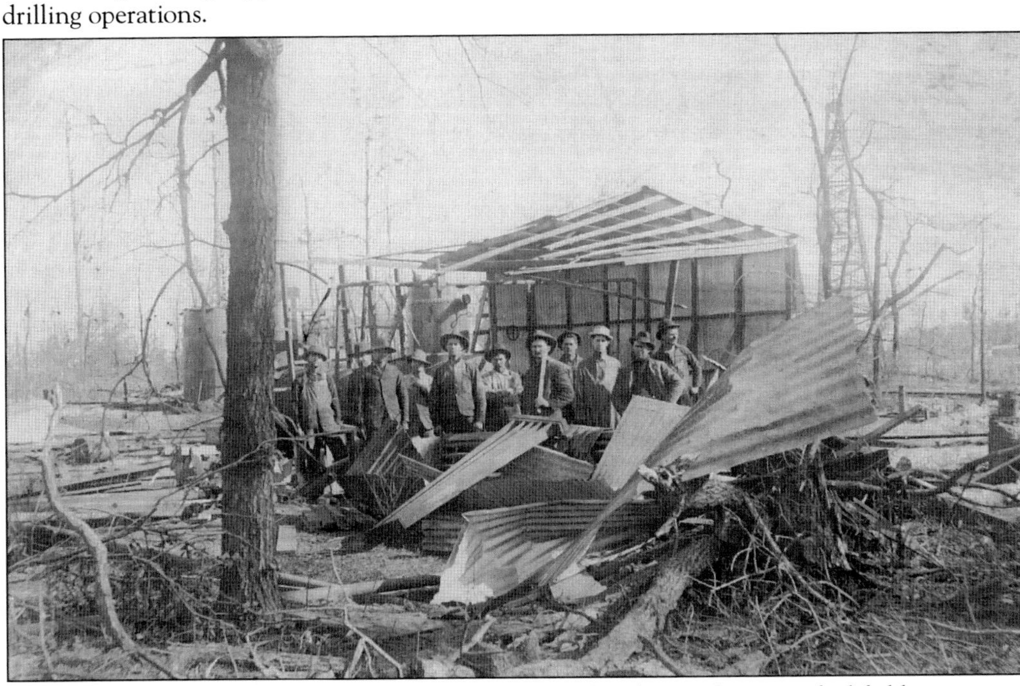

MISHAPS IN THE OIL FIELD. In the 1900s, there was no local manufacturer of oil-field equipment. Most equipment was either homemade or consisted of a piece of manufactured equipment doing a job it was not originally intended to do. Shown here is the result of a boiler explosion, which was a common occurrence.

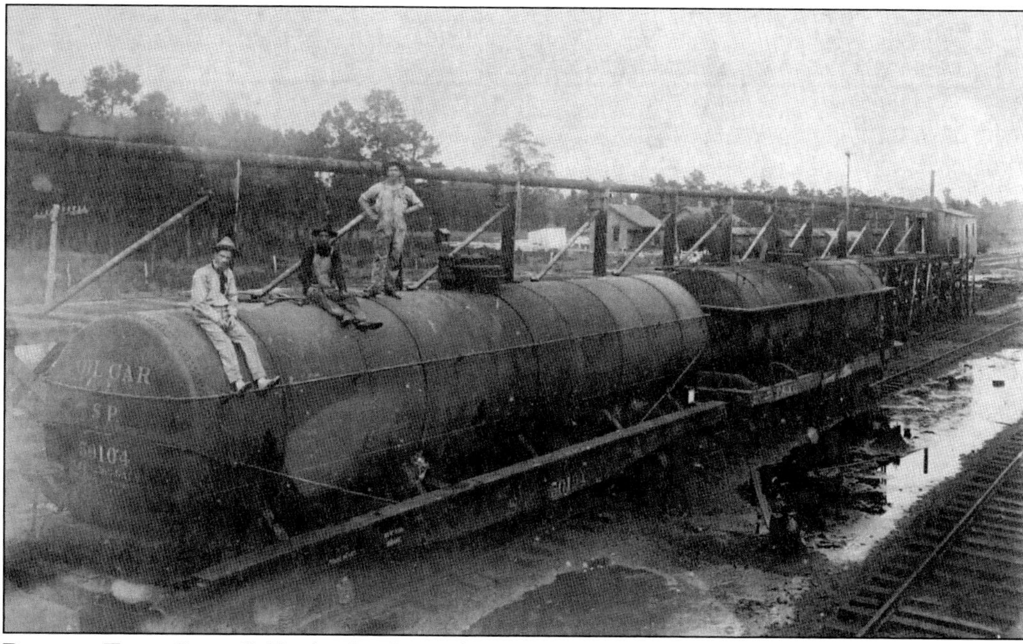

Railway Tank Cars. Oil had to be shipped to town via mule teams and then loaded into railway tank cars for transportation to the refineries. Without paved roads, getting the oil to town was a slow and tedious process. To be more efficient, oil companies eventually built pipelines to transport the oil from the field directly to the refinery.

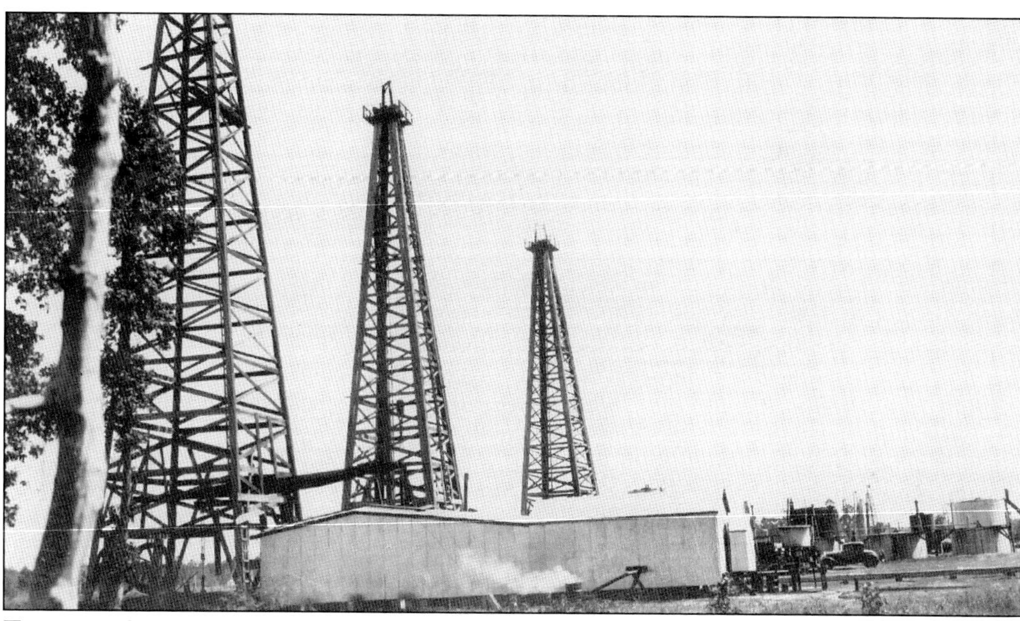

Towering Oil Derricks. Oil derricks dominated the landscape at Moonshine Hill. The wooden oil derricks from the first oil boom were eventually replaced by steel ones. The steel derricks remained at Moonshine Hill for many years after the last oil boom, rusting and falling apart before finally being dismantled.

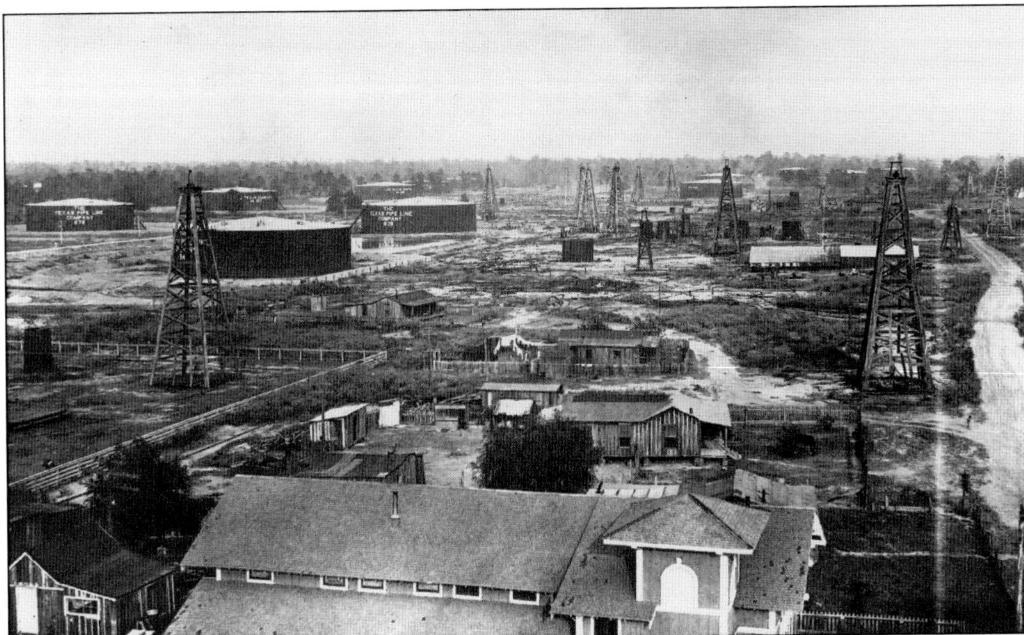

Aerial View. This photograph was taken from atop an oil derrick at Moonshine Hill. Visible in the upper part of the photograph are the large oil storage tanks belonging to the Texas Company, which is better known today as Texaco. The roof of the Union Church can be seen at the bottom of the image.

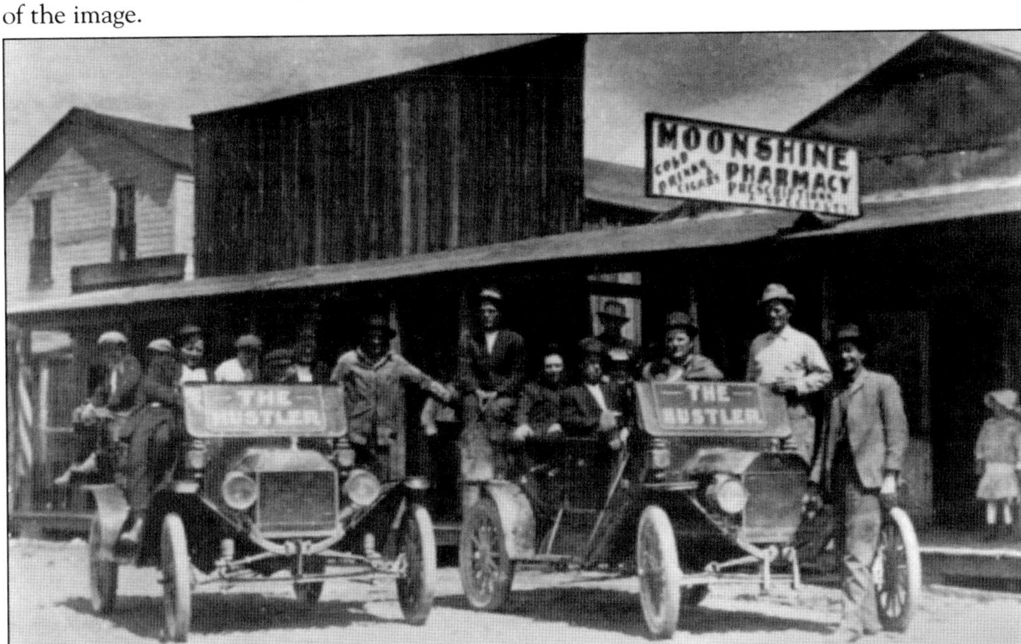

Moonshine Pharmacy. Starting around 1915, the Moonshine Pharmacy was operated by Phil Beavins and Bernard E. Rhodes. The establishment had a soda fountain, a cigar counter, and a long counter where residents could buy drugs and sundry items. Beavins served on the Humble ISD School Board from 1919 to 1923. "The Hustler" was a jitney, or taxi service, used to transport people between Humble and Moonshine Hill.

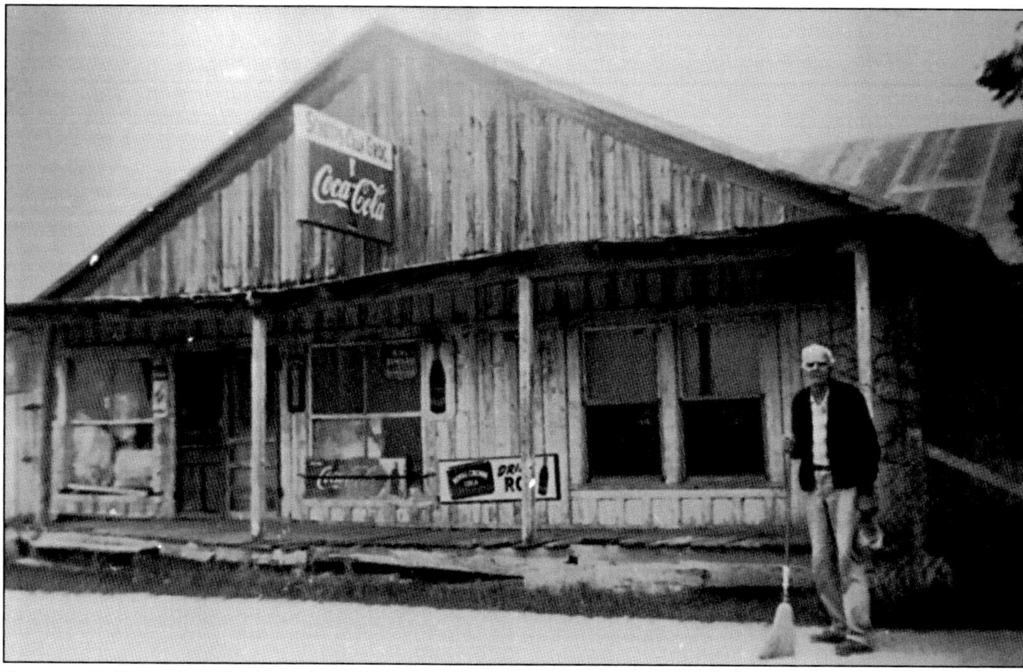

Schott's Grocery Store. A.O. Schott and Harry Rogers opened this store at Moonshine Hill in the 1920s. Residents could shop at the store, and Schott would also deliver groceries via his Model T Ford. He eventually bought out Rogers's share of the business. The Schotts also operated a store in Humble. The Moonshine Hill store was closed in 1962.

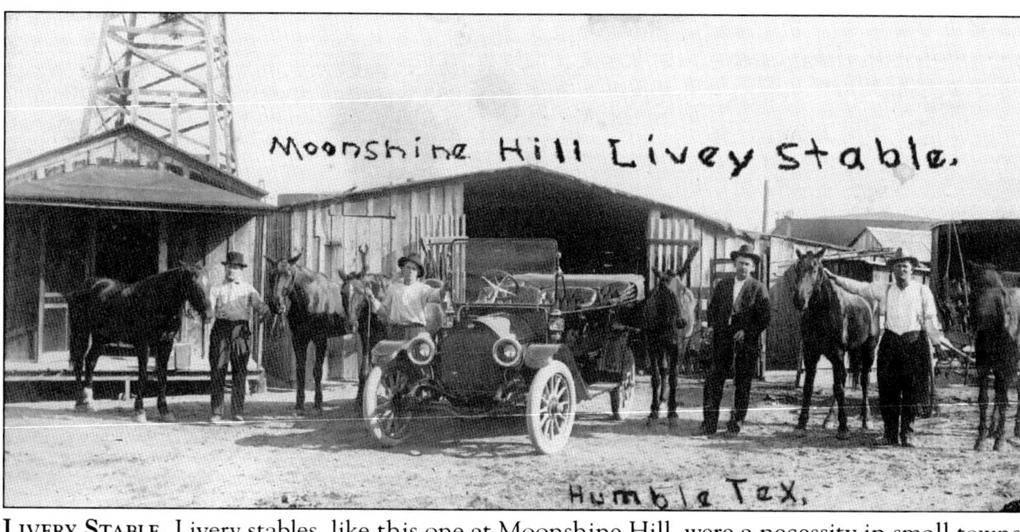

Livery Stable. Livery stables, like this one at Moonshine Hill, were a necessity in small towns. From these stables, horses, teams, and wagons could be hired. Privately owned horses could also be boarded for a short time. Prior to the common use of automobiles and the creation of concrete roads, horse-drawn wagons were the only way to move equipment across the oil fields.

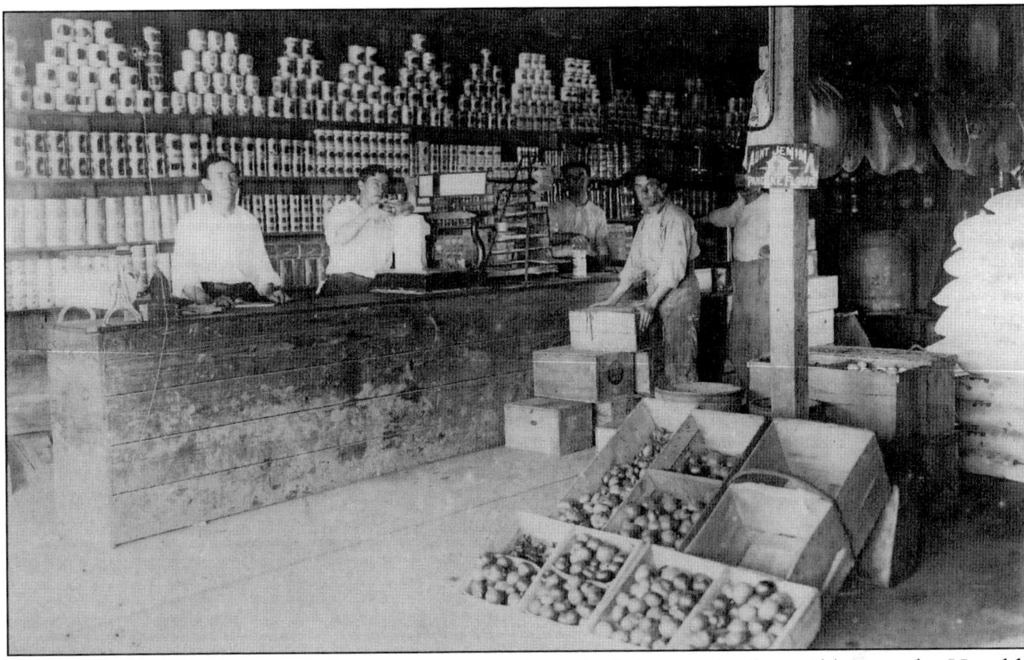

Humble Grocery Company. Located at Moonshine Hill during the first oil boom, the Humble Grocery Company was owned by Will and Morris Jamison. Most grocery stores of that era were owned by local residents, not corporations. Many products, such as coffee and tea, would come to the store in bulk, to be repackaged by the store clerk to a convenient size for the customer.

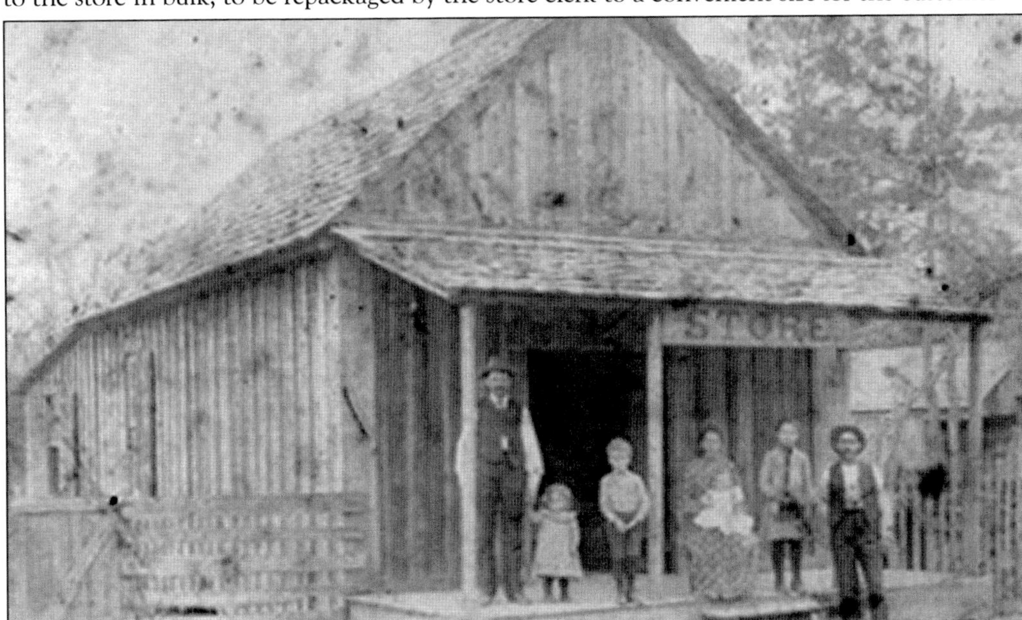

Charpiot Store. E.S. Charpiot operated a store at Moonshine Hill around 1904. He assisted Charles E. Barrett in obtaining drilling tracts in the area. Charpiot had other dealings with individuals in the gas and oil business over the years, and he formed the Evening Star Oil Company of Texas in 1908, which was eventually absorbed by other oil companies. (Courtesy of Margaret Byron.)

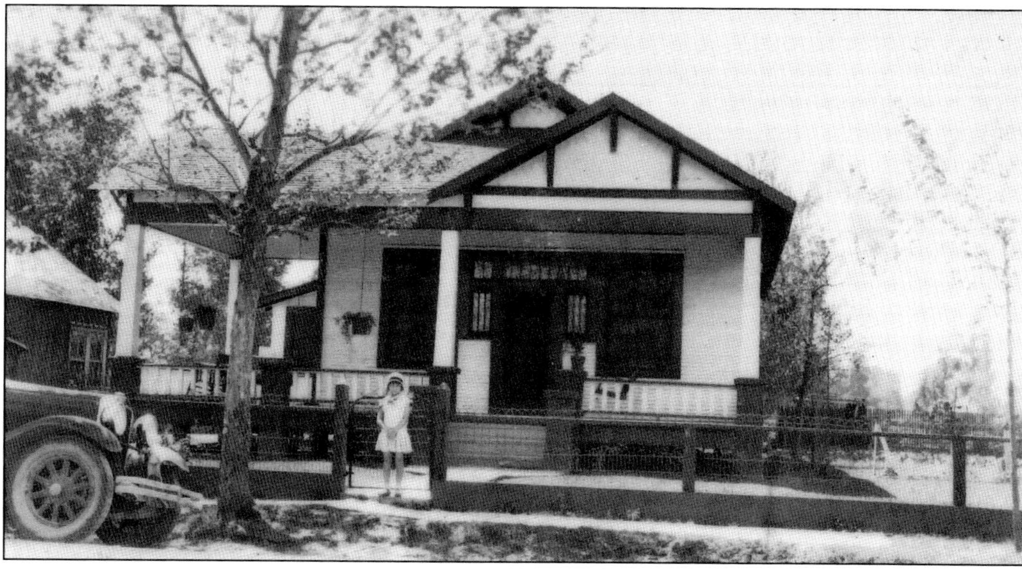

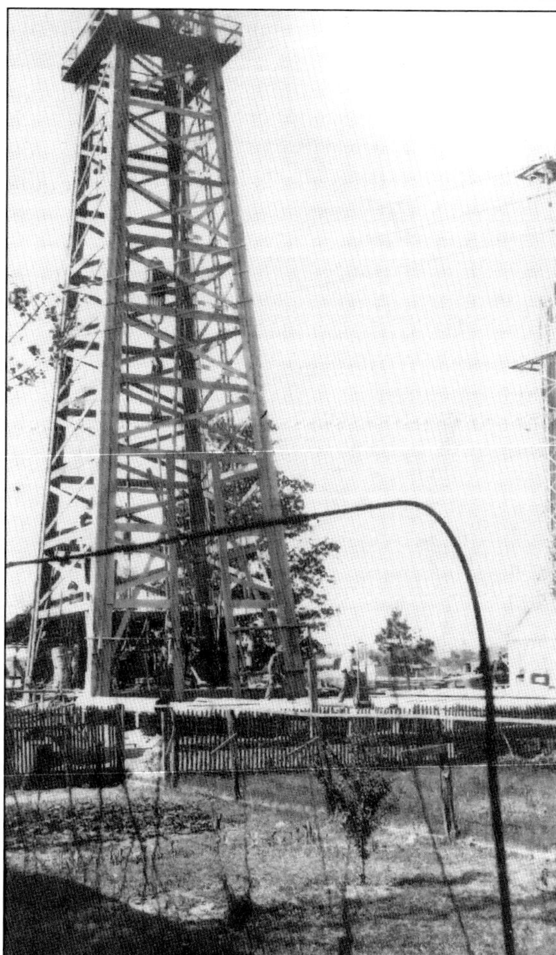

Oil All Around. Oil wells were not limited to Moonshine Hill. They were all over the town. The Pursley family owned and operated the Humble Pharmacy. Their home (above) was on Staiti Street in the downtown area. A visitor walking out the back door would see an oil well (left). The wells were very noisy and ran all hours of the day and night. The installation and operation of an oil well usually destroyed everything around it (landscaping, gardens, etc.). However, residents tolerated it while dreaming of riches to come. Most wells turned out to be dry.

Three

Businesses

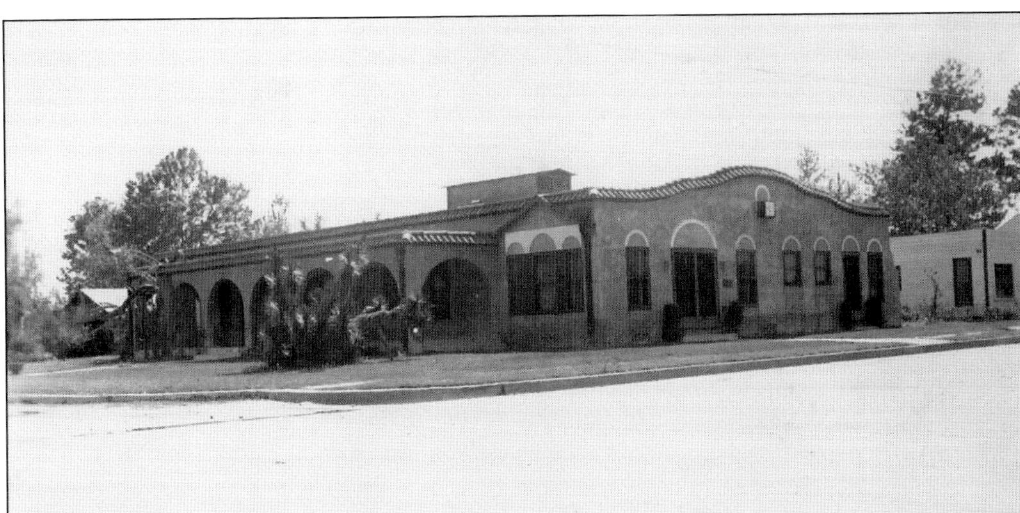

Humble Funeral Home. Established in 1932 by Kelcy and Leona Isenberg, this funeral home opened in a small residence on First Street and Avenue D. In 1936, it was moved to a better facility in the 700 block of Main Street (shown here). The Isenbergs opened the Humble Flower Shop (white building on the right) next door in 1938. Kelcy Isenberg served on the Humble ISD School Board for many years.

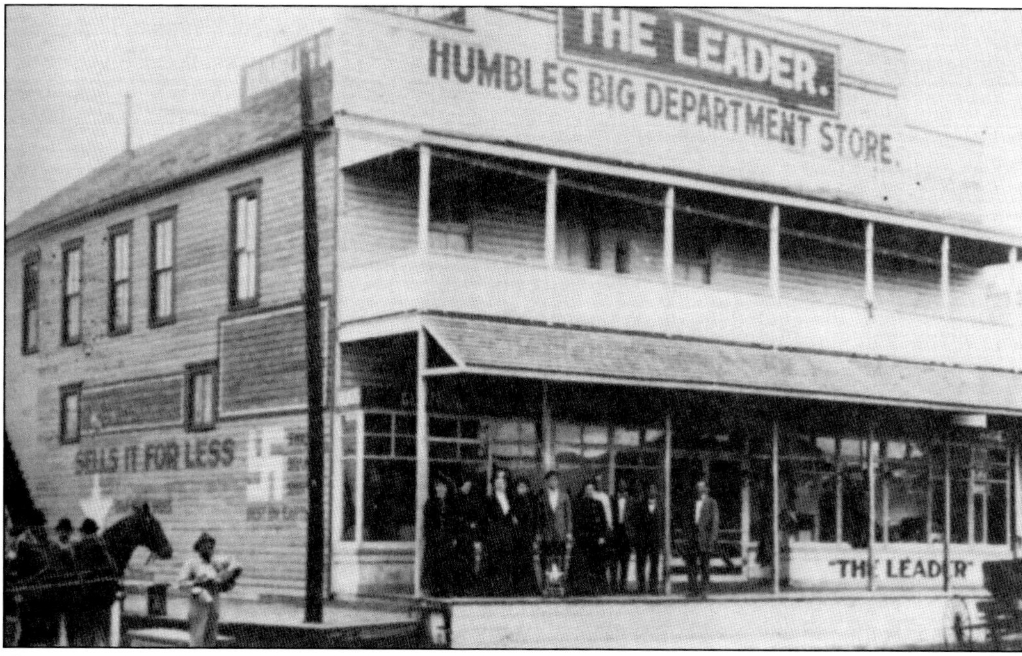

THE LEADER. Humble's largest department store during the early years was The Leader, established in 1903 and operated by the Grossman family. It later became the J. Grossman Dry Goods Store. The building was located on the corner of Barrett Street (Main Street) and Avenue B, where the Humble Bank State Building was built after 1912. (Courtesy of the James Tull Chapter of the Daughters of the American Revolution.)

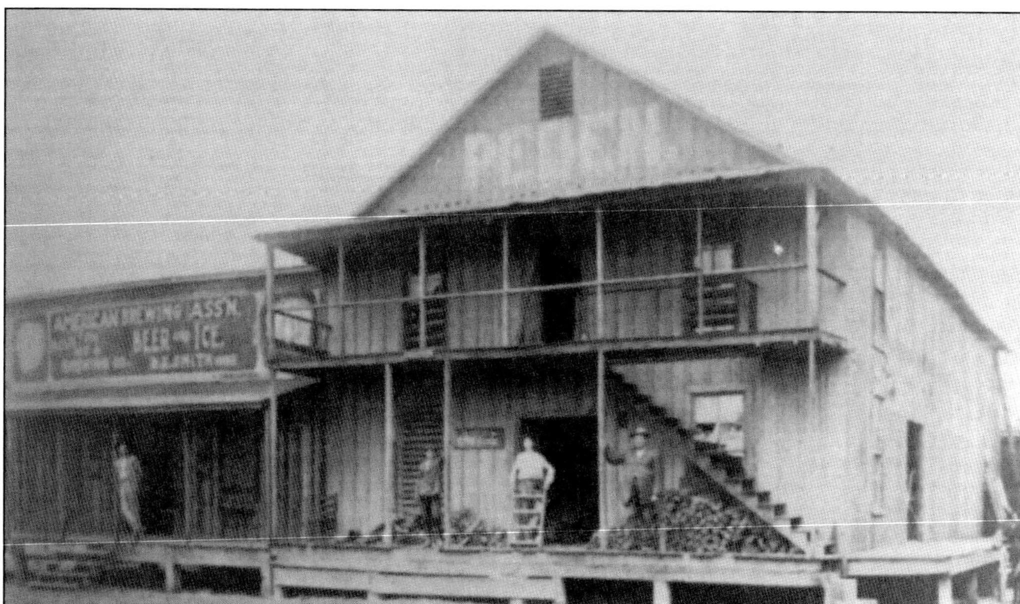

ROSS STERLING FEED STORE. Ross Sterling was operating feed stores in three other oil boomtowns before he came to Humble. In 1904, he purchased several lots in downtown Humble and opened up a store under the name R.S. Sterling & Co., Grain and Hay. (Courtesy of the James Tull Chapter of the Daughters of the American Revolution.)

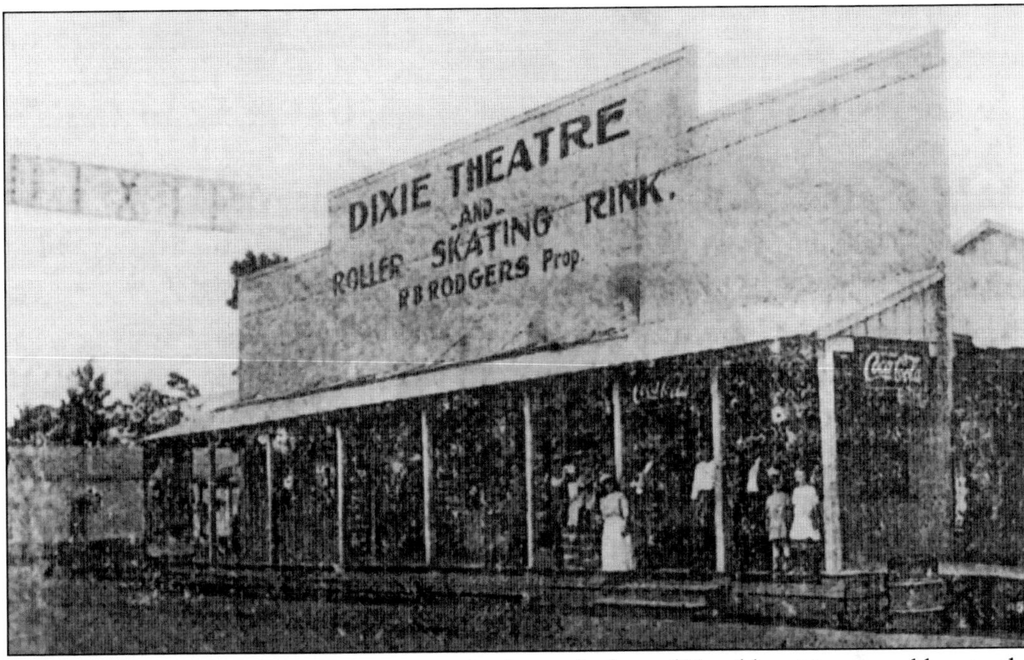

Dixie Theatre, 1912. For entertainment in the early days of Humble, citizens could go to the Dixie Theatre and Roller Skating Rink, owned by R.B. Rodgers. The name was changed to the Star Theatre in the 1920s. When E.N. Collins was the owner in the 1930s, it became known as the Lindell Theatre.

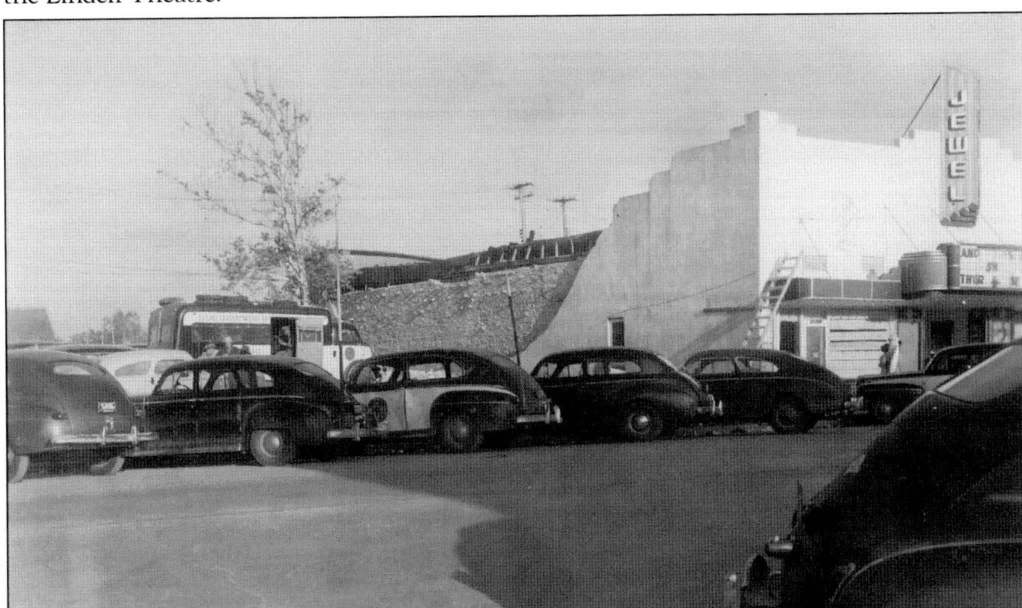

Jewel Theatre in Texas City, 1947. In 1947, E.N. Collins sold Humble's Lindell Theatre to the Long Theatre Circuit. That same year, the Jewel Theatre in Texas City, also owned by the Long Theatre Circuit, was damaged during the 1947 Texas City Disaster. The circuit's owner had the Jewel Theatre sign moved to Humble. (Courtesy of Special Collections, University of Houston Libraries.)

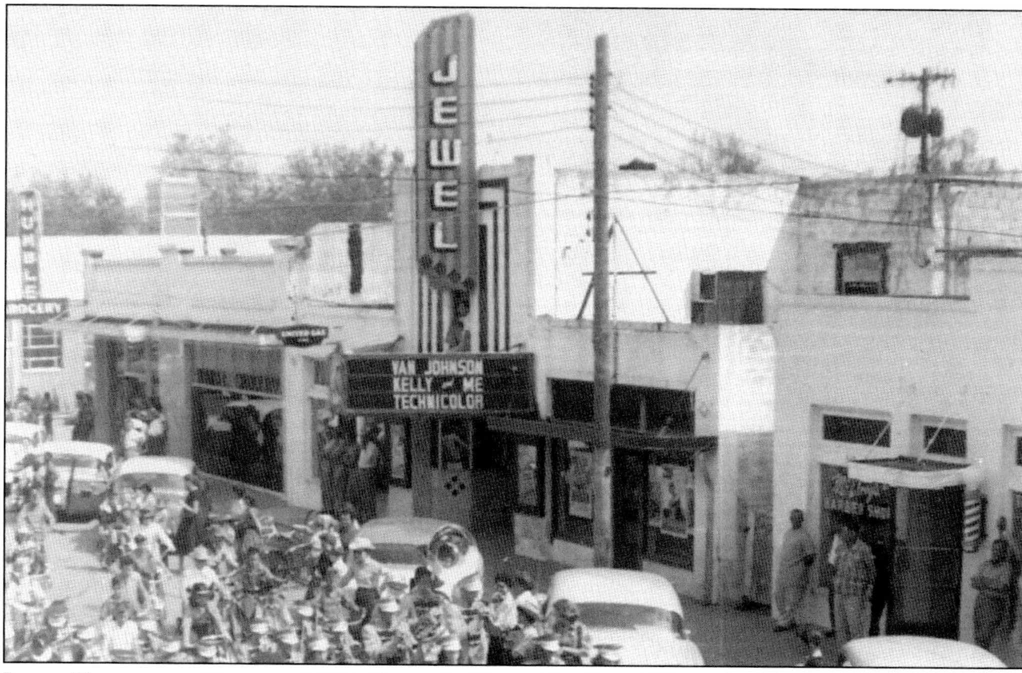

Jewel Theatre in Humble, 1957. Once the Texas City Jewel Theatre sign was moved to Humble, the Lindell Theatre was renamed the Jewel Theatre. In this photograph, a parade in Humble passes by the Jewel Theatre in 1957. The marquee announces that *Kelly and Me*, starring Van Johnson, is showing.

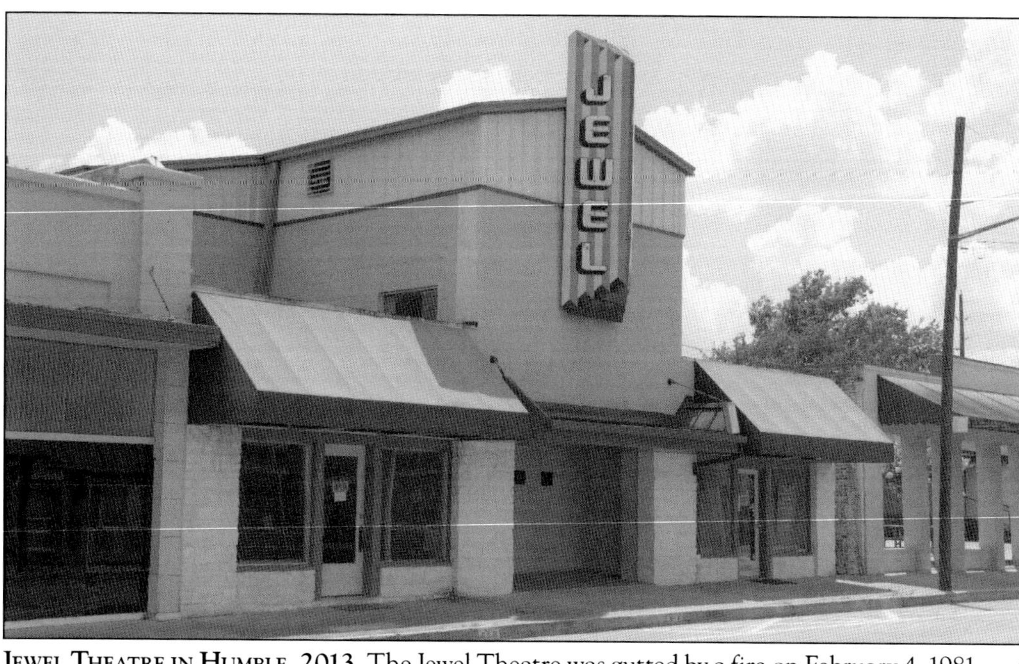

Jewel Theatre in Humble, 2013. The Jewel Theatre was gutted by a fire on February 4, 1981, and was eventually remodeled for use by businesses. Humble businesses and citizens worked to restore the original sign, and it was again lighting up Main Street in 2007. (Courtesy of Scott Meaux.)

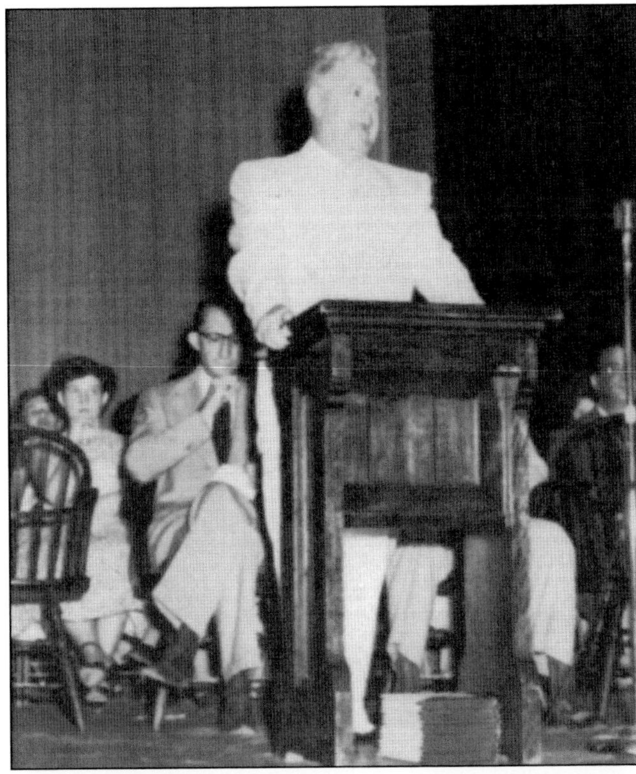

Robert Everett Smith. R.E. Smith (1894–1973) attended the Humble School, but quit by 1911 to work in the oil fields. He eventually became successful in oil, real estate, and cattle ranching. He was instrumental in acquiring the Colt .45s baseball team (later the Astros) for Houston. Smith was awarded an honorary degree from Humble in 1948. He died in 1973 with a fortune of $500 million.

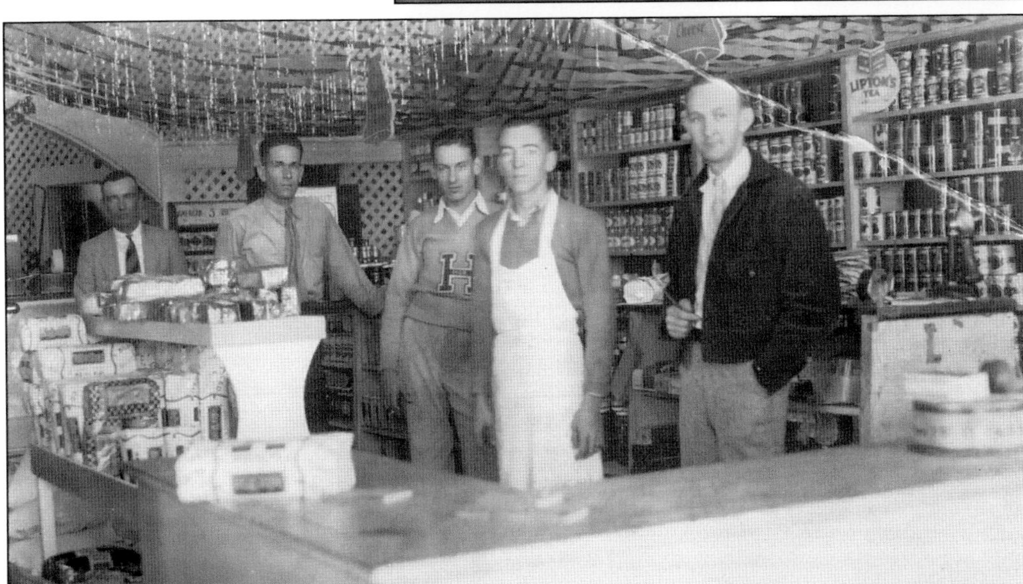

Schott's Grocery. In July 1929, Hilton Schott, with the help of his father, purchased the Red and White Grocery Store on the corner of Main Street and Avenue C. H.F. Bozarth ran the meat market in the store. Pictured from left to right are Hilton Schott, Lennon F. Timme, Joe L. Koinm, Billy Lomax, and Chester Johnson.

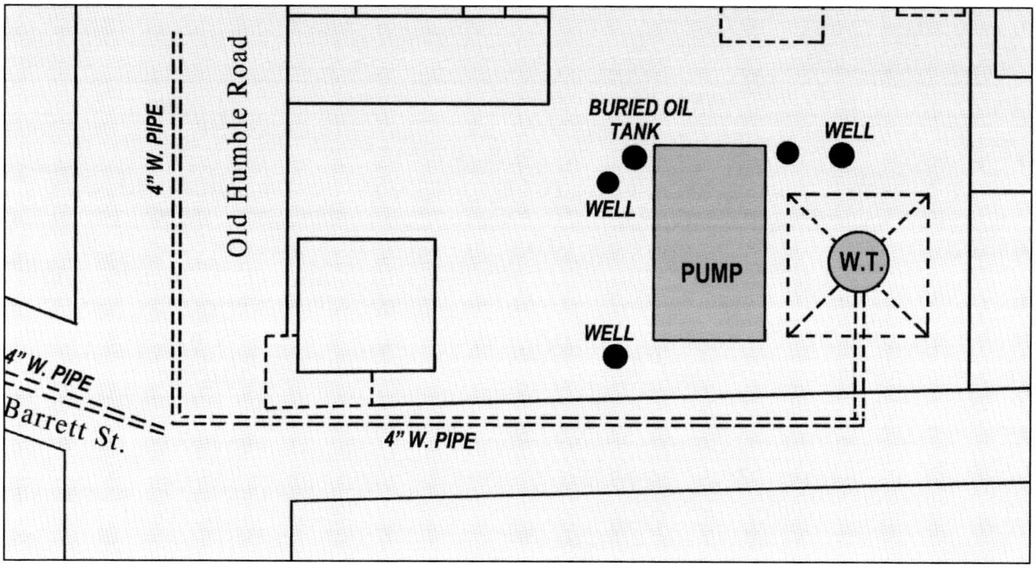

Humble Water Works. The 1926 map above shows the Humble Water Works, located on Barrett Street (Main Street), where the Humble Swimming Pool is now located. Nick Lambrecht was president and superintendent, and Alfred Lambrecht was the general manager. A pumping station (pictured below) was used to move water from the well up to the top of the water tower. From the tower, gravity moved water through pipes to different locations around town, typically to very affluent customers that could afford to have pipes installed at their homes. Residents without water pipes could purchase barrels of water from Lambrecht for $3. The City of Humble took over water operations in 1933.

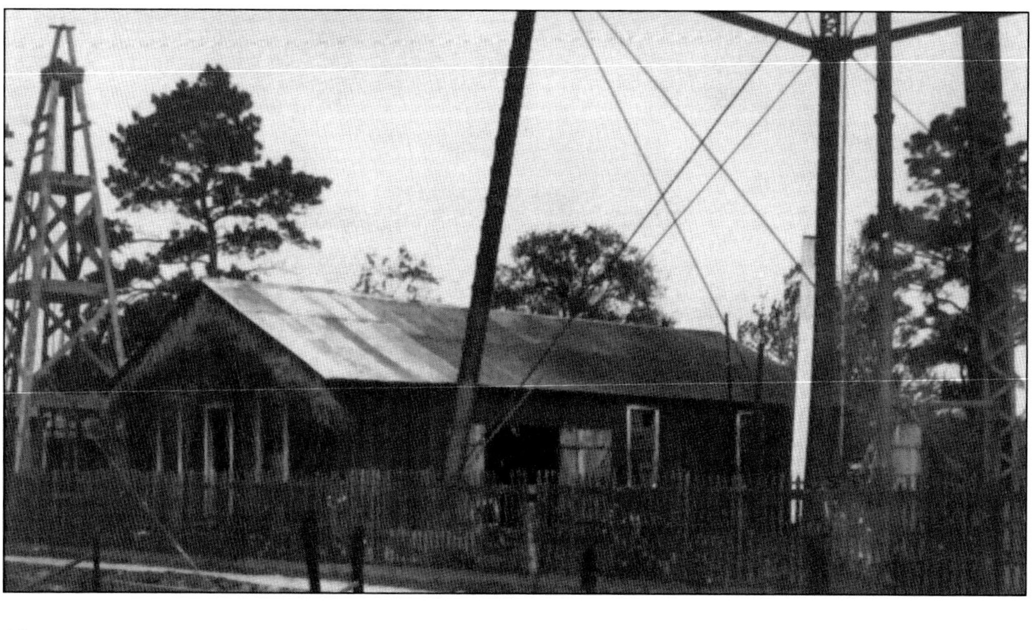

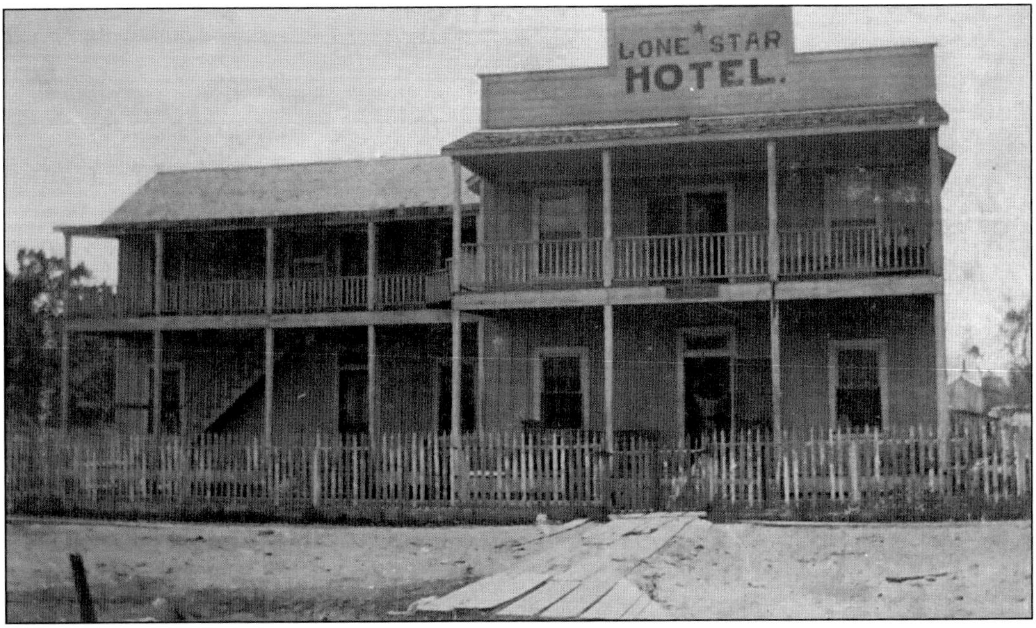

Lone Star Hotel, 1917. This hotel was built in the early 1900s, during the oil boom, to accommodate the influx of people to Humble and Moonshine Hill. It was located on the west side of the railroad tracks, south of Barrett Street (Main Street). Owner Martha Presswood was born in 1863 in Louisiana. She married a Mr. Shelton and, at a later date, married Andy Sayers. After Sayers, died, Martha married a Mr. O'Connor. Known as Martha O'Connor by the Humble residents, she ran the Lone Star Hotel until her death in December 1949. The garden at the rear of the hotel (below) provided fresh produce for the guests. The hotel was demolished in the 1940s, and a large, two-story brick home was constructed on the site by Martha's son, Matt Sayers.

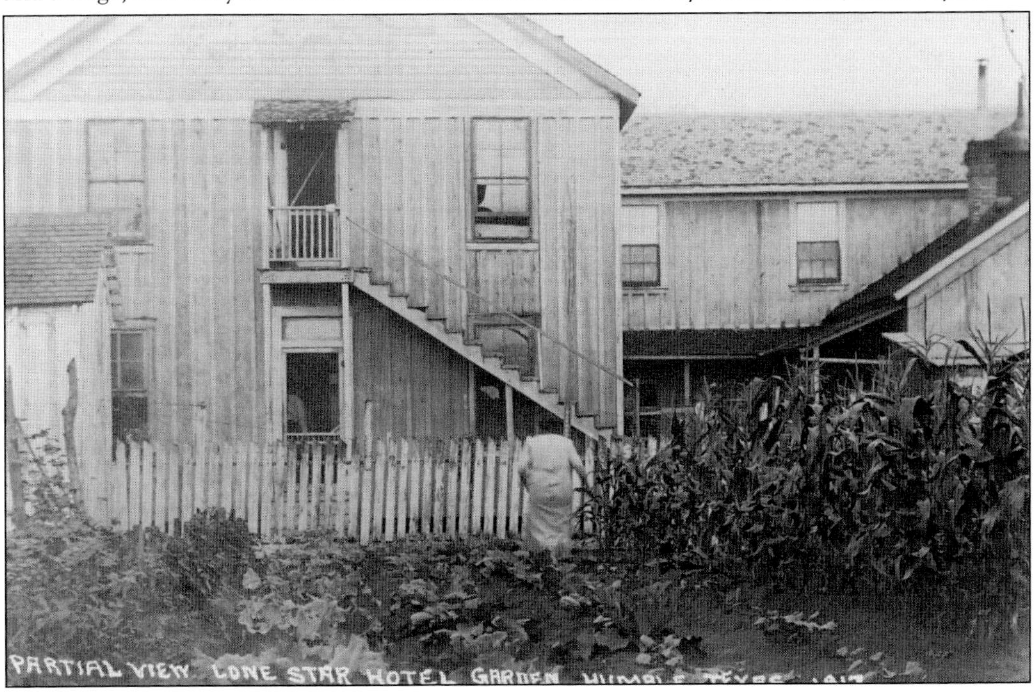

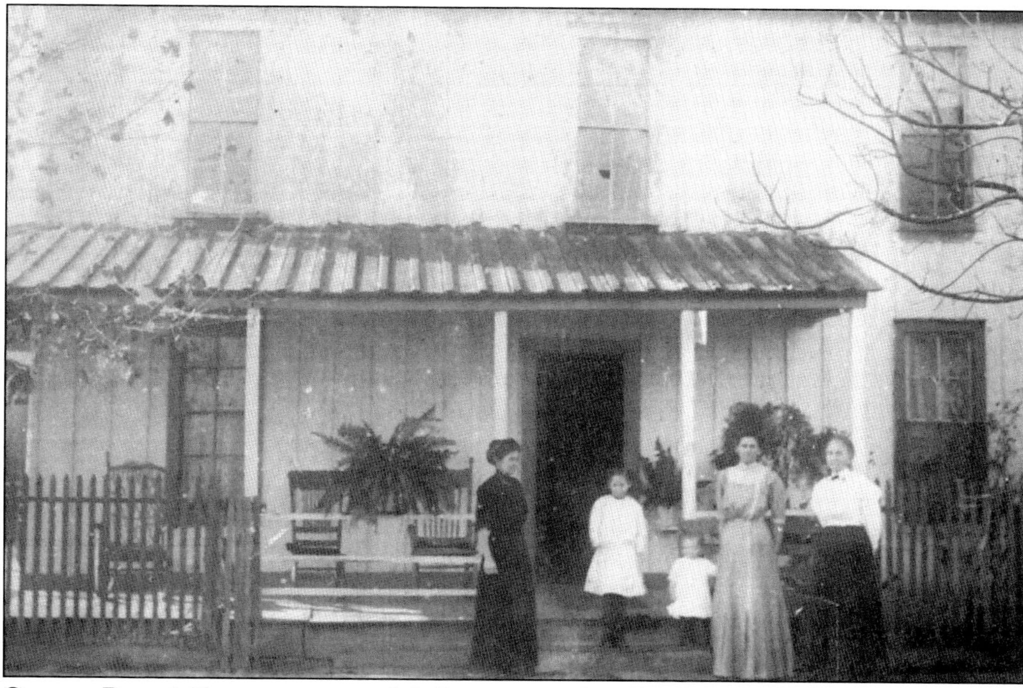

GRANNY PAYNE'S BOARDINGHOUSE. Ada Payne was widowed in June 1900, at 49 years of age. She purchased lots on Granberry Street and had a boardinghouse built. She managed the establishment until her death in September 1938. Pictured from left to right are Maude Heard, Wilma Hare, Mildred Hare, May Hare, and Ada Payne.

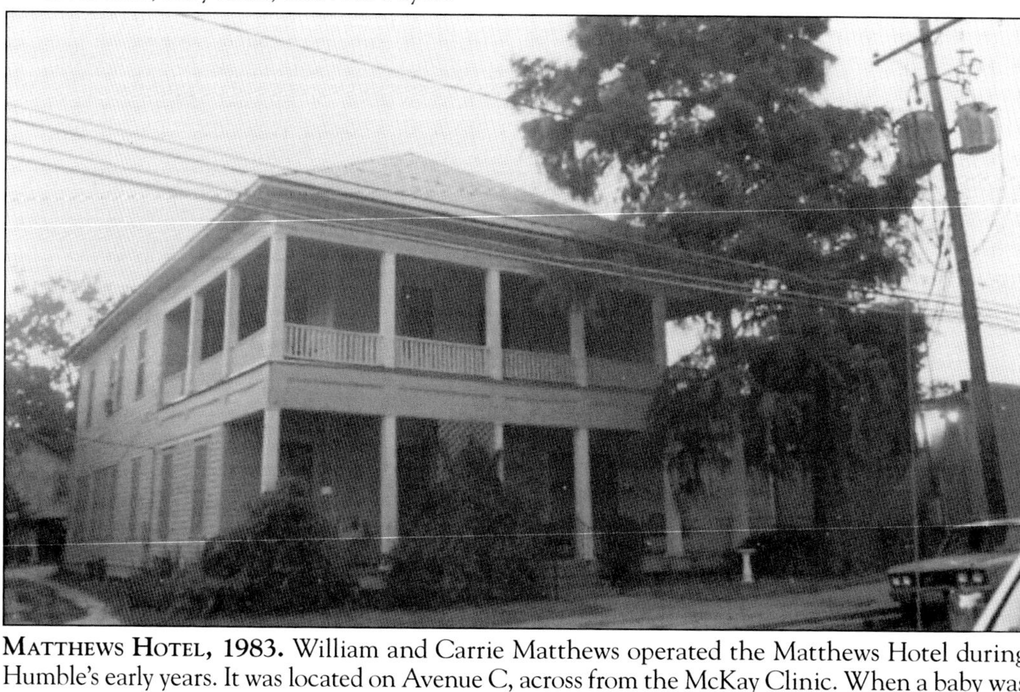

MATTHEWS HOTEL, 1983. William and Carrie Matthews operated the Matthews Hotel during Humble's early years. It was located on Avenue C, across from the McKay Clinic. When a baby was delivered at the clinic, the mother would stay the night in the clinic, and meals would be brought over from the Matthews Hotel. Later, this became the home of Mr. and Mrs. H.V. Wooten.

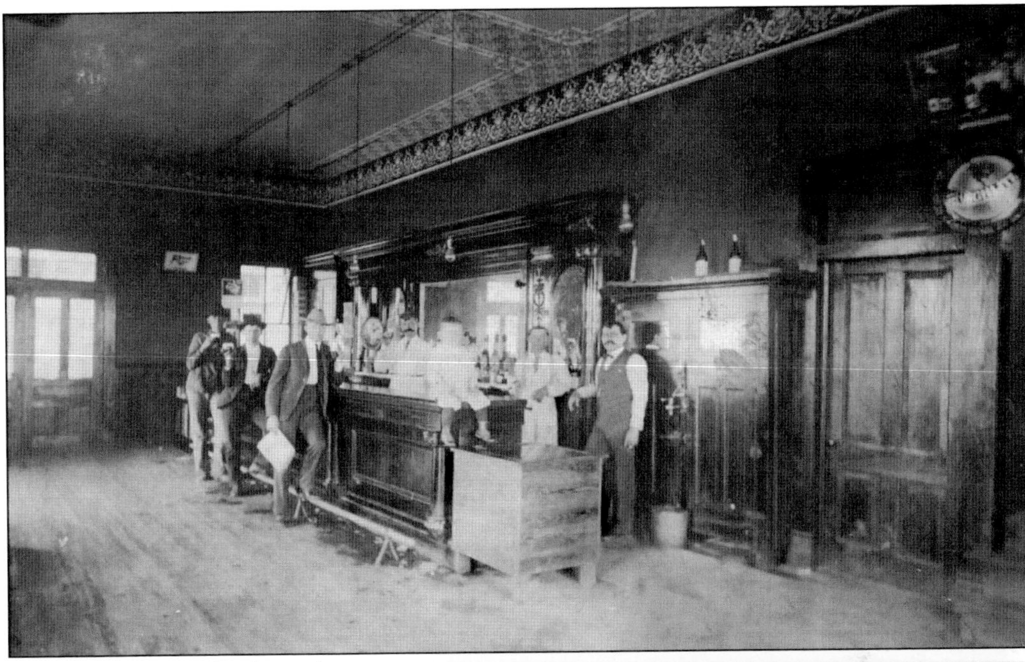

SALOONS. During the first oil boom in Humble, the town was infested with saloons. The number of saloons has been reported to be as high as 76 on Barrett Street (Main Street) alone. Many oil-field workers took refuge from their long work hours by visiting saloons before and after work, and the town doctors were kept busy by sewing up men injured in bar fights.

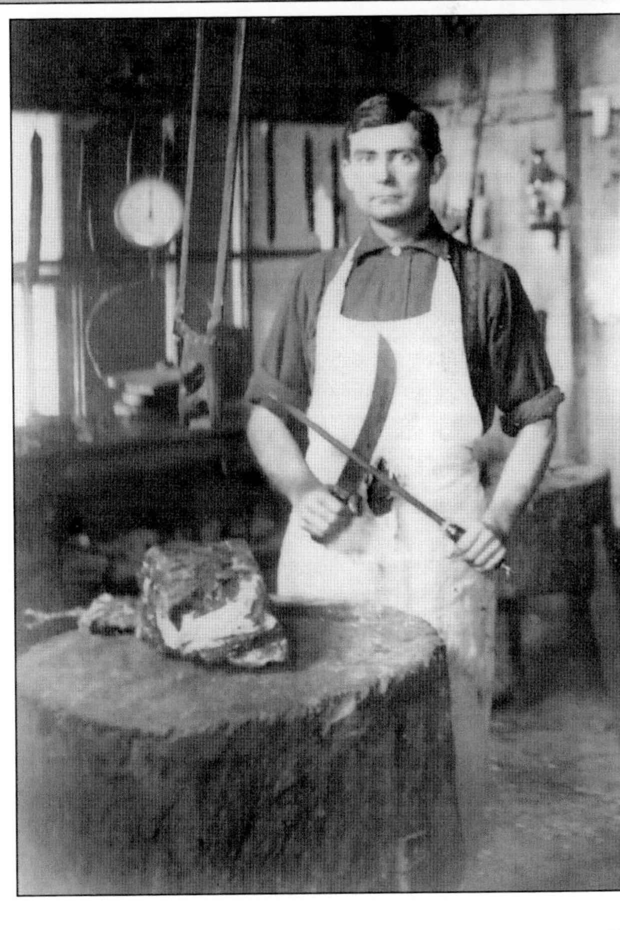

HORACE FRANCIS BOZARTH. Bozarth (1882–1960) was a vice president of the Humble State Bank under Ross Sterling. Bozarth worked as a butcher in several stores and owned a meat market in the McLaughlin Building, which was destroyed by a fire in February 1918. He married Amna Emily Isaacks, a daughter of E.M. "Booge" Isaacks. Bozarth served on the Humble ISD School Board from 1919 to 1923.

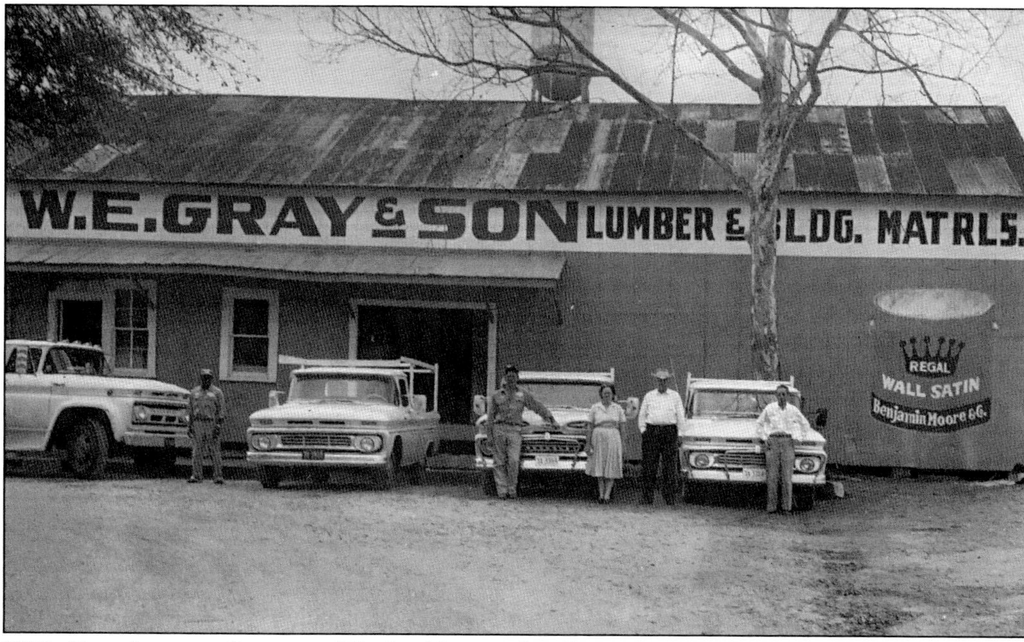

W.E. Gray Lumber Company. The building in the above photograph, originally the R.S. Smith Feed Store, later became the Lindley Lumber Company, which was managed by W.E. Gray. It was located on Railroad Avenue, next to the tracks, where the City of Humble Public Works department now stands. W.E. Gray served as the mayor of Humble in 1945, was president of the Humble Fat Stock Show & Rodeo in 1963, and was president of the Humble ISD School Board for many years. In the below photograph are, from left to right, Jack Fatheree, Max Ellis, Dale Gray, and W.E. Gray.

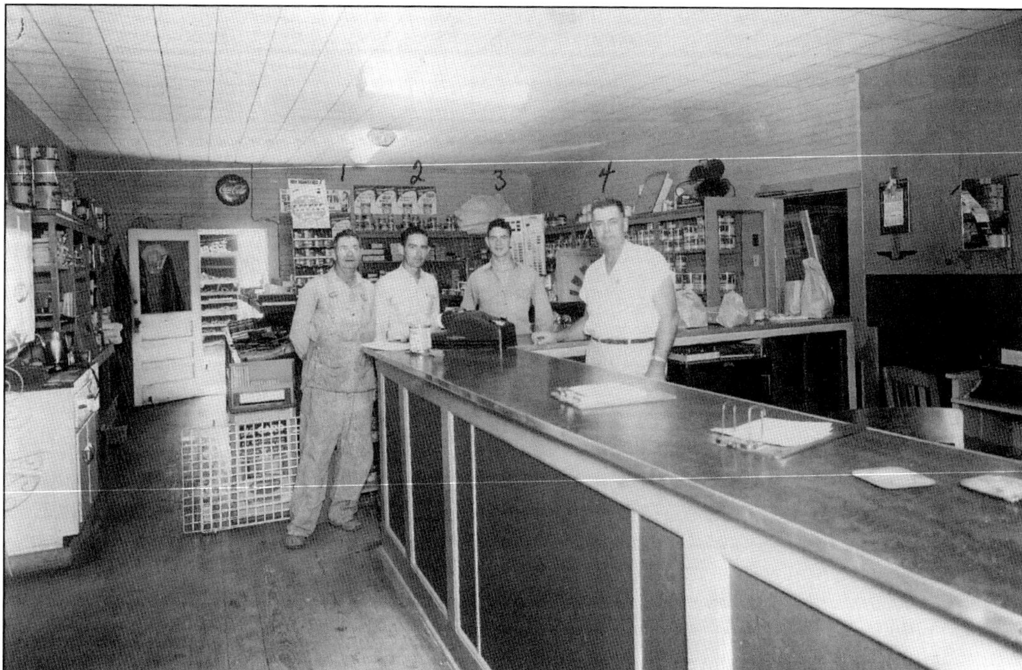

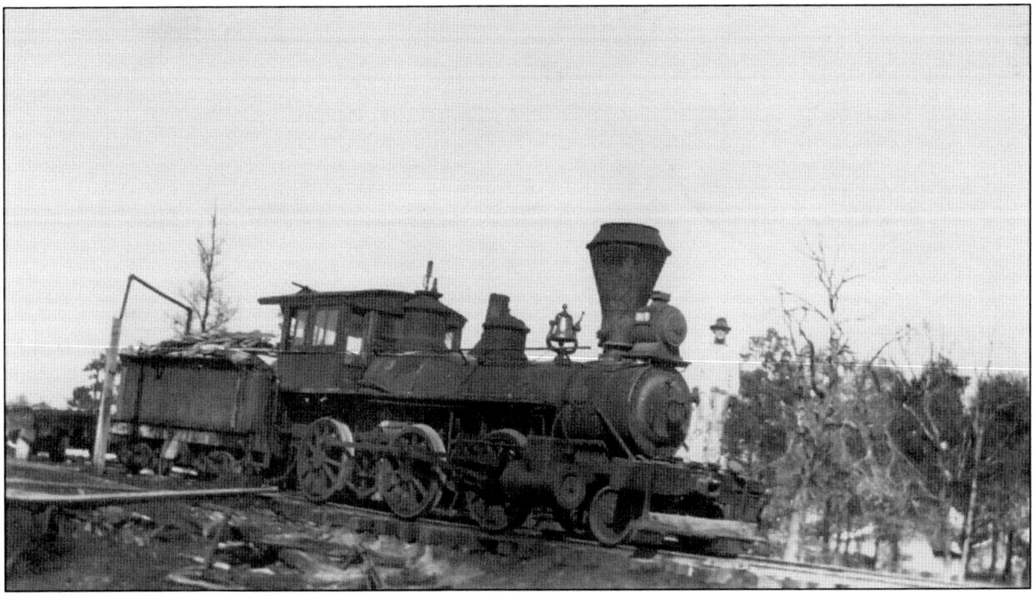

C. Bender & Sons Log Train. Charles Bender operated his sawmill in Humble under the name of C. Bender & Co., and later as Bender & Sons. His log trains roamed the countryside, gathering trees for lumber. After the death of Charles Bender in 1906, the company became Bender Bros. Frank Bender and Eugene Bender constructed the 10-story Bender Hotel in downtown Houston, which later became the San Jacinto Hotel.

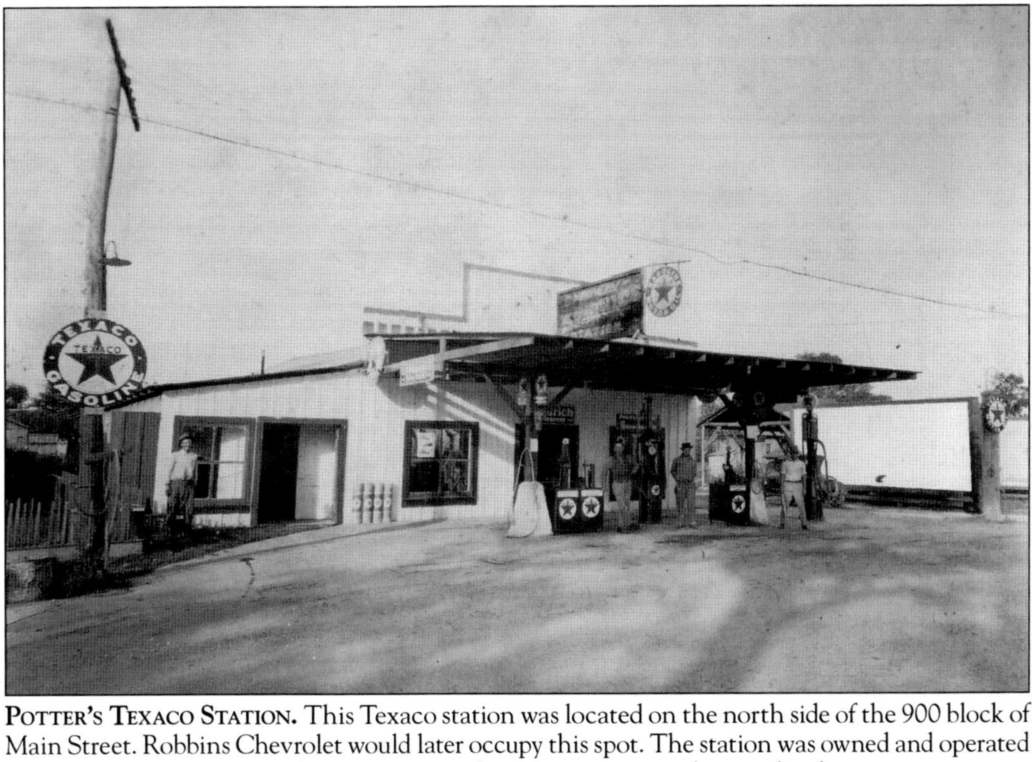

Potter's Texaco Station. This Texaco station was located on the north side of the 900 block of Main Street. Robbins Chevrolet would later occupy this spot. The station was owned and operated by Lewis Potter in 1926 and 1927. Potter is the center man standing under the awning.

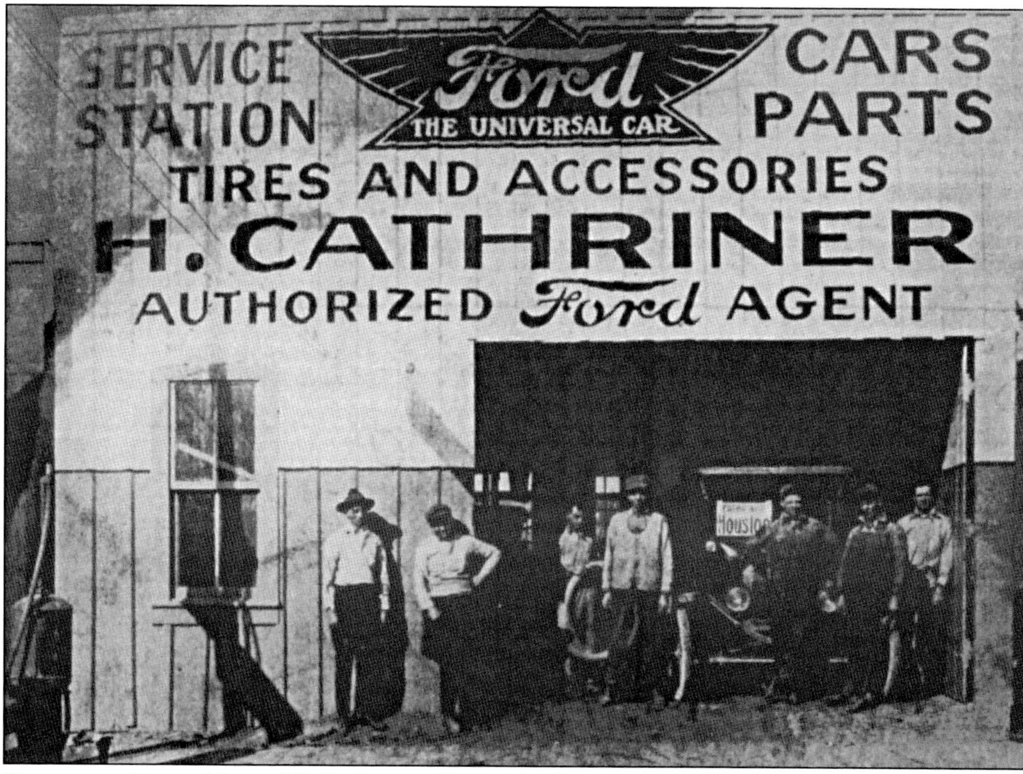

CATHRINER FORD. Henry W. Cathriner (1880–1966) moved to Humble in 1906 and opened an automobile repair shop. In 1911, he started a passenger-carrying business between Humble and Houston. Cathriner opened a Ford dealership in Humble in 1913, one of the first Ford dealerships in Harris County. Mrs. Cathriner acted as the parts manager. He expanded and opened additional Ford dealerships in Crosby, Baytown, and Goose Creek.

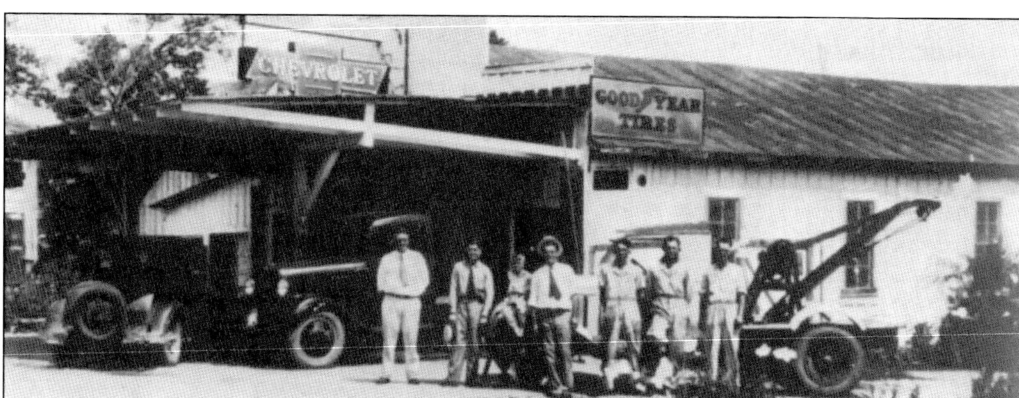

ROBBINS CHEVROLET, 1932. Robbins Chevrolet began as a Chevrolet dealership in Coldspring, Texas, in 1928. It was owned by William Cleveland Robbins, Sam Roberts, and Ed White. The dealership was brought to Humble in 1932 and was located on Barrett Street (Main Street), near the Old Humble Road (now South Houston Avenue). By 1935, Robbins had bought out Roberts and White.

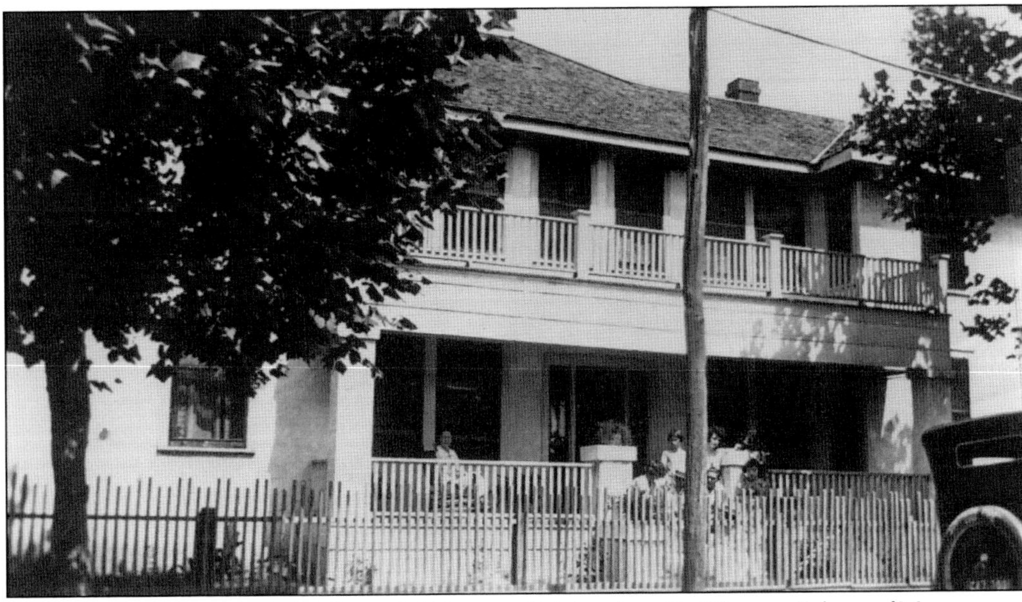

Falvey Hospital. In 1918, Dr. Jerry C. Falvey and his brother, Dr. Thomas Falvey, of Montgomery County built the Falvey Hospital at the corner of Higgins Street and Avenue D. In 1920, Dr. James Dameron and Dr. Haden McKay Sr. acquired and operated the facility as the McKay-Dameron Hospital. Ray and John Tooke purchased the building in 1924 and turned it into a teachers' dormitory. At one time, 15 female teachers lived in the building.

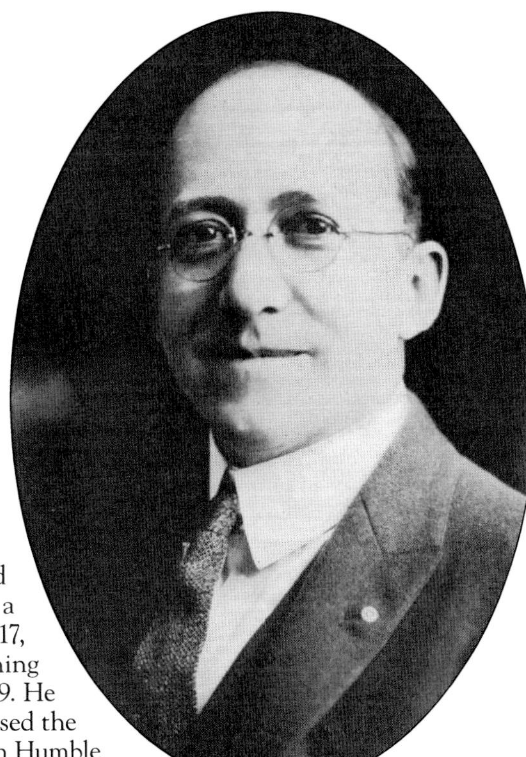

Dr. James H. Dameron. Dr. Dameron moved his family to Moonshine Hill in 1915, leaving a successful medical practice in Mississippi. In 1917, he served in the Army Medical Corps. Returning home, he moved his family to Humble in 1919. He and his cousin, Dr. Haden McKay Sr., purchased the Falvey hospital in 1920. Dameron moved from Humble to Orange in 1923.

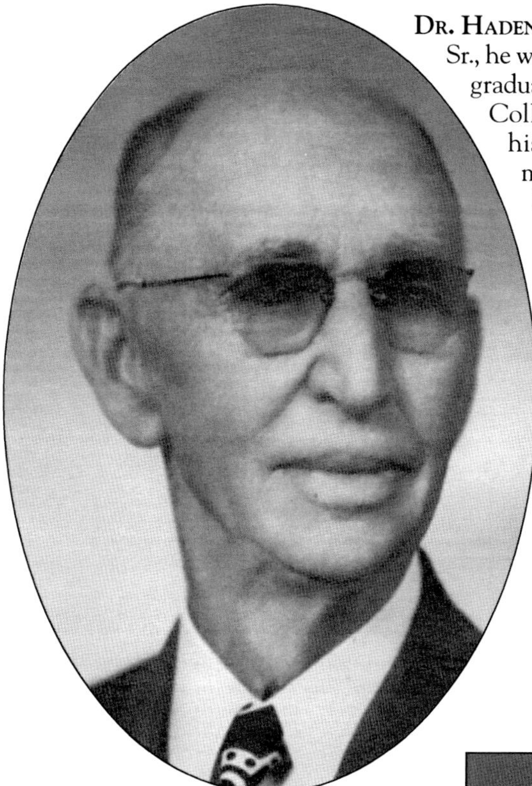

DR. HADEN EDWARDS MCKAY II. Referred to as Dr. McKay Sr., he was born in Mississippi, the son of a physician. He graduated from the University of Louisville Medical College in 1893. Dr. McKay (1870–1949) brought his family to Humble in 1919, and he practiced medicine there. He served on the Humble ISD School Board from 1924 to 1926. The McKay Bridge across Lake Houston is named in his honor.

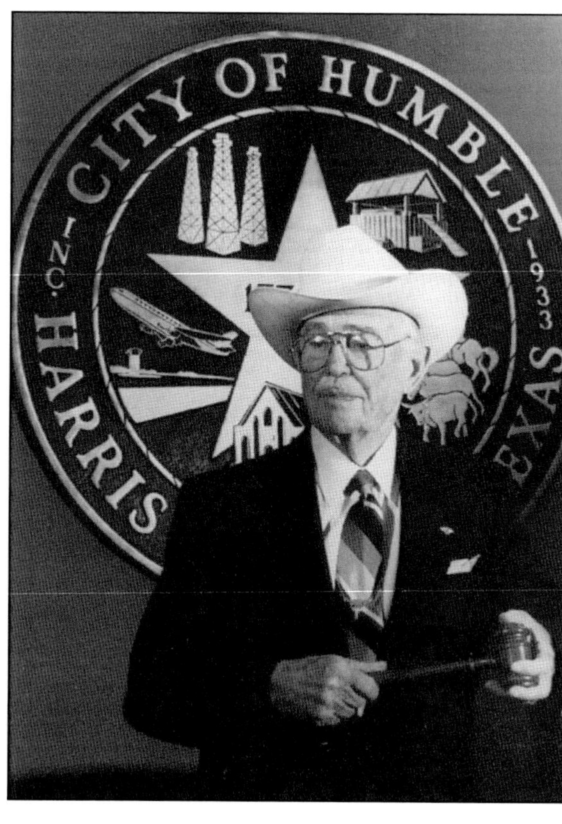

DR. HADEN EDWARDS MCKAY III. Dr. McKay Jr., as he was known, came to Humble with his parents in 1919. He followed in his father's footsteps by becoming a physician, graduating from the Chicago Medical School in 1936. He started practicing medicine in Humble in 1938 and continued to see patients until his death. Dr. McKay Jr. (1908–1996) served as the mayor of Humble for 24 years.

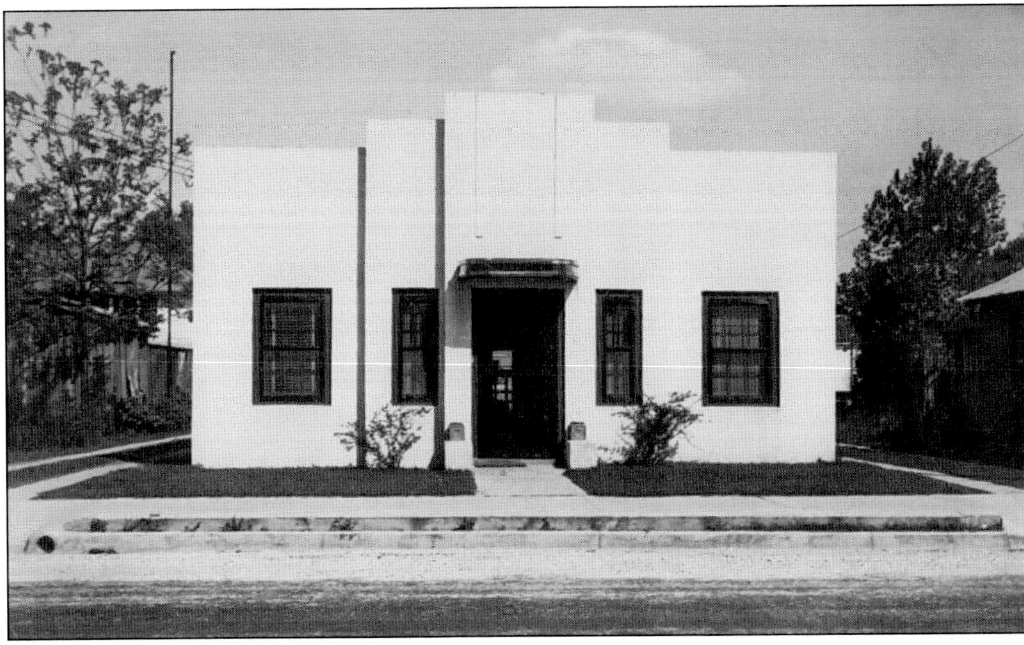

McKay Clinic. Located on Avenue C, between Main Street and Higgins Street, this medical clinic was built in 1938 by Dr. Haden E. McKay Sr. and Dr. Haden E. McKay Jr. It was reportedly the first fireproof building constructed in Humble. An apartment was included in the back of the building, where Dr. McKay Jr. lived during his bachelor years. Upon his marriage to Lillian Janda, he built a home next to the clinic (at left in the below photograph). The clinic included examination and delivery rooms, sterilizers, prescription-compounding equipment, and an X-ray machine. Dr. McKay Jr. saw patients at the clinic until his death in 1996. Mrs. McKay graciously deeded the McKay Clinic to the Humble Museum as a memorial to her husband and his father.

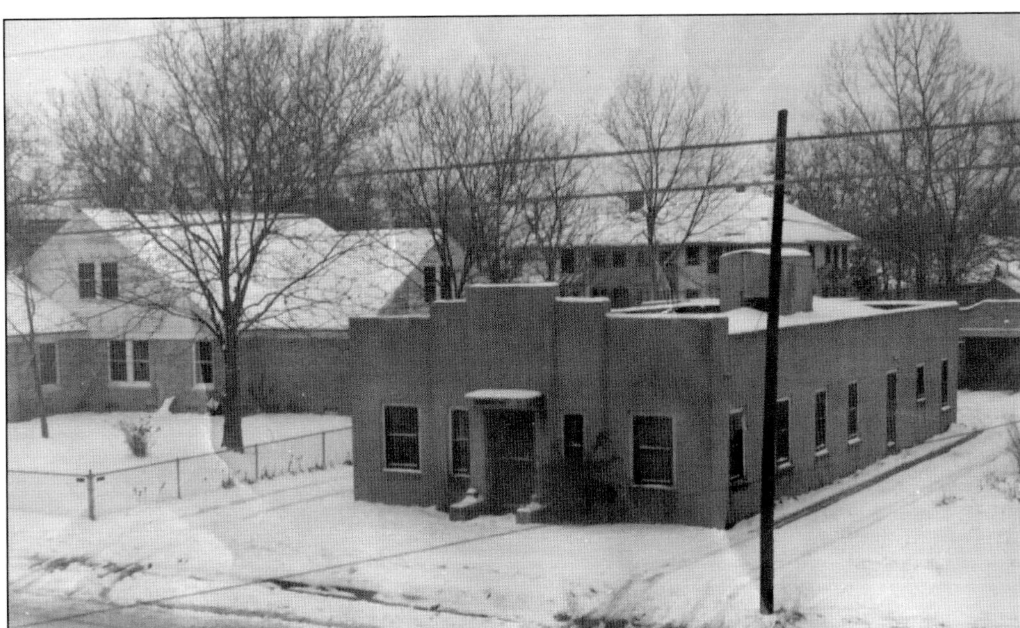

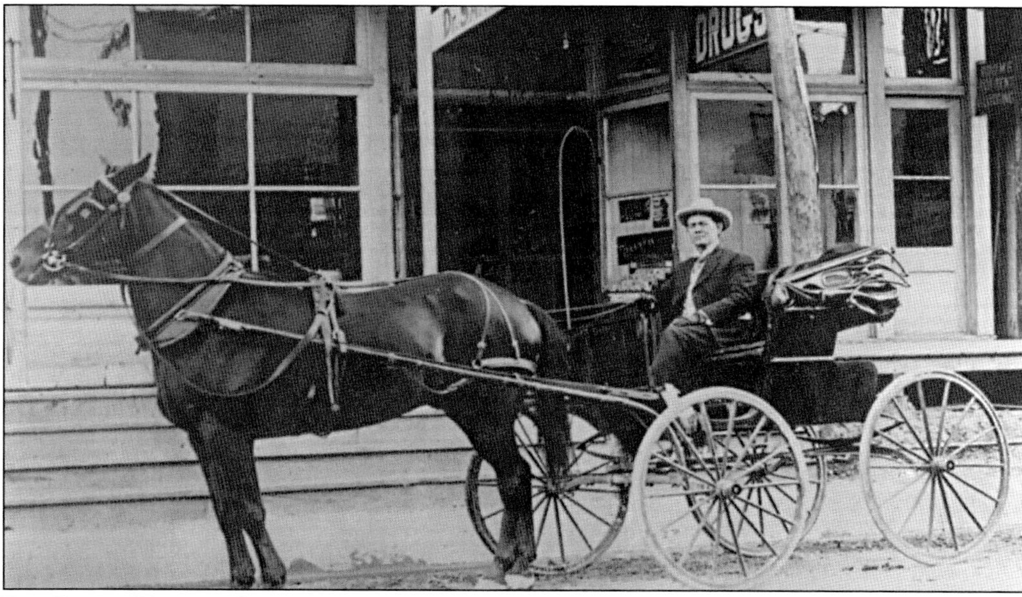

DR. JAMES WILLIAM SANDLIN. Dr. Sandlin (1877–1951) was one of the earliest physicians in Humble, maintaining a practice in town for 53 years. He operated the Sandlin Drug Store on Barrett Street (Main Street), which was a gathering place for many oilmen from Moonshine Hill. He delivered thousands of babies during his days in Humble, and worked on many injured oil-field workers and accident victims.

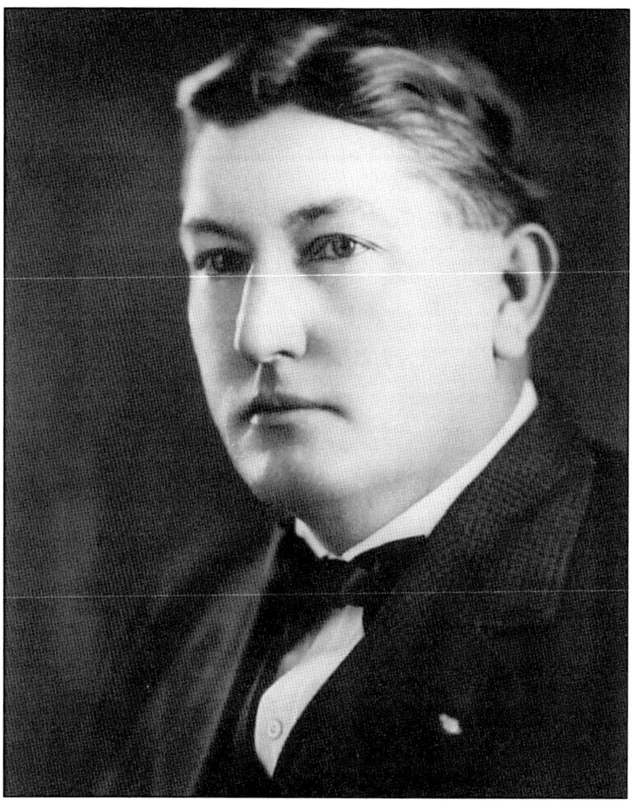

DR. JOHN DUBOSE. Born in Angelina County, Texas, Dr. DuBose moved to Humble in 1903. At that time, he was serving as the doctor of the Southern Pacific Railroad. DuBose served on the school board for Humble ISD from 1919 to 1924 and was president of the board for four years. He also served as the first mayor of Humble in 1933.

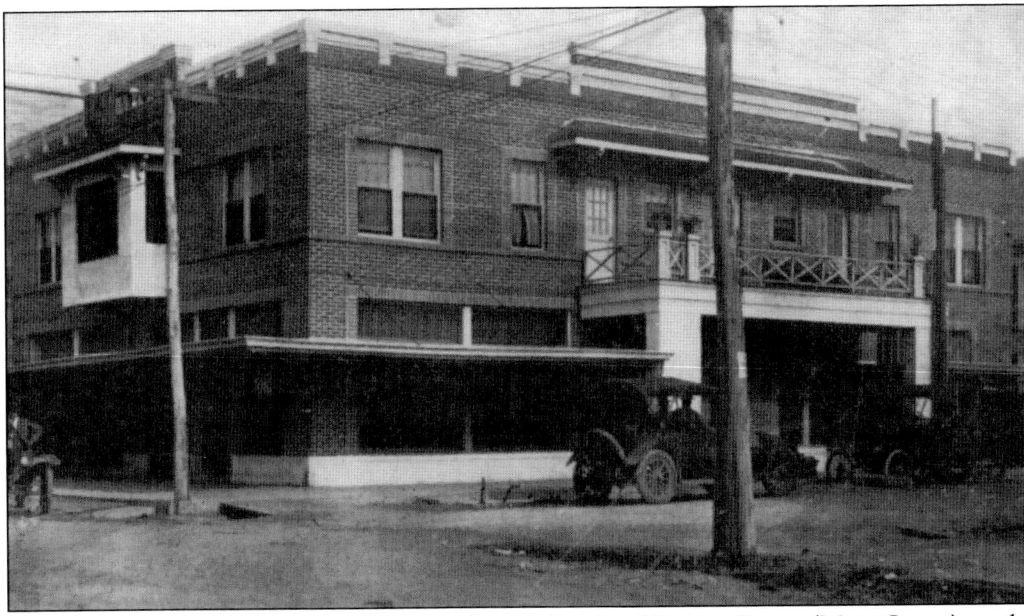

Guaranty State Bank, 1919. Built on the north side of Barrett Street (Main Street), at the corner of Avenue C, this building was home to the Guaranty State Bank. The town's dentist, Dr. Manning, had his practice in this building. From 1932 to 1950, this building was the home of the A&P Grocery Store.

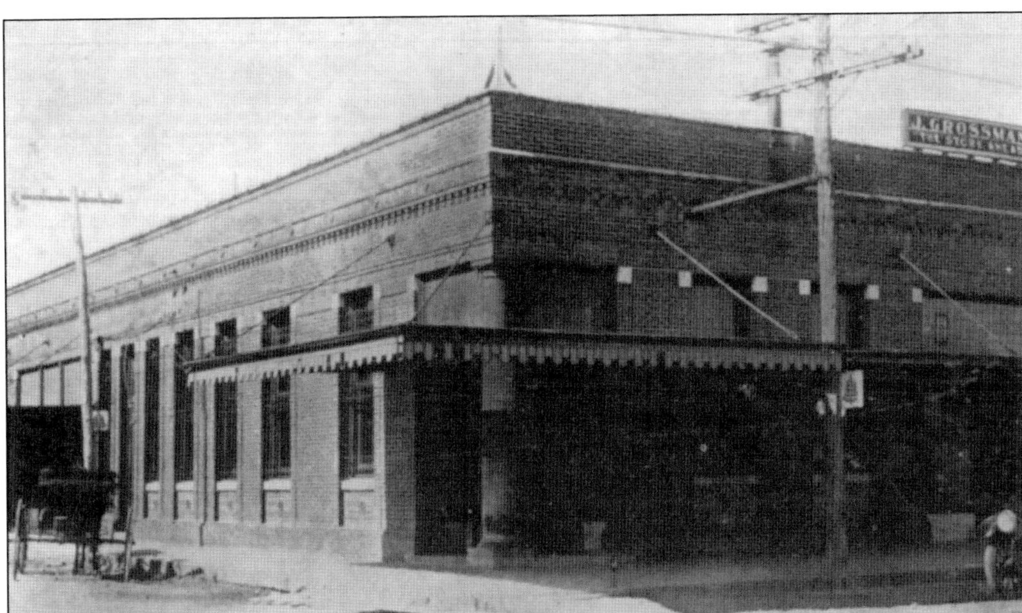

Humble State Bank, 1919. Built in 1912 on the south side of Main Street, at the corner of Avenue B, this structure still stands. It has been used by various businesses over the years. Ross Sterling had this structure built to replace the original Humble State Bank building that burned down in the Humble fire of 1912. The Humble Masonic Lodge building stands on the location of the original bank building.

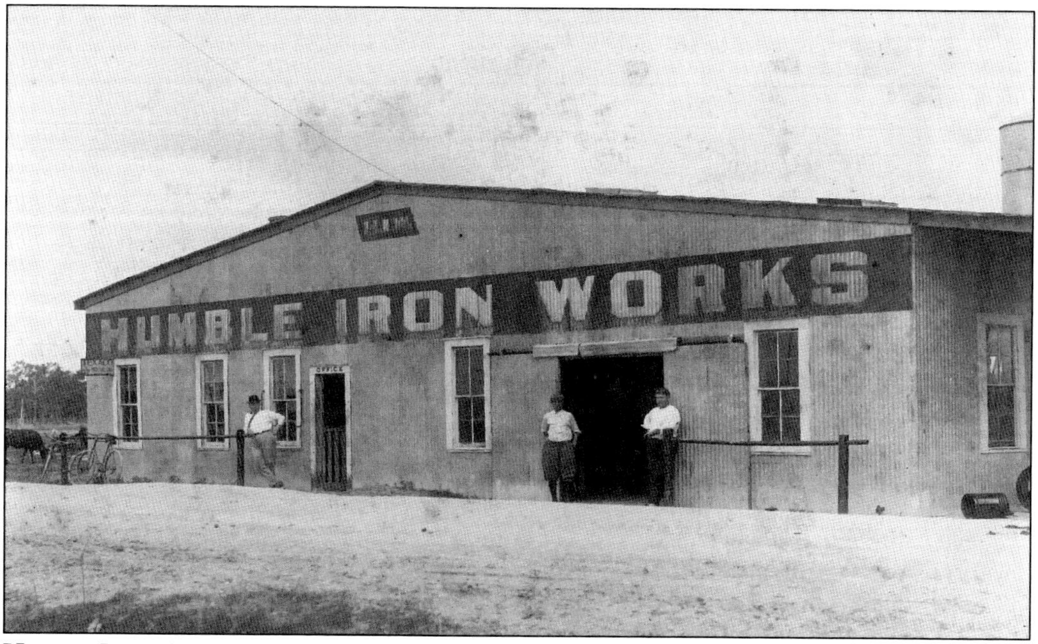

Humble Iron Works. Organized in 1913 by Harry S. Cameron, the Humble Iron Works began primarily as a machine shop. Cameron repaired drilling rigs and was good at forging high-grade steel. Oilman James Abercrombie bought a controlling interest in the company in 1920. The two men formed the Cameron Iron Works and developed a blowout preventer for oil wells in 1922.

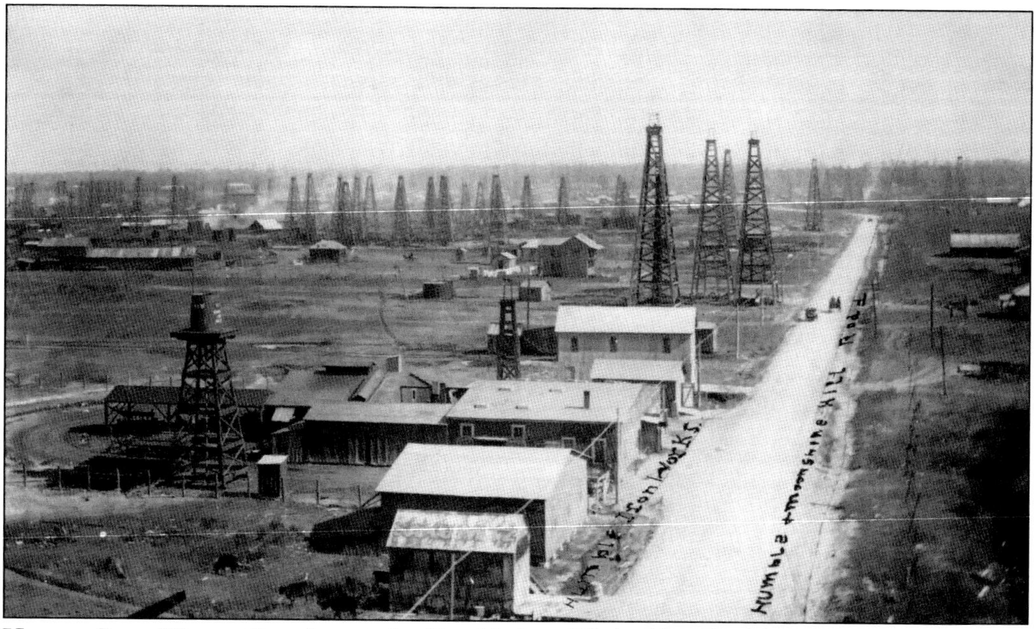

Humble Iron Works. Seen here is the Humble Iron Works (third building from the bottom) on the Humble-Moonshine Hill Road. The turn in the road, seen near the horizon, is the beginning of Moonshine Hill Loop. Note the large number of oil derricks on the landscape. (Courtesy of Jeff Spencer.)

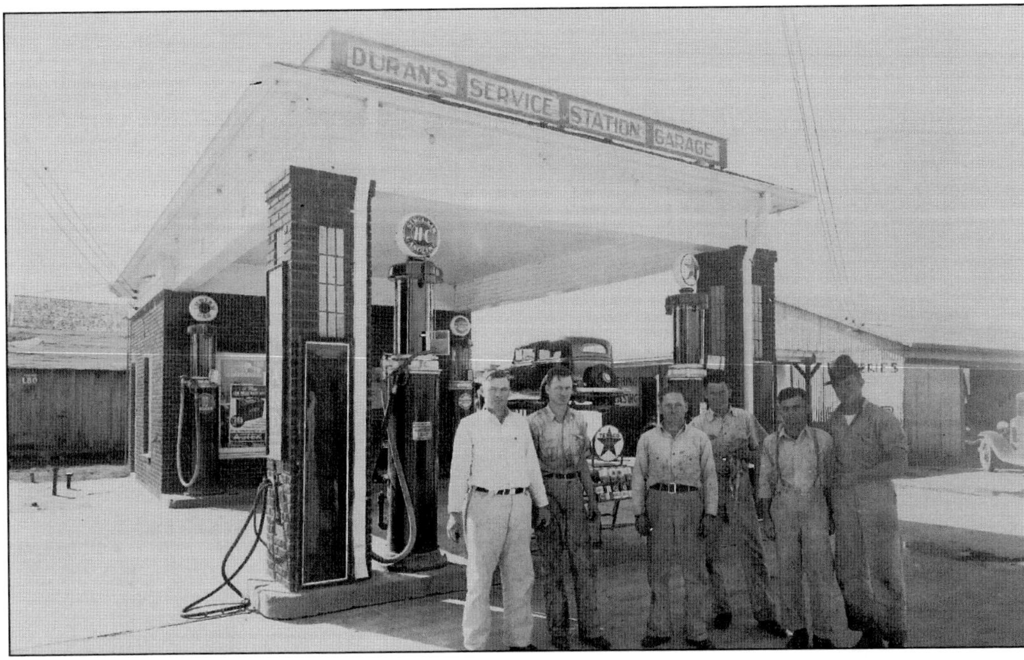

Duran's Service Station and Garage. Alton Duran operated a service station on the corner of Avenue A and Higgins Street. Above, posing at the Higgins Street location around 1931 are, from left to right, Alton Duran, Homer Duran, Siegal Cammack, unidentified, Dalton Pope, and Ernest Scheible. Below, Alton (left) and Homer Duran pose in their service station garage. In 1939, Alton Duran took a chance by being one of the first business owners to move to Highway 35 on the west side of downtown Humble. The lone gas station on the highway became a welcome sight for travelers. With the location, and being open 24 hours a day, the volume of business at Duran's Texaco service station increased dramatically.

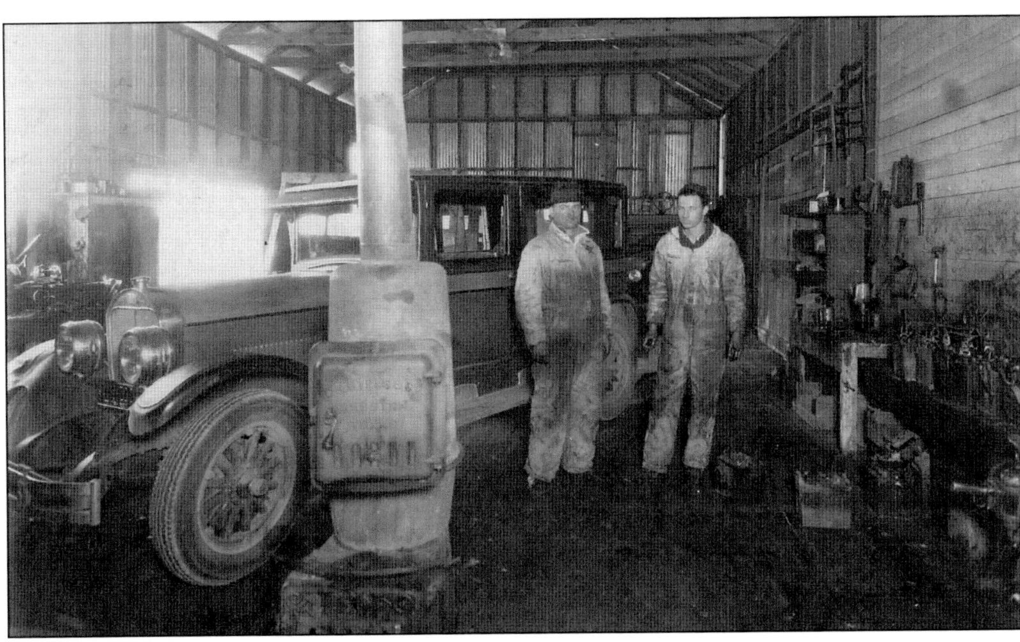

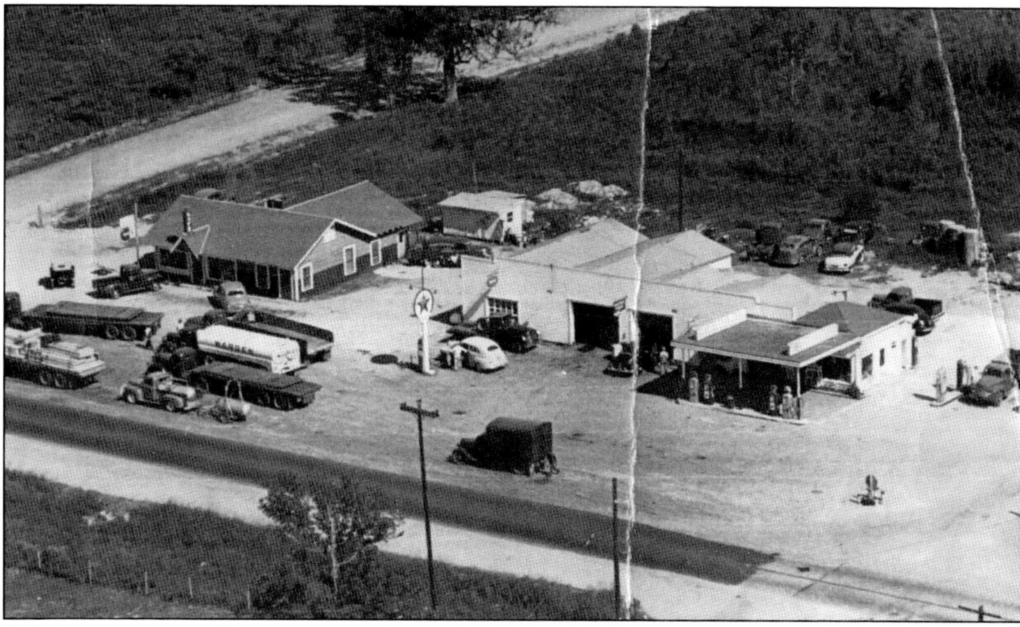

US Highway 59. When a new highway opened west of the railroad tracks, passing traffic no longer stopped in Humble, hurting local businesses. In 1939, Alton Duran took the risk of moving his Texaco service station to the highway. Many ridiculed that his business would falter. Instead, it thrived off of travelers looking for a convenient place to fill their cars with gas. The following year, Bertha and Roy Bass opened a drive-in café next to Duran's Texaco station (below). To drum up business, Roy's Café featured all-female carhops wearing majorette-type uniforms. Teens from outlying villages began to hang out at Roy's, exposing local boys and girls to teens from New Caney and Aldine. The name of the highway was changed from 35 to US Highway 59. The above photograph shows Roy's Café and Duran's Texaco station on US Highway 59, between Higgins Street (left) and Main Street.

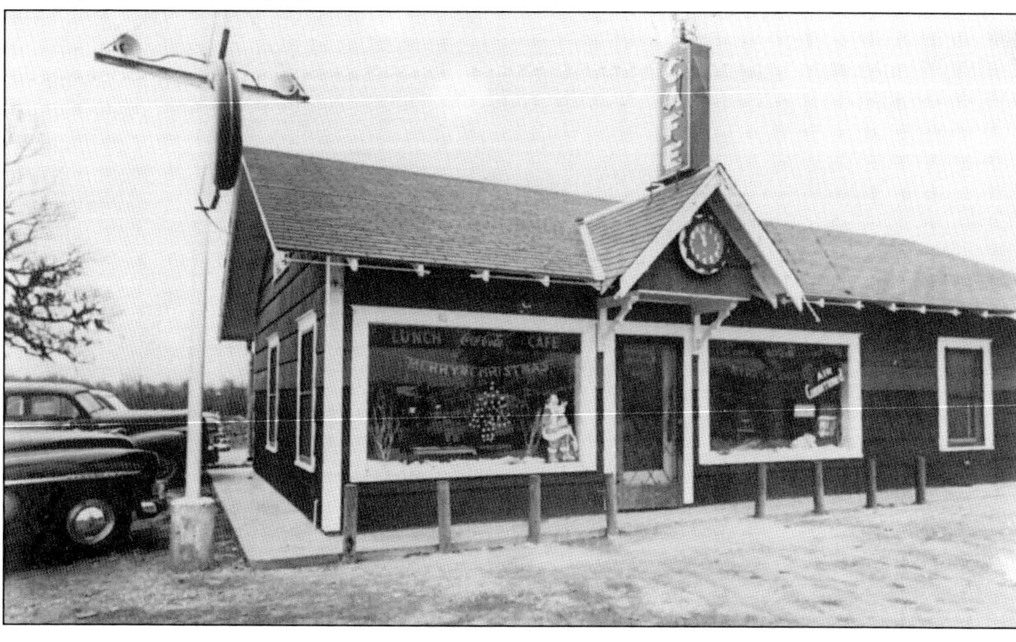

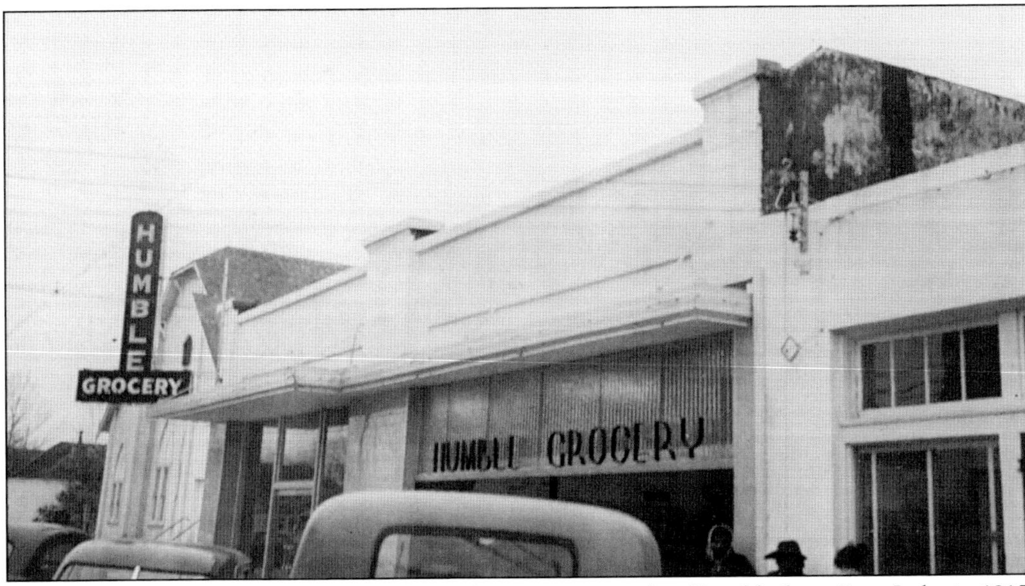

Humble Grocery. Oliver Frank and his wife, Hattie, moved to Humble from Sour Lake in 1915. Oliver opened a grocery store on Barrett Street (Main Street) in November 1915. In 1921, Oliver's brother John left the Navy and moved to Humble. He became a partner in the Humble Grocery Store with Oliver in 1923. About this time, John married Adele Womack, who was working as a teacher in Humble. In 1943, Oliver and John purchased the M.L. Carpenter building (above), on the corner of Barrett Street and Avenue C. This building was the original location of Tooke's Drug Store before it was moved in the 1920s to Main Street and Avenue B. The inside of the Humble Grocery Store is shown in the below photograph. The Frank brothers retired from the business in 1961.

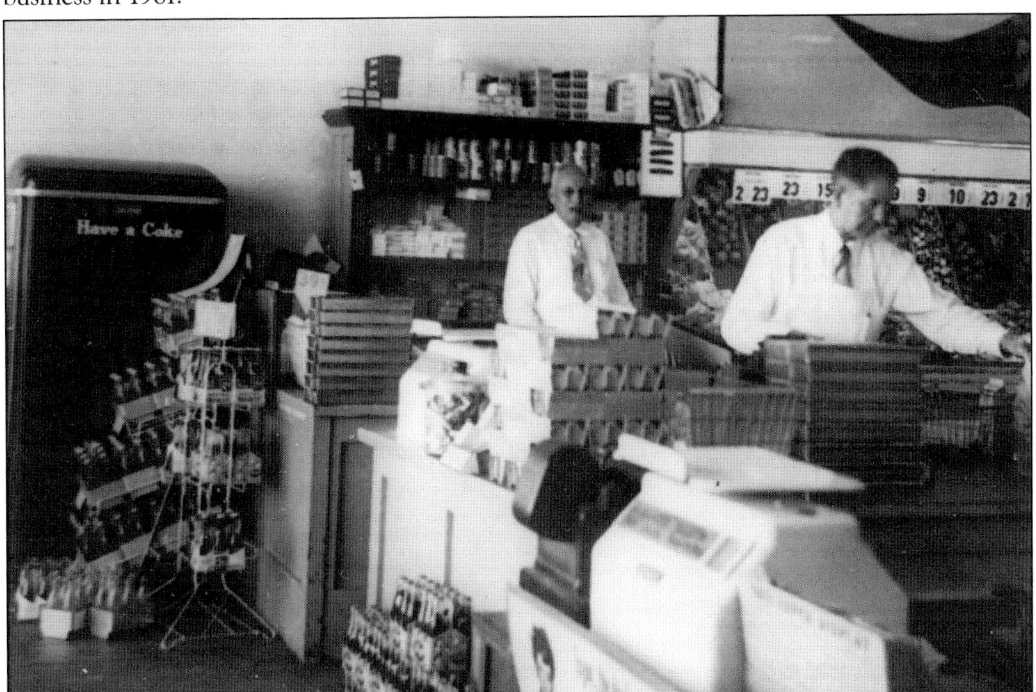

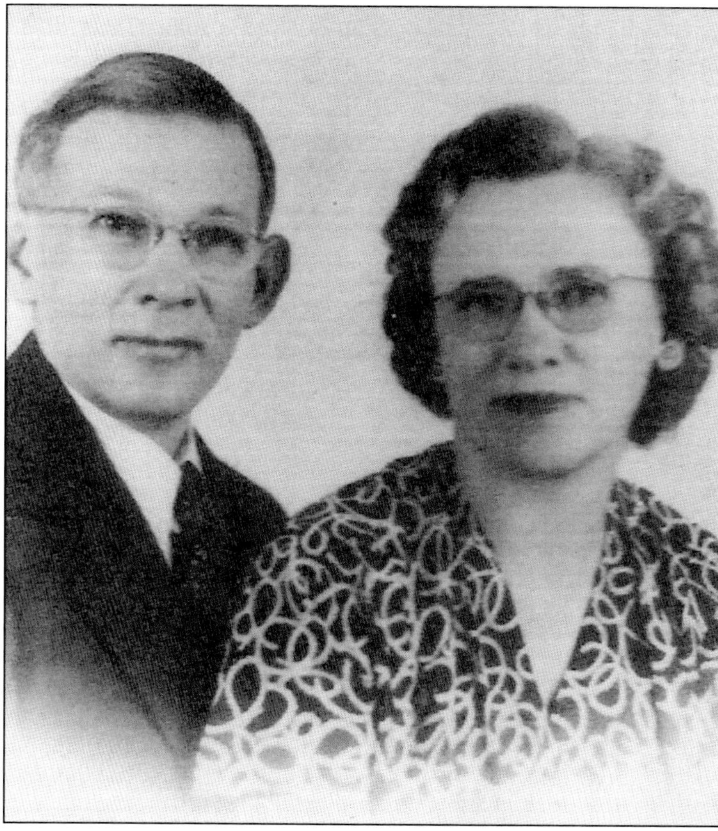

HUMBLE PHARMACY. Herndon and Anna Pursley came to Humble in 1918. Herndon had received a pharmacy degree from Baylor University in Dallas, and he started working at the Humble Pharmacy in 1918. It was owned at the time by Dr. Bennett. In 1923, the Pursleys became part owners of the pharmacy, and they later became full owners. The pharmacy, located in the 200 block of Barrett Street, was a gathering place for Humble citizens. Herndon Pursley had the first movie camera in Humble, and he enjoyed recording his family and the town's residents. He sold the pharmacy in the early 1950s due to ill health.

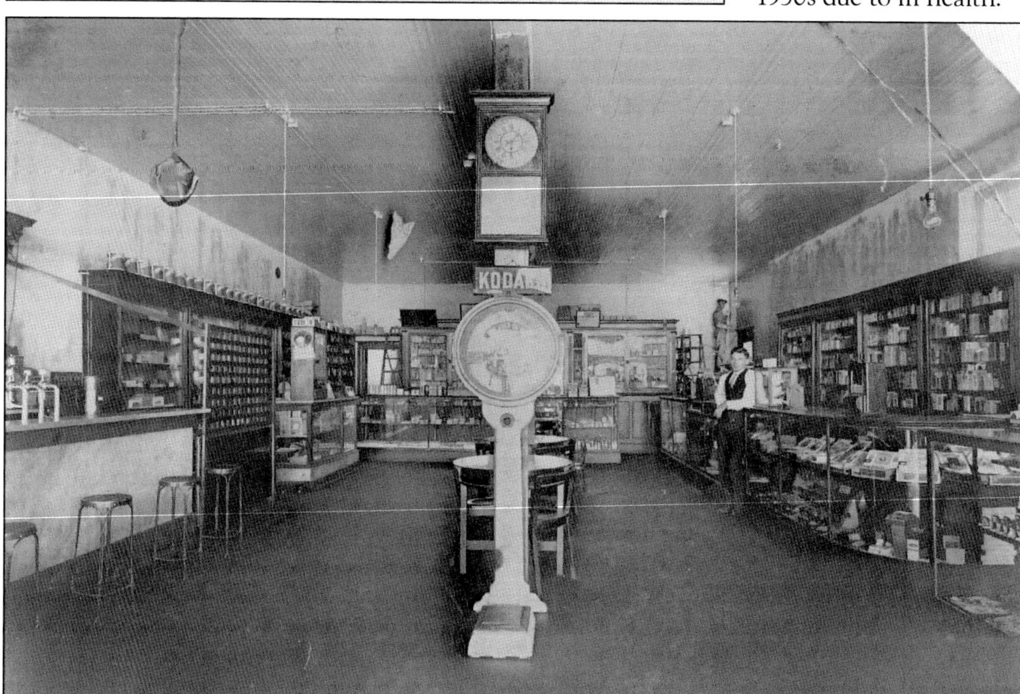

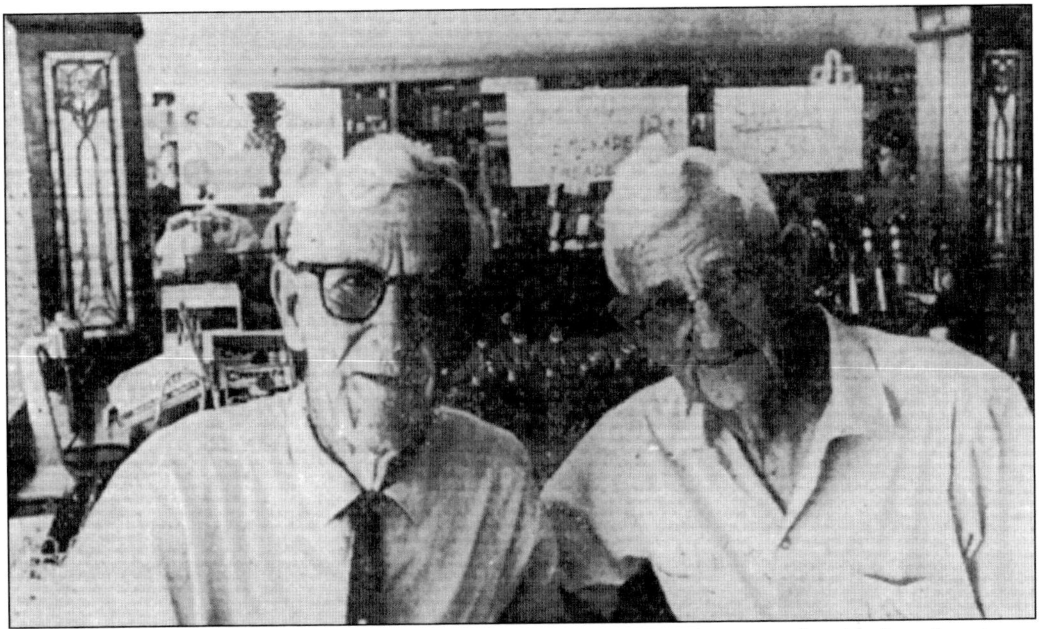

Ray and John Tooke. John Tooke (right) worked in a Texas City drugstore shortly after a hurricane almost destroyed the town in 1915. While working at that pharmacy, he met and married Q'Bell Clayton. They left Texas City and moved to Humble, where John (1883–1969) and his brother, Ray (left, 1888–1965), opened Tooke's Drug Store in August 1916. (Courtesy James Tull Chapter of the Daughters of the American Revolution.)

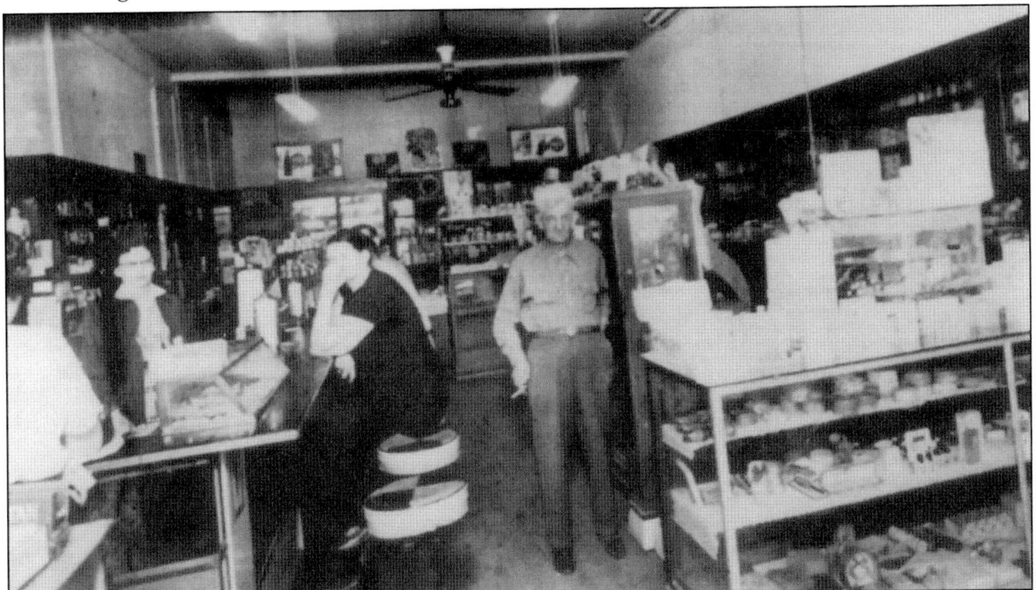

Tooke's Drug Store. Opened in August 1916 by brothers John and Ray Tooke, the drugstore was a favorite hangout for local residents. The Tooke brothers were especially kind to neighborhood children, patching them up when hurt, giving them extra scoops of ice cream, and letting them read the comics and magazines as long as they liked. The brothers sold the store to J.M. Keller in May 1963. Ida McElroy is pictured standing behind the counter at the left; John Tooke is standing in the center of the store.

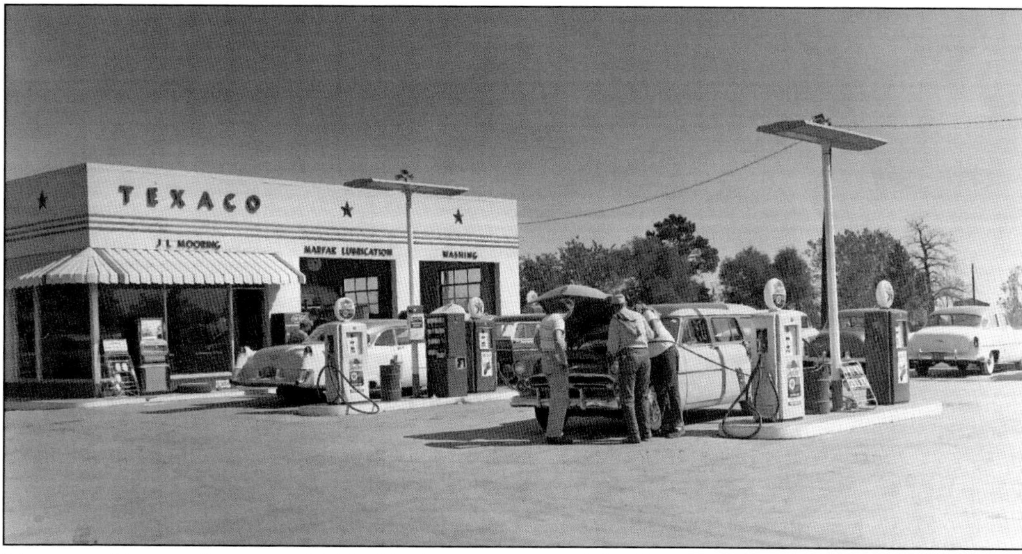

MOORING TEXACO STATION, 1950S. J.L. Mooring owned the Texaco station on Main Street (across from the Humble Swimming Pool) in the early 1950s. He later moved to this newer building, located on Business FM 1960 and North Houston Avenue, across from the Artesian Well. He and his wife, Brookie, were socially active in the Humble community for many years.

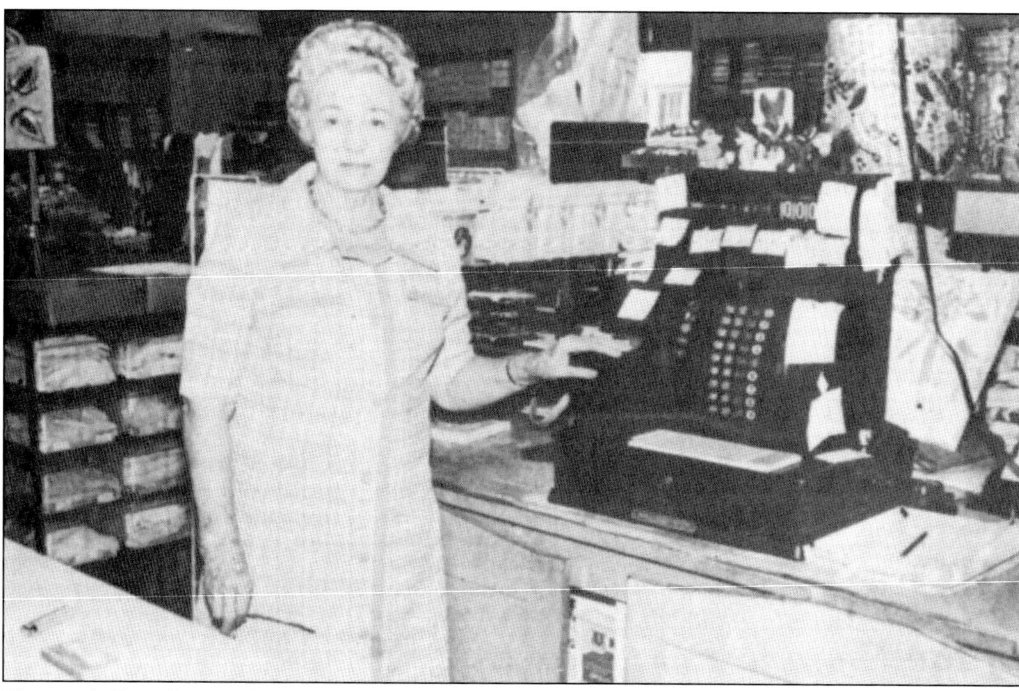

KATTAR'S DRY GOODS STORE. Joe Kattar purchased a store, established in Humble in 1915, from his uncle prior to 1918. Myrtle Powers started working at the store in 1918, and she married Joe Kattar in 1923. The store moved to the 300 block of Barrett Street (Main Street) in the 1930s. As owner of the store, Myrtle Kattar worked there until it closed in 1977.

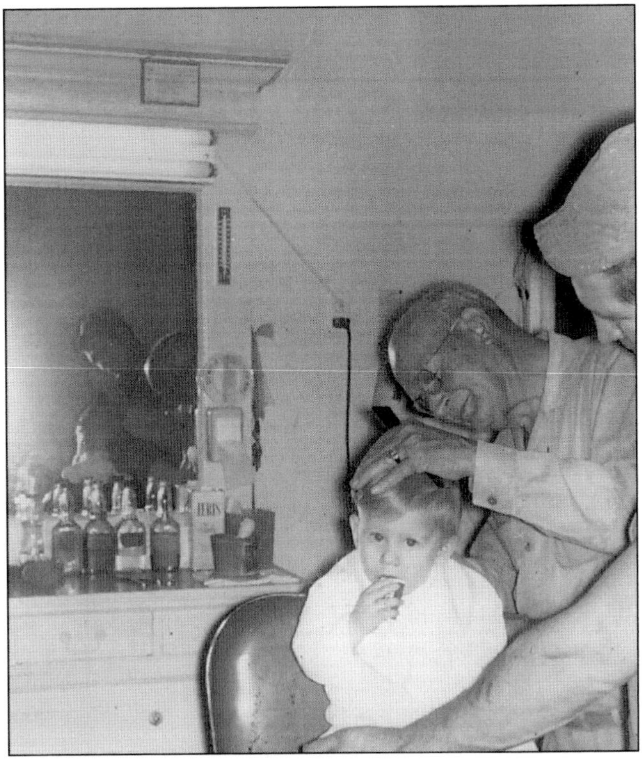

Shuler's Barber Shop, 1964. The barbershop was located in a two-story building in the 400 block of Main Street. Jake Shuler, a longtime Humble resident, is remembered as a friendly and kind country barber. He was in business for 43 years. In this photograph, Jake Shuler is cutting Sonny Buford's hair.

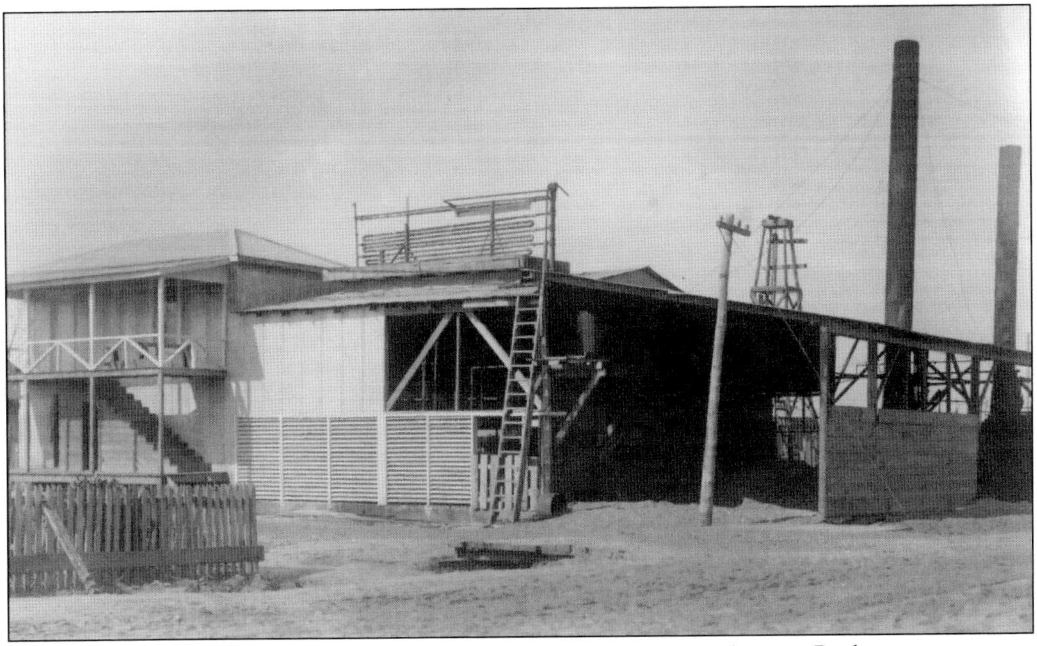

Humble Ice and Power Company. Located on Higgins Street at Avenue B, this company was originally called the Humble Light and Water Company when it was started by Frank Albert Peters in 1907. The ice plant was added in 1912. In 1923, a bottling plant was built and put into operation, but was later discontinued. Frank Peters was active in the community, serving as the president of the Humble Chamber of Commerce.

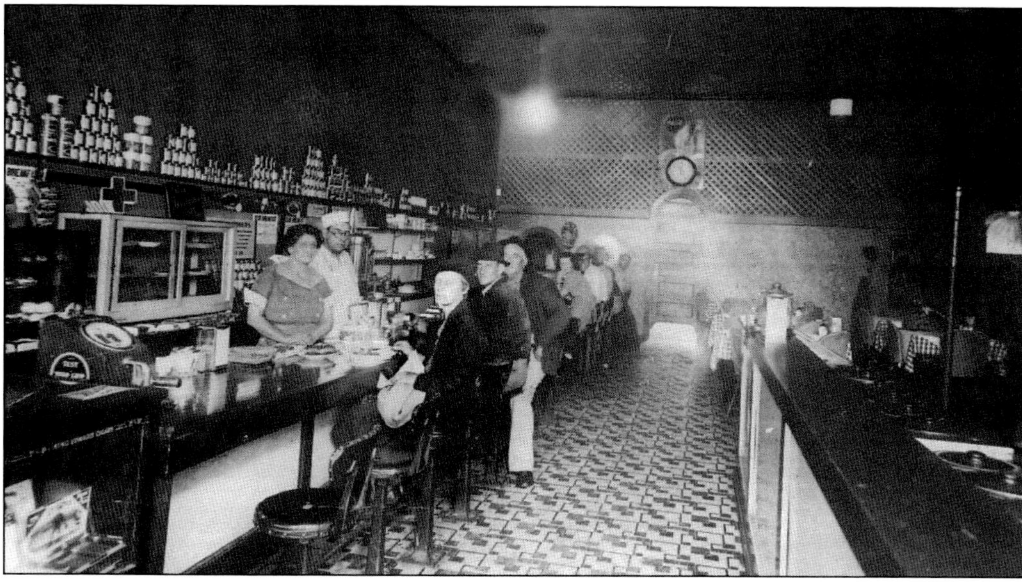

HUMBLE CITY CAFÉ, 1931. Joe and Rosa Bernardino, natives of Italy, were married in Louisiana and moved to Humble in 1929. They owned the Sandwich Shop next to the theater and, eventually, bought the City Café on Barrett Street (Main Street). To accommodate oil-field laborers who worked 12-hour shifts, the Humble City Café was kept open 24 hours a day.

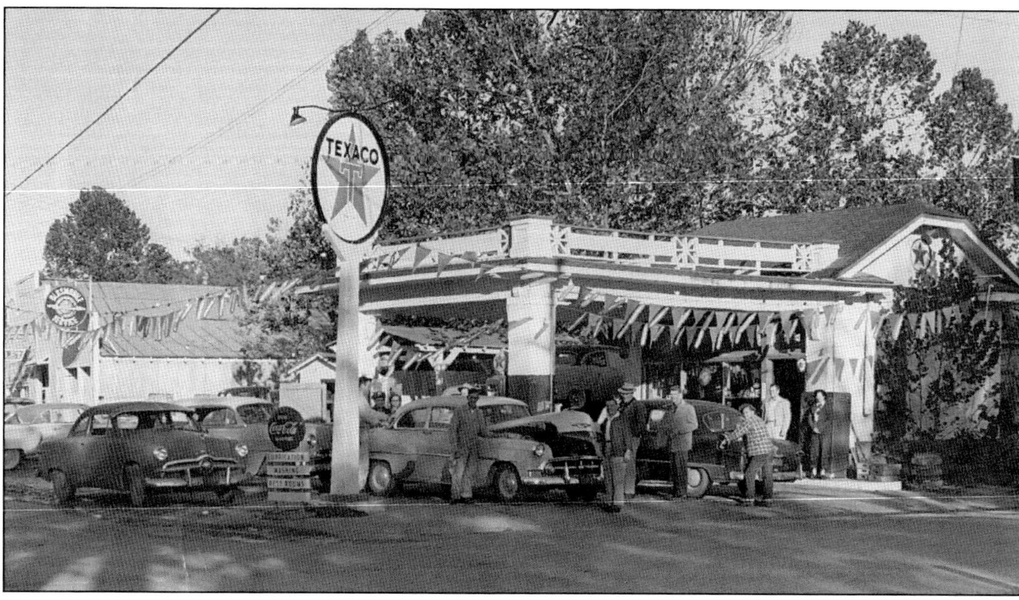

MAIN STREET TEXACO STATION, 1950S. This Texaco station was located at the corner of Main Street and Old Humble Road, across from the Humble Swimming Pool and next to Robbins Chevrolet. The station was operated by the Moorings in the 1950s, and by Robert Lee Brock in the early 1960s.

Four

Schools

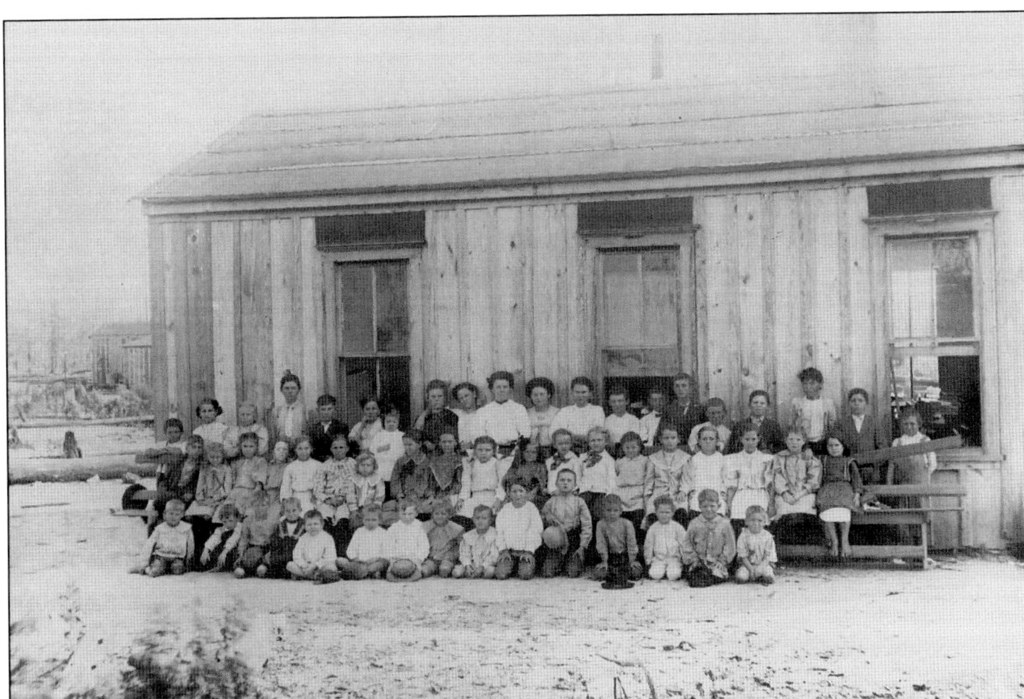

West River School, 1904. This school was built in 1888 at the corner of Old Humble Road (now South Houston Avenue) and Isaacks Road for Harris County Common School District No. 28. The land was sold by Harris County constable William S. Humble (son of Humble founder Pleasant S. Humble) for $5. Rose Hamblen, Lilah Dunnam, and Katie Deady were the school's first teachers.

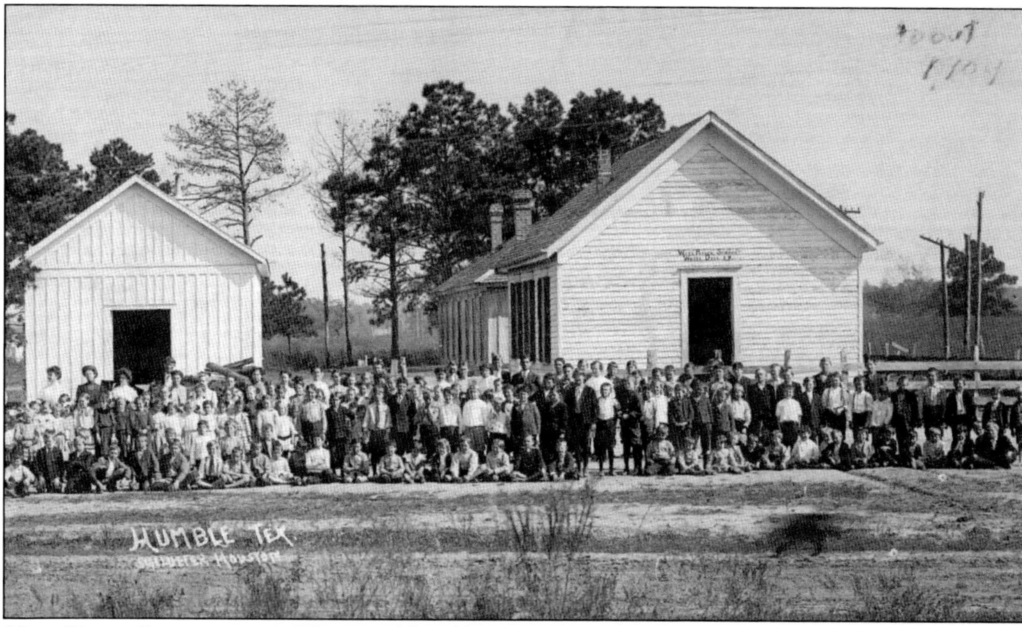

West River School, 1909. The Humble oil boom resulted in a large increase in student enrollment, from 50 students in 1904 to 250 students in 1909. To accommodate this influx of students, a new brick schoolhouse was built on Higgins Street in the summer of 1909. The West River School was closed, and the land was eventually sold to the Humble Cemetery Association.

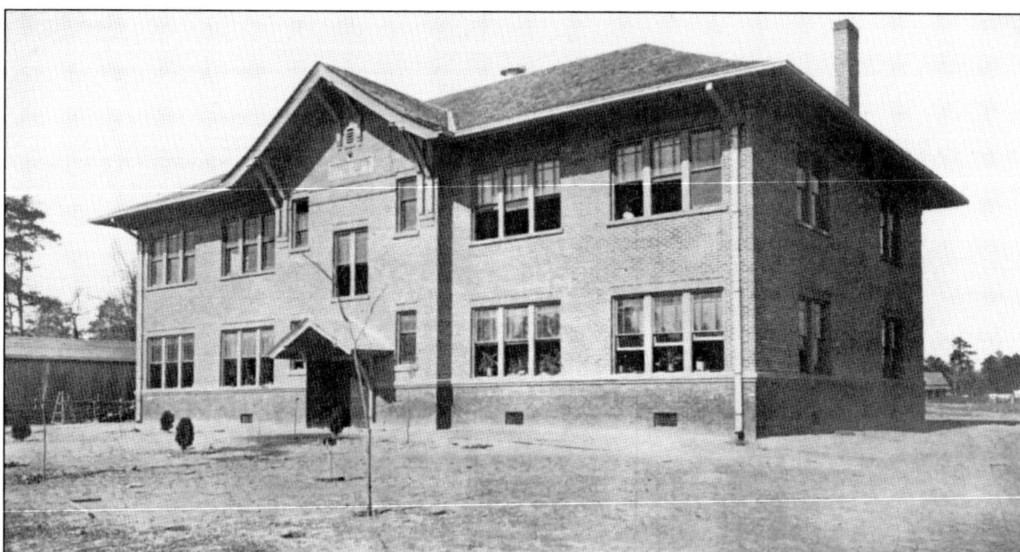

The Humble School, 1909. The first brick schoolhouse in Humble was built at the corner of Higgins Street and Avenue F. It was a two-story building with six classrooms that housed grades one through nine. The county paid the Charles Bender estate $450 for the land, and a $10,000 schoolhouse bond was passed by the citizens of Humble to pay for the building's construction. (Courtesy of the Houston Metropolitan Research Center.)

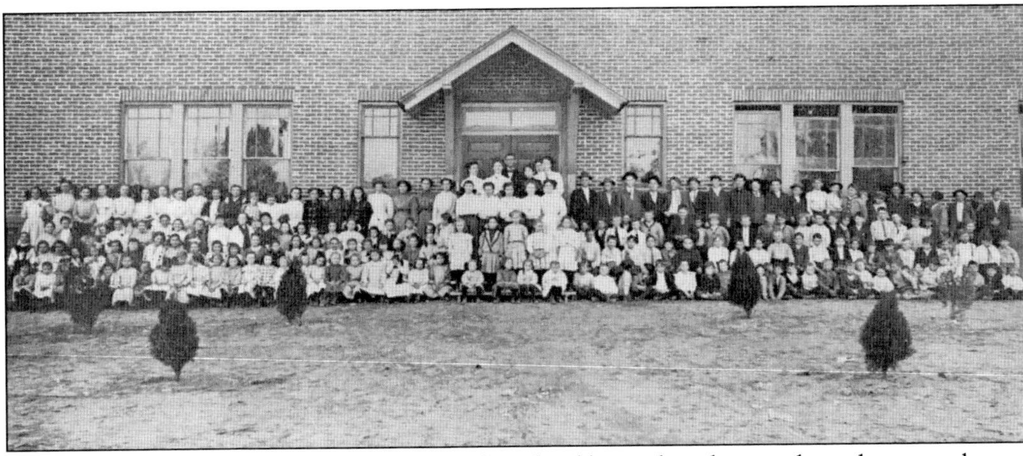

Students at the Humble School, 1910. The school housed grades one through seven, plus two grades of high school (grades eight and nine). Daniel Henry Womack (1867–1957), the district's first superintendent (1909–1911), served as principal of the school. Grades 10 and 11 were added in 1911, when the Humble School became a county high school. (Courtesy of the Houston Metropolitan Research Center.)

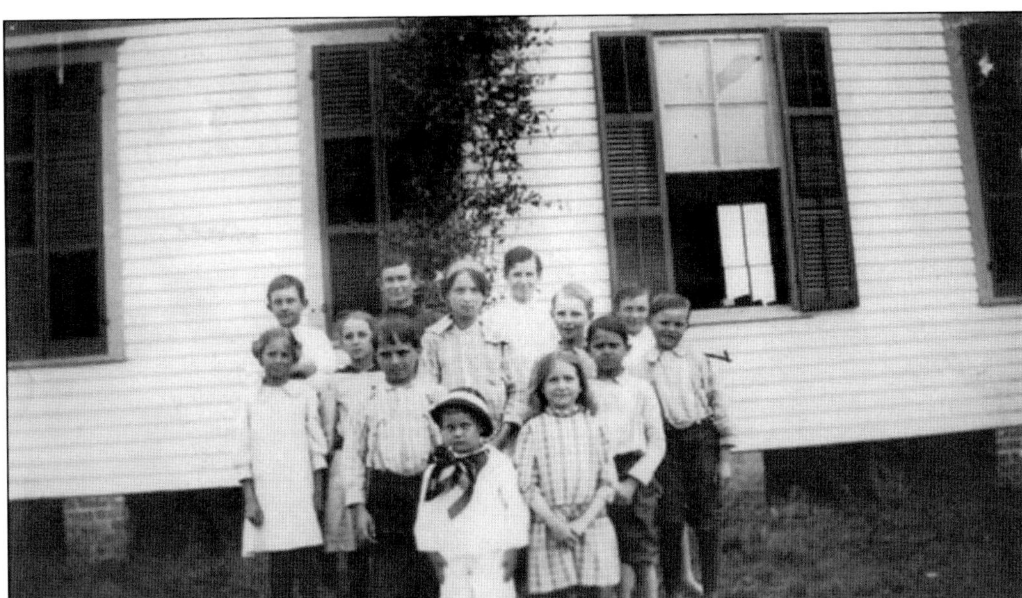

Singleton School, 1912. Originally called Joe Dunman's Schoolhouse, the school opened in 1873 on the Atascocita Road. It became the Dunman's Prairie School in 1888, when District No. 35 was created. In 1903, after the death of Joe Dunman, the school was moved farther west on Atascocita Road and renamed the Singleton School. The building housed grades one through seven. (Courtesy of Margaret Byron.)

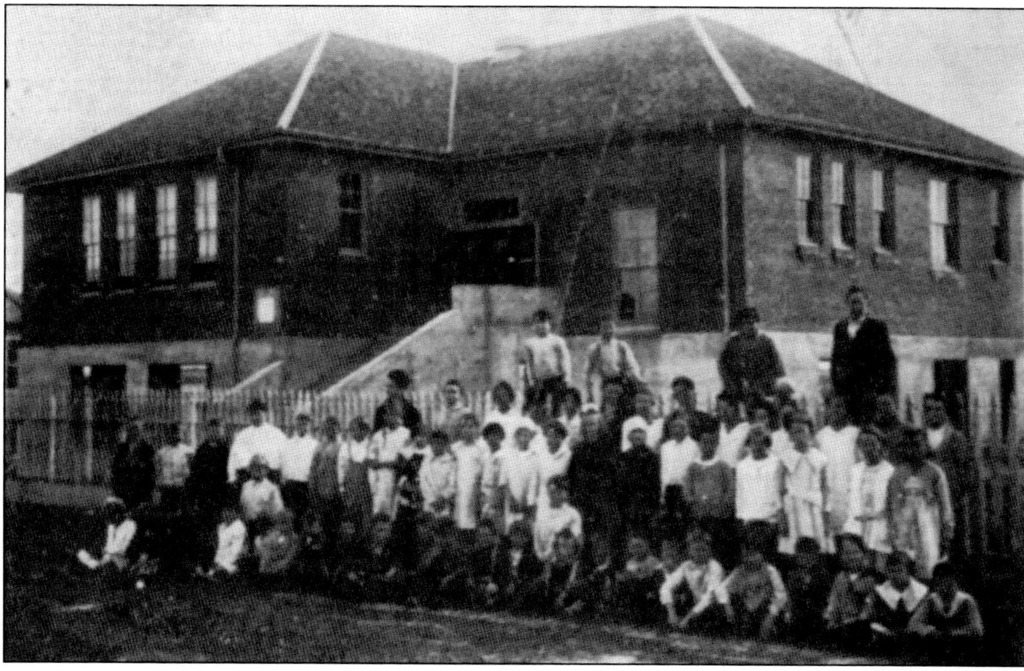

Singleton School, Brick Building, 1918. The school was named for Reed Singleton, a local landowner and frequent election judge. District No. 35 erected this brick building to replace the wooden schoolhouse during the 1917–1918 school year. In the summer of 1918, District No. 35 was merged with District No. 28 to create District No. 50.

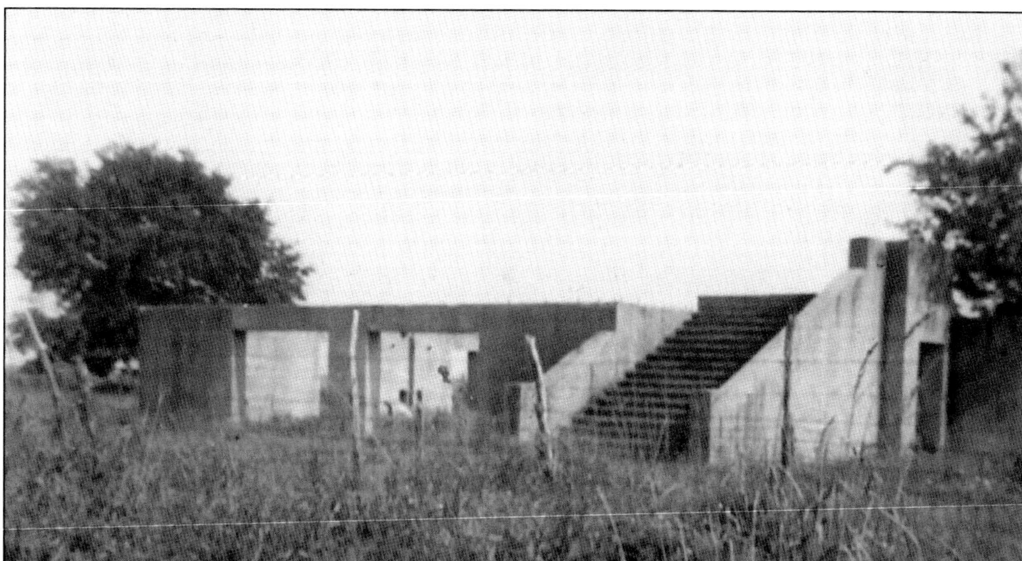

Singleton School Remains. Humble ISD closed the Singleton School in 1926 due to low enrollment. The building was sold in 1937 and partially demolished in the 1940s. The lower structure remained standing in a field for many years. The site is now part of the Waste Management Landfill on Atascocita Road, near Wilson Road.

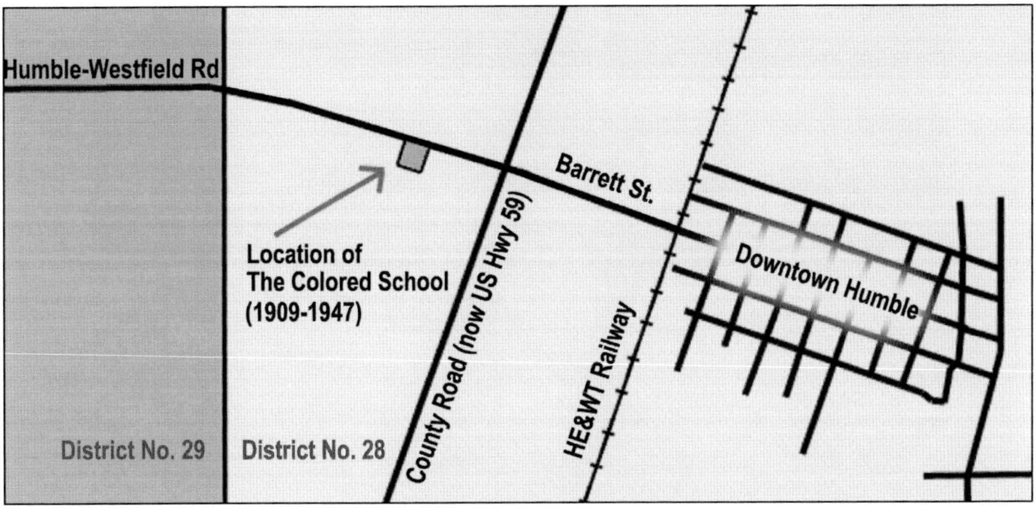

The Colored School. Humble had a school for African American students starting in 1886. It was originally called Dunman's No. 2 and became the Narrow Gauge School. Later, it was called the Pleasant Grove School. In 1909, a new schoolhouse was built near present-day Bordersville. The school was never given a name but was simply referred to as the Colored School. It was destroyed in a fire in 1947.

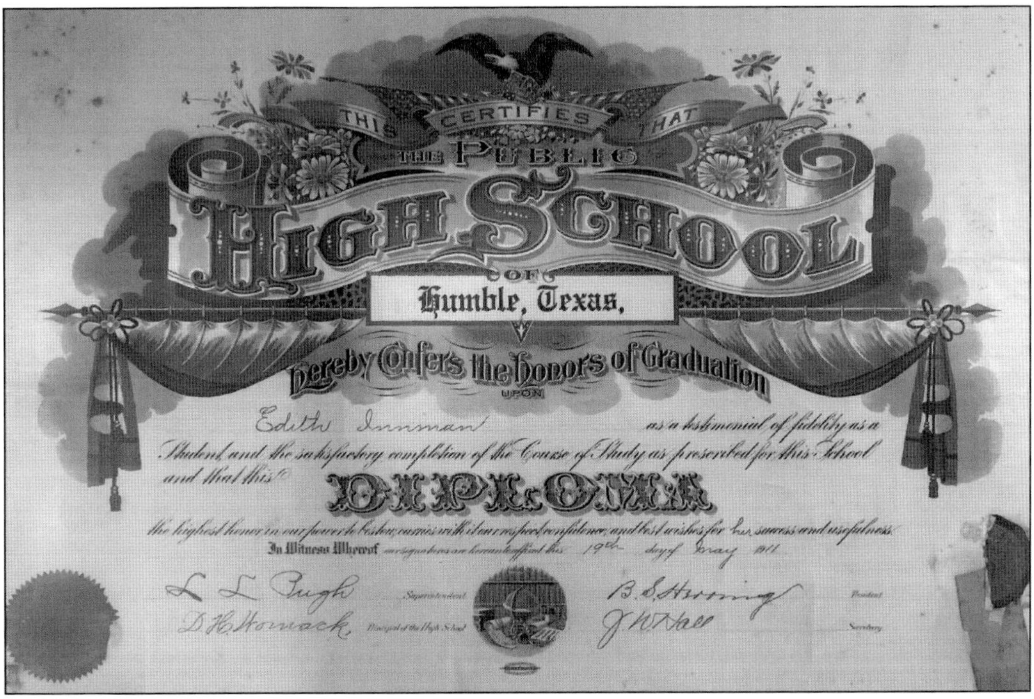

Edith Inman Diploma, 1911. The Humble School became a county high school in 1911. As part of that process, grades 10 and 11 were added to the curriculum. The first two students to receive a high school diploma from Humble were twins Edith and Ethel Inman, in May 1911. The 12th grade was not added to the Texas curriculum until 1941.

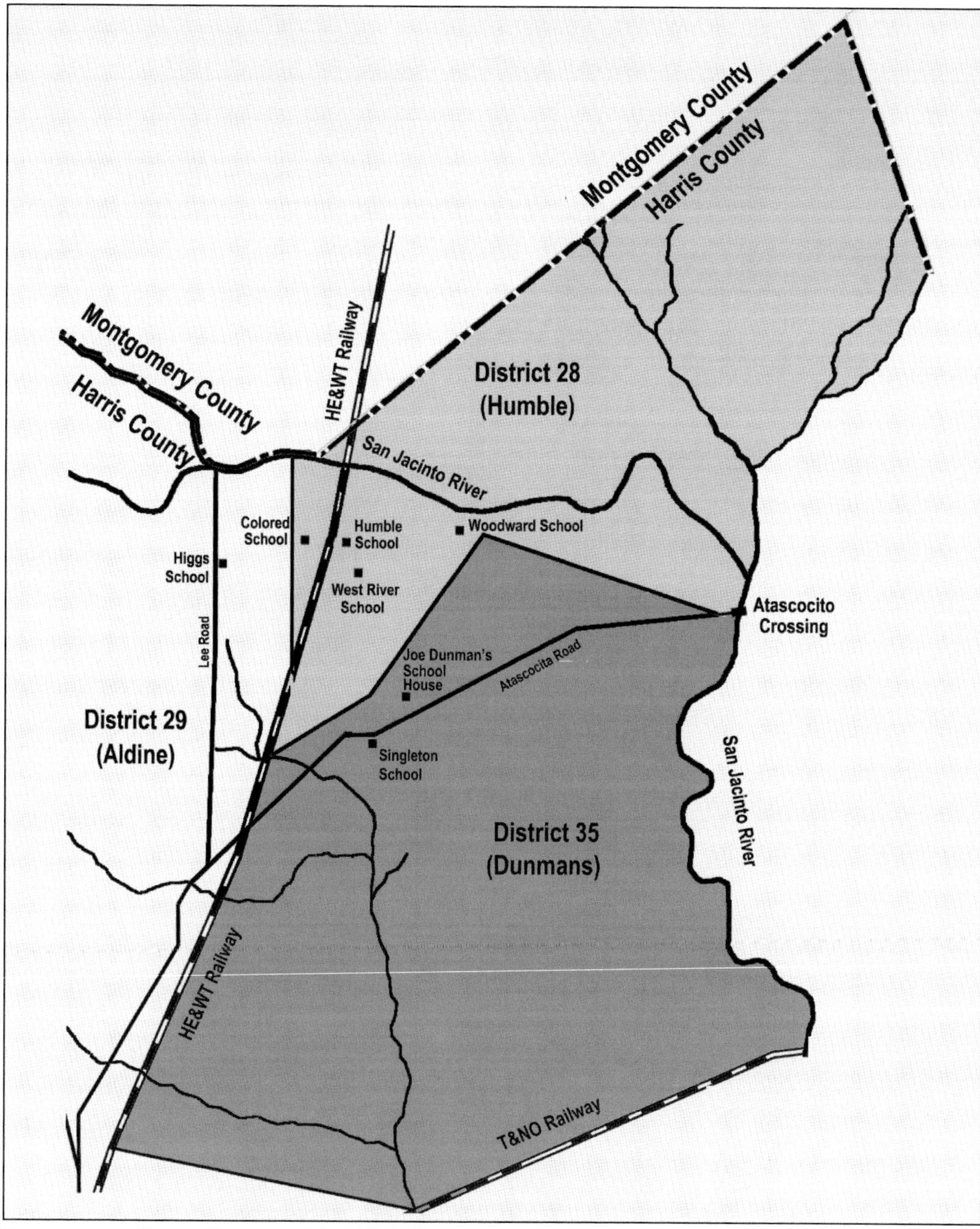

Location of Early Schools. Humble ISD started out as Harris County Common School District No. 28 in 1884. In 1888, the district was split into two parts: The northern section remained as District No. 28, and the southern portion became District No. 35. In 1918, the two parts were combined into District No. 50, which became Humble ISD a few months later. The schools indicated on this map are the following: Joe Dunman's Schoolhouse (1873–1903); West River School (1888–1909); Singleton School (1903–1926); Woodward School (1909–1932); Humble School (1909–1929); and the Colored School (1909–1947). The Higgs School, near Humble, was in District No. 29.

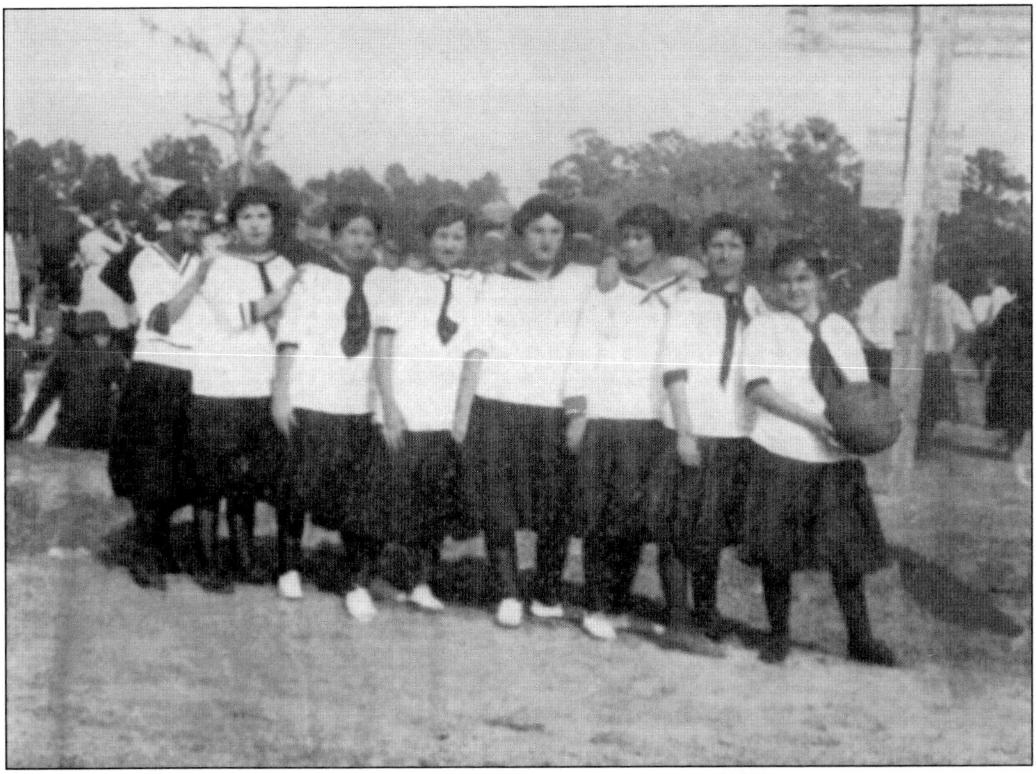

Humble Girls' Basketball Team, 1914. During the 1913–1914 school year, Harris County held its first interdistrict sports competition. The girls' basketball team from the Humble School competed, doing well in the competition. This is the earliest-known sports team from the Humble schools. (Courtesy of the Houston Metropolitan Research Center.)

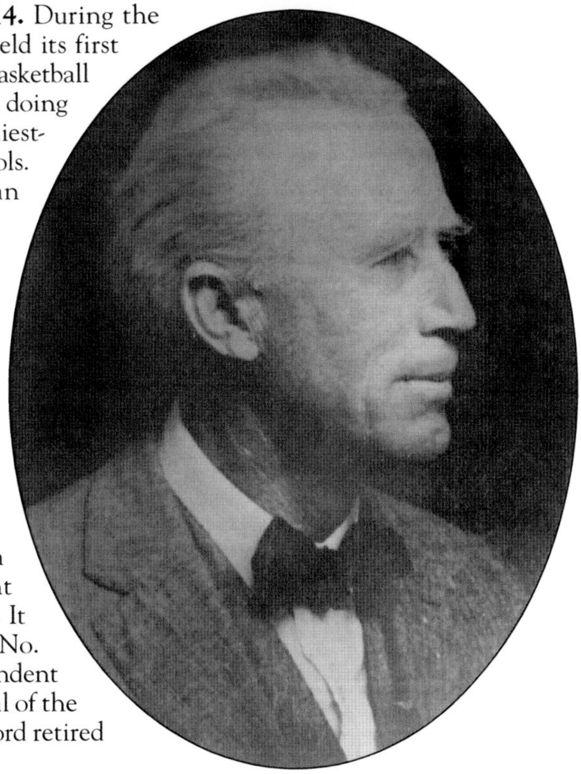

John Franklin Crawford. Crawford (1860–1930) was the second school superintendent for Humble, serving from 1911 to 1919. The school system went through many changes during that time. It started as District No. 28, then District No. 50, and then became the Humble Independent School District. He also served as principal of the Humble School from 1911 to 1914. Crawford retired in May 1919.

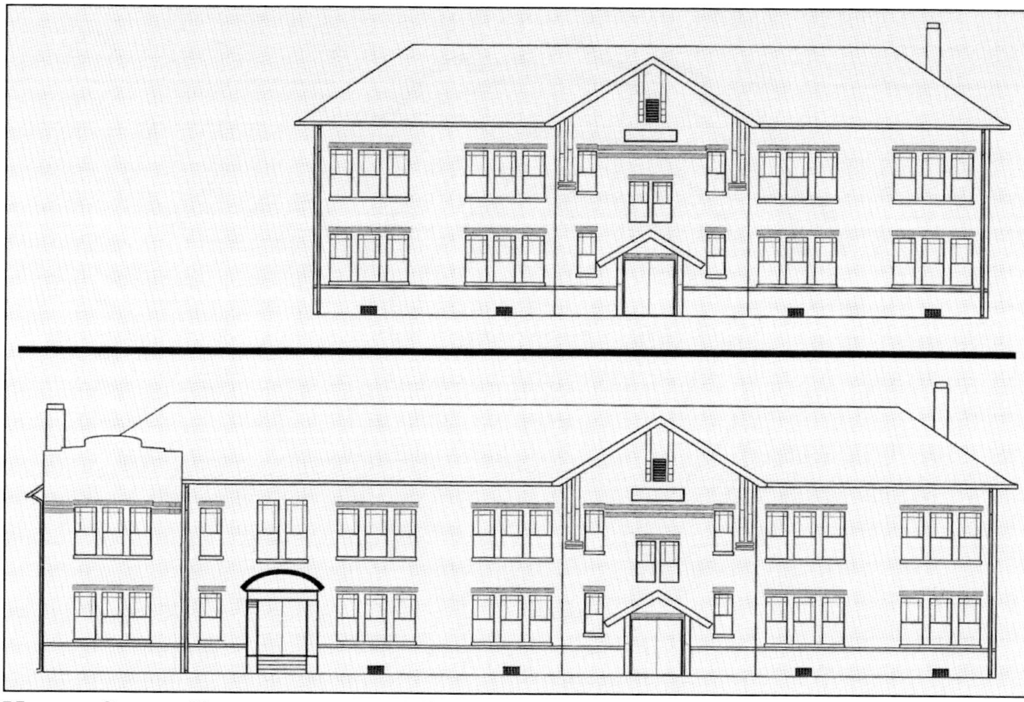

HUMBLE SCHOOL RENOVATIONS, 1915. District No. 28 expanded the size of the Humble School in the summer of 1915. When the school was built in 1909 (top diagram), only 250 students were enrolled. By 1915, there were 600 students attending the school. A $10,000 schoolhouse bond was passed in April 1915 to expand the school (bottom diagram).

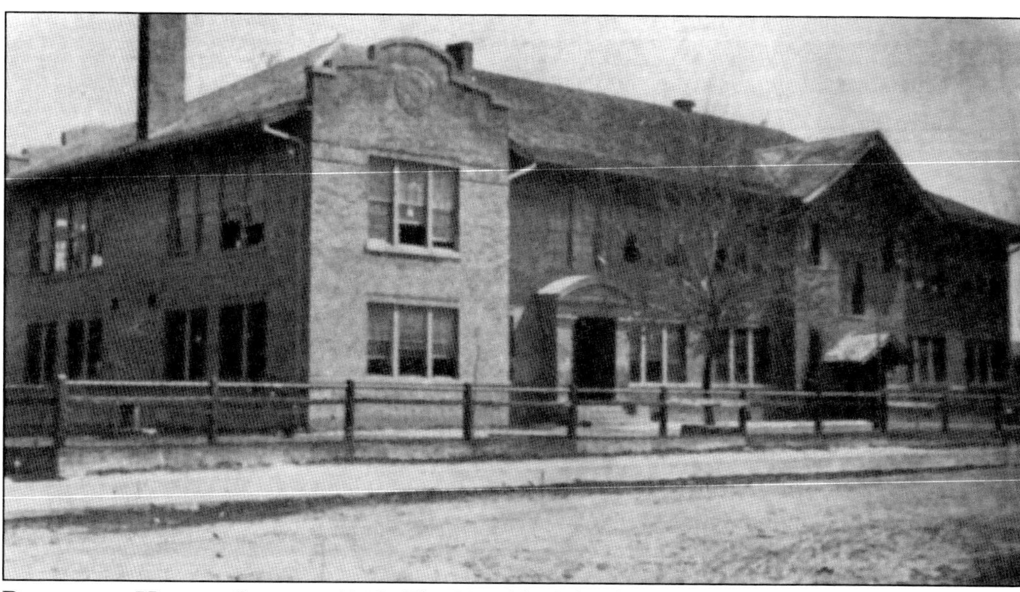

RENOVATED HUMBLE SCHOOL, 1919. The Humble School is seen here after being renovated in 1915. A fence was also built around the school to prevent animals from entering the schoolyard, as Humble did not have a stock law in those days. One day, a hog trying to steal a little boy's lunch grabbed the boy's leg by mistake. Several children chased the hog until it let go of the boy.

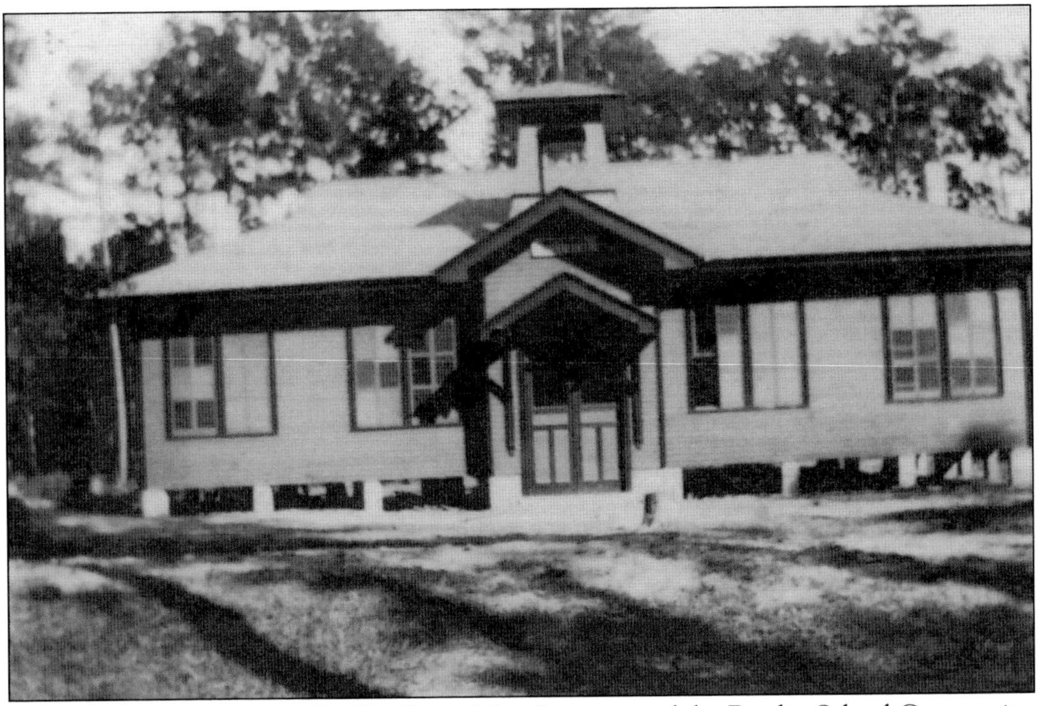

Higgs School, District 29. The Higgs School was part of the Durdin School Community, established in 1876 by G.L. Durdin, Pleasant Humble, and H. Smith. Located on Lee Road near the Humble-Westfield Road (present-day FM 1960), it was later consolidated with the Westfield School Community to become District No. 29. In 1935, District No. 29 became the Aldine Independent School District. Several early Humble students attended this school.

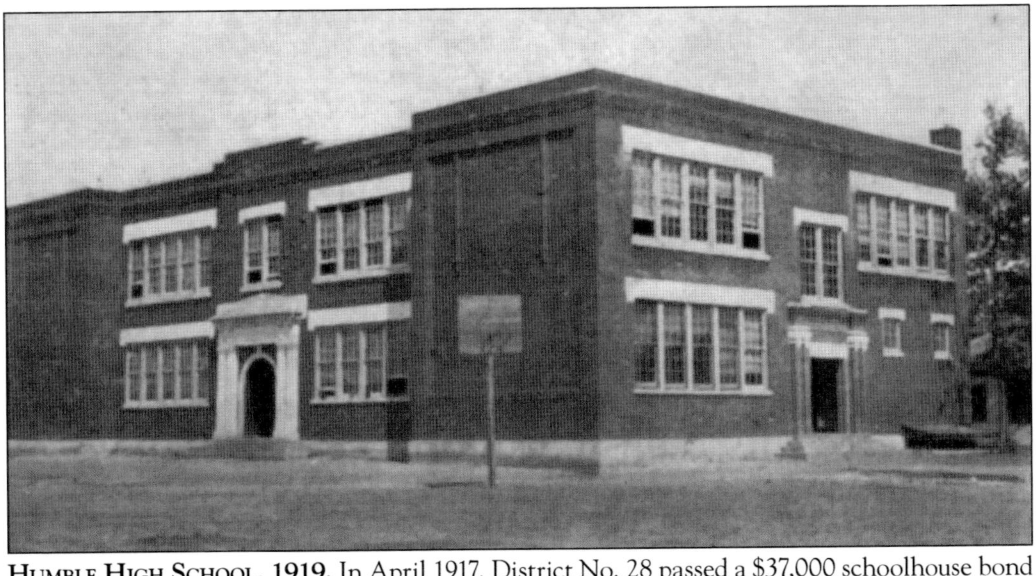

Humble High School, 1919. In April 1917, District No. 28 passed a $37,000 schoolhouse bond to construct a new high school building. Architect Oscar F. Holcombe designed the building, along with a new masonry Woodward School building at Moonshine Hill. Holcombe later quit his construction-firm job and served as mayor of Houston for a total of 22 years.

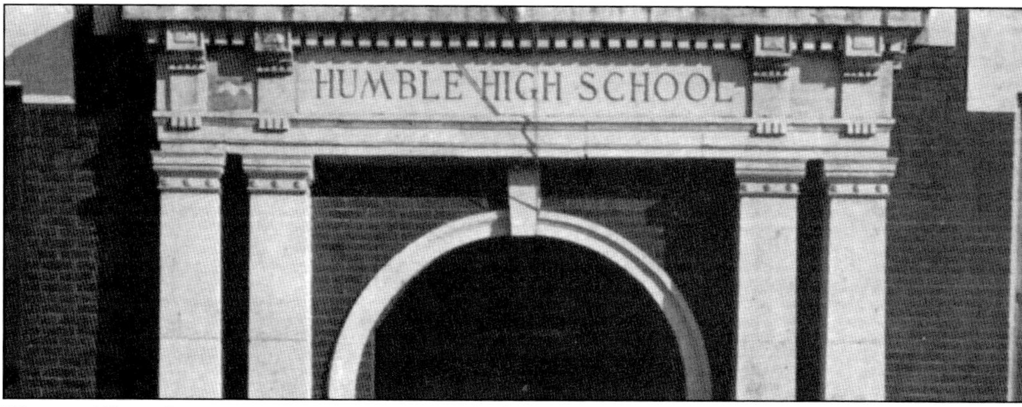

Humble High School Doorway, 1919. To build the new high school, District No. 28 purchased the block next to the Humble School, on the corner of Higgins Street and Avenue D, from the Bender estate. The street between the two schools was closed in the mid-1920s. The contract to build the school was given to the firm of Reynolds and Etty.

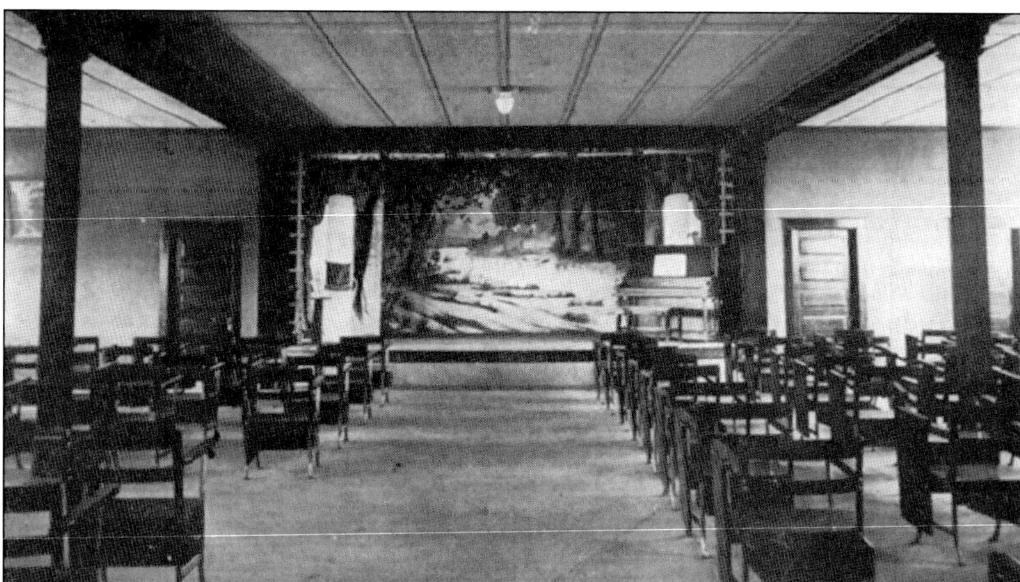

Humble High School Auditorium, 1919. Humble High School opened in September 1918. Frances R. Hyde served as the first principal. In addition to classrooms, the building had an auditorium, a superintendent's office, a principal's office, and a home economics room. As was common in those days, there was no cafeteria. Students brought their lunch, walked to one of the local restaurants, or went home to eat.

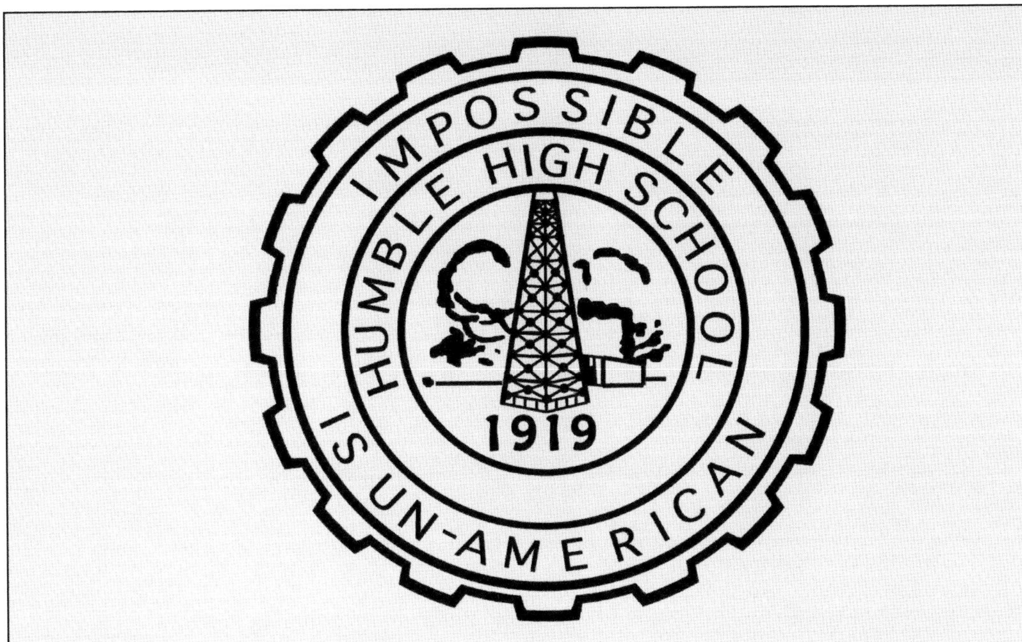

School Motto, 1919. "Impossible Is Un-American" was the motto for Humble High School when it opened in 1918. The logo is featured on each page of the 1919 yearbook, *The Gusher*. The motto would resurface during the building of Charles Bender High School in 1929.

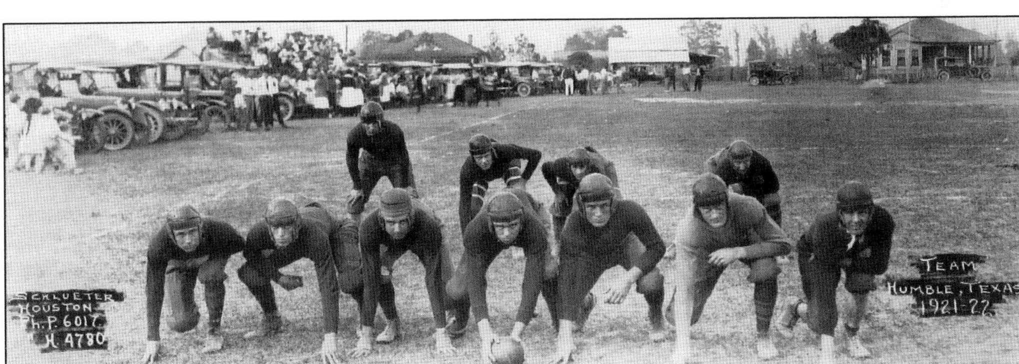

Humble Football, 1921. Football became a popular sport in the 1920s. According to Humble sports historian Donald Wilkins, the first team was called the Tigers, but the name and team color changed each year. In 1924, the student body voted for purple and white as the permanent school colors. They also chose the Wildcat as the permanent mascot, because of its perception as a ferocious animal.

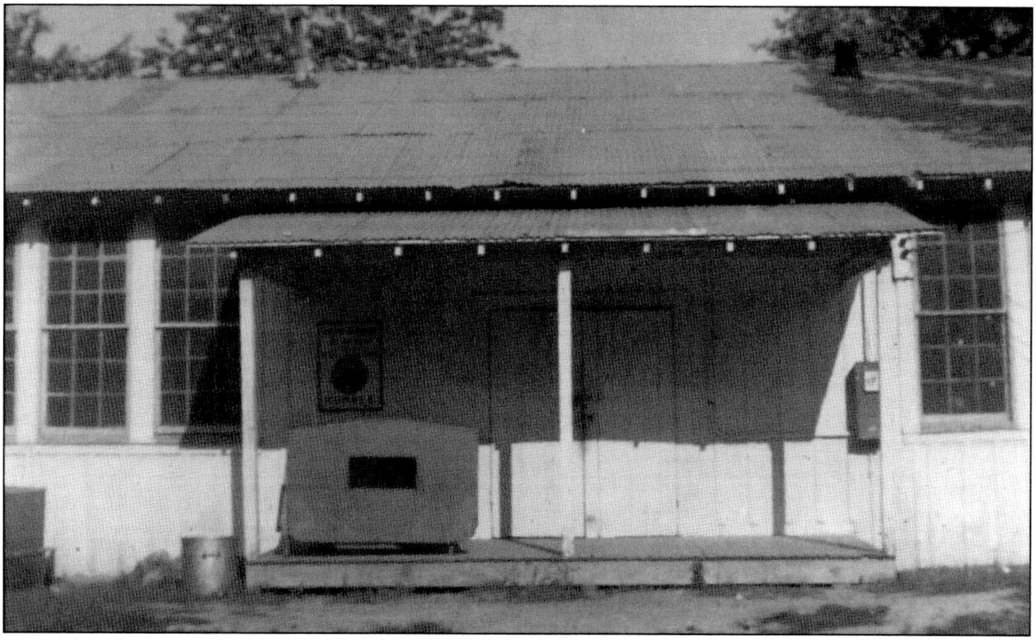

Primary School Building. The district erected a primary school building in 1921 to house first and second grades. It was located on the southeast corner of Hermann Street and Avenue F, across from the Humble School. By the 1940s, the building was used as a government sewing room, part of the Works Progress Administration program. In the 1950s, it was converted into the Vocational Agriculture building (seen here).

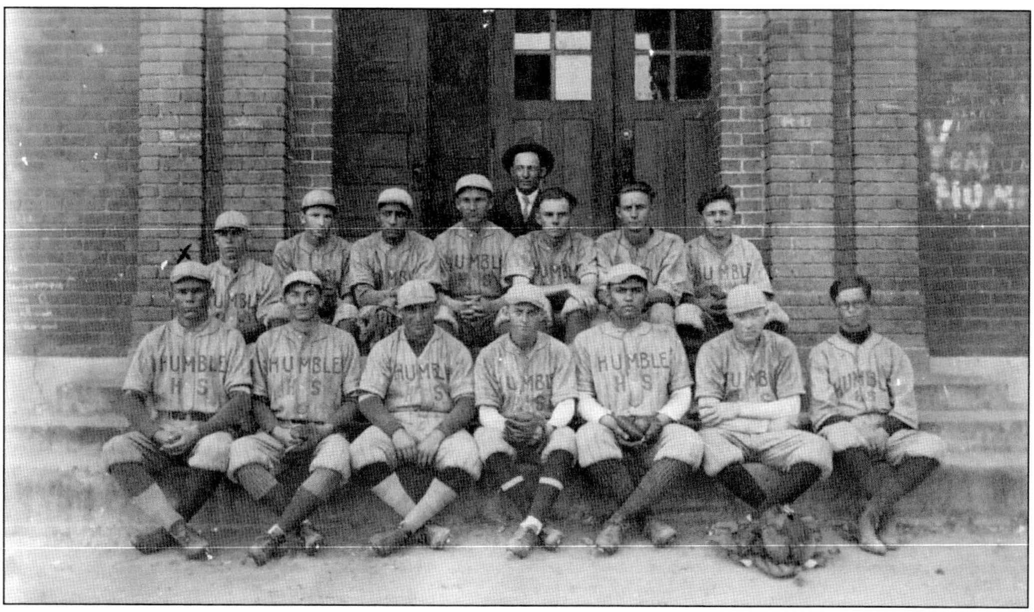

Humble High School Baseball, 1923. The oil companies had baseball teams that played in the Humble area. Humble High School also had a baseball team, which competed in several county meets. During county meets that lasted more than a day, visiting athletes were housed overnight with local families. The University Interscholastic League started managing interschool sports competitions, beginning with football in 1920, then basketball in 1921 and baseball in 1947.

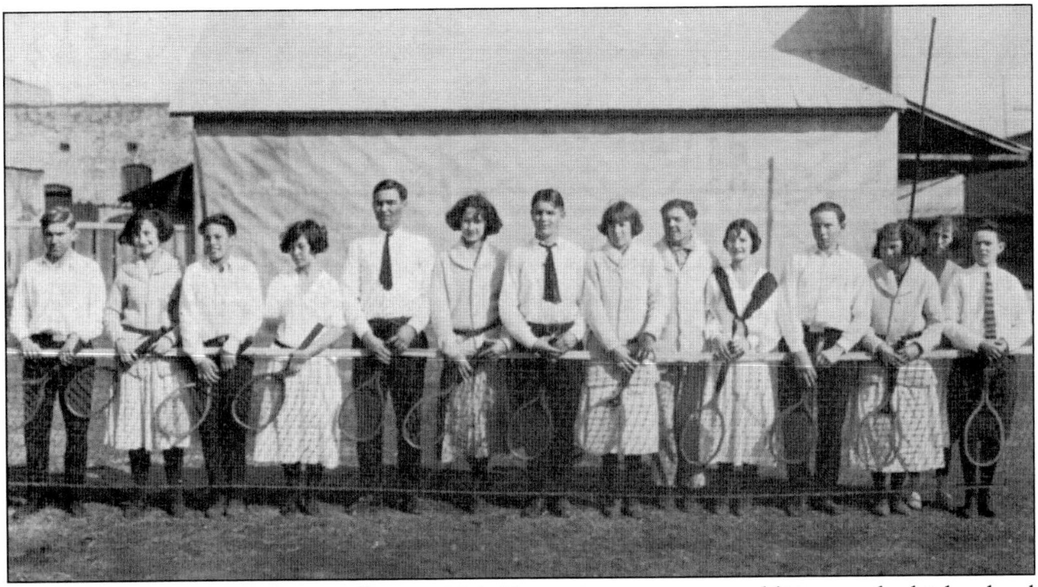

Humble High School Tennis Club, 1924. Tennis is not a recent addition to the high school sports curriculum. The Humble High School Tennis Club started in the early 1920s. Coached by W.G. Stephens, the team won half of its matches at the county tournament in 1924. John Holbrook (ninth from left) and Jack Defee (seventh from left) were the top players from 1924 to 1926.

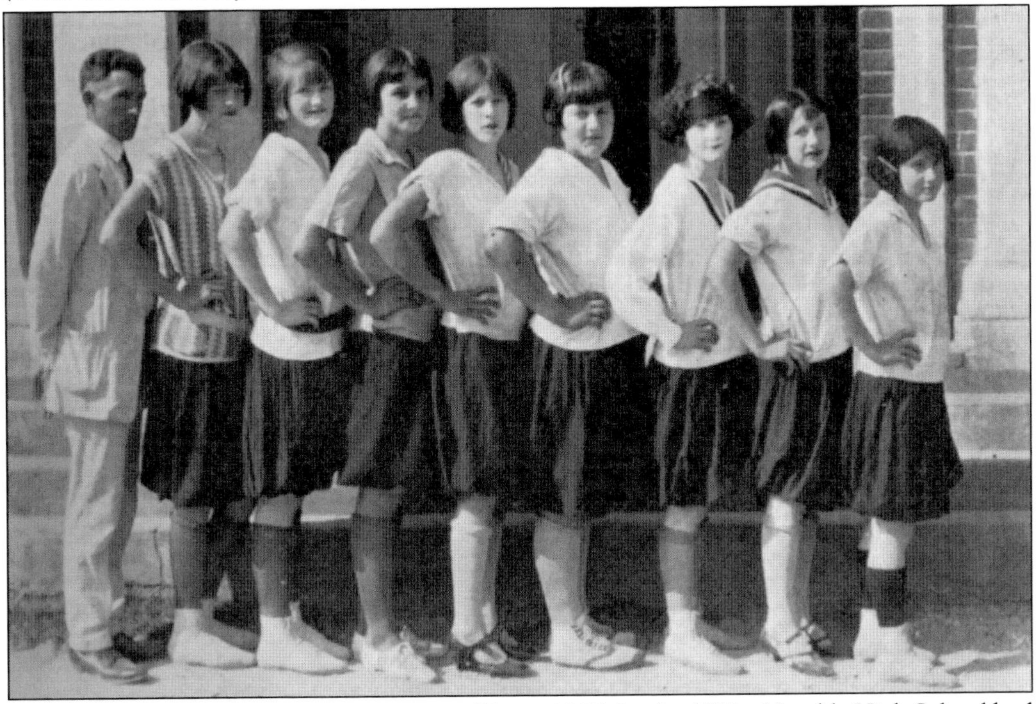

Humble High School Girls' Volleyball Team, 1925. In the 1920s, Humble High School had many of the same sports teams that schools have today. Football, baseball, basketball (both girls and boys teams), track, tennis, and girls' volleyball were being played at Humble High School in the 1920s. The 1925 girls' volleyball team (shown here) was coached by principal Hugo Hartsfield (far left).

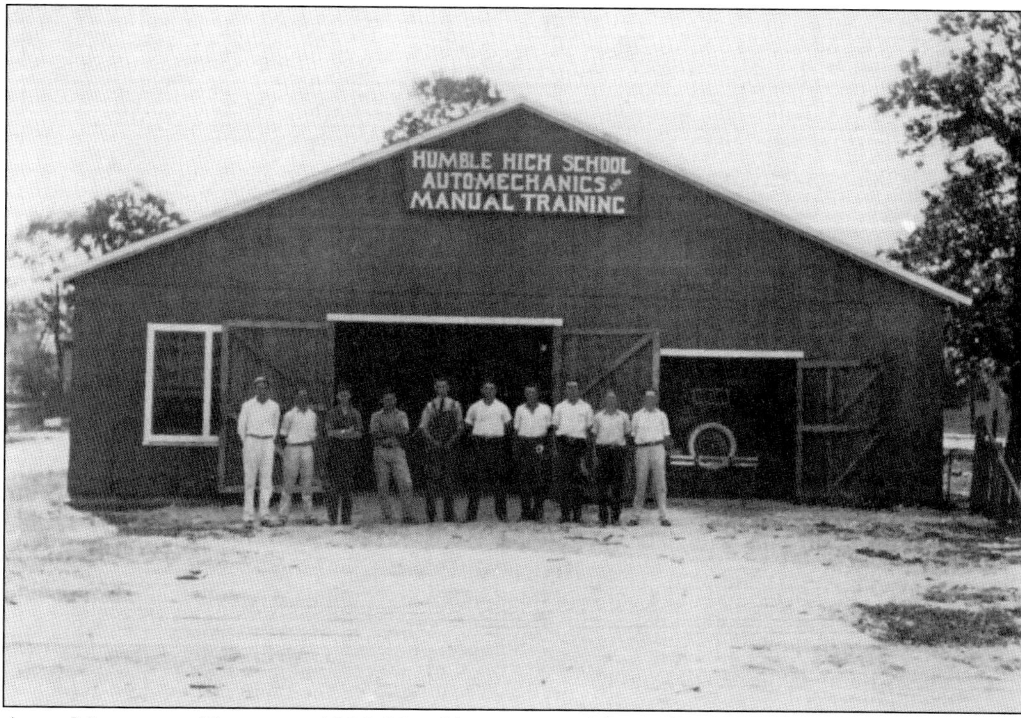

AUTO MECHANICS BUILDING, 1925. Humble was one of the earliest schools in the county to offer classes in automobile mechanics, starting the program in 1924. The Texas State Department of Education praised Humble for the quality of the school's Auto Mechanics and Manual Training program. Mr. Dunham was the auto mechanics teacher. The school board voted to discontinue the program at the end of the 1926–1927 school year, due to the low number of students enrolled and the high cost each student had to pay to be in the program. The Auto Mechanics Building was located on the northwest corner of Hermann Street and Avenue D. The district would later use this property as the location of the superintendent's home.

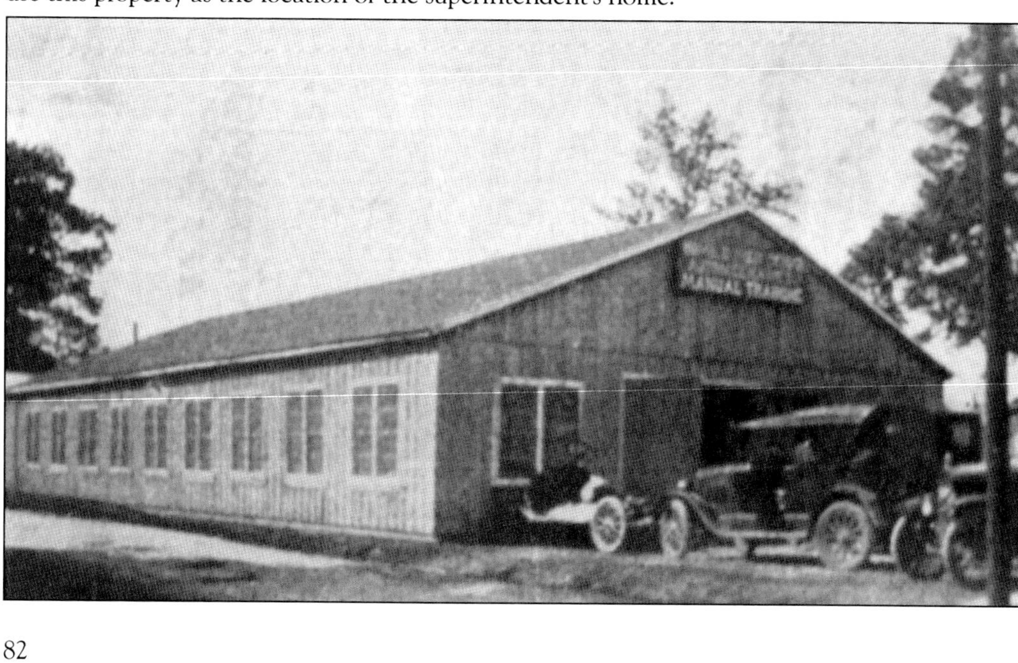

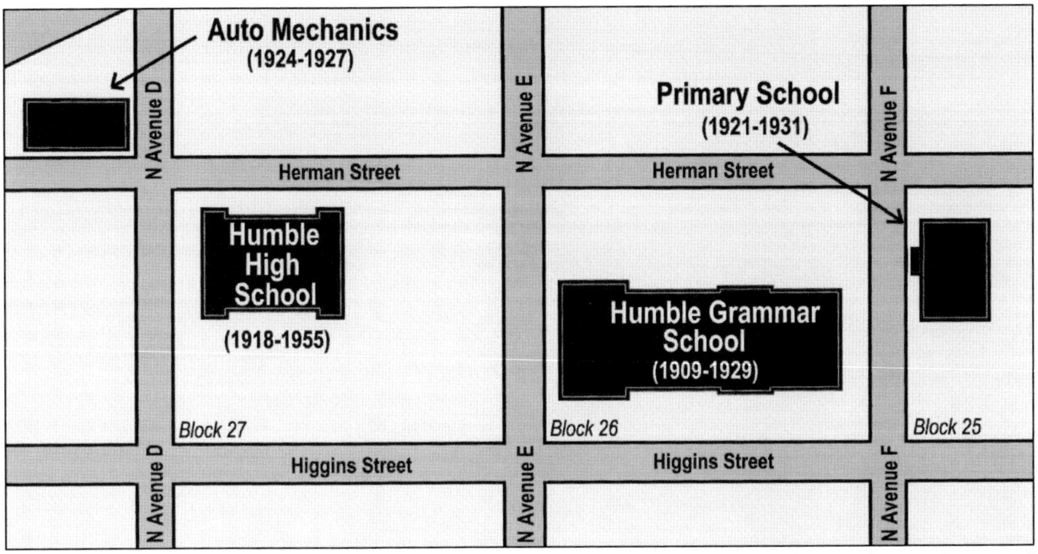

HIGGINS STREET PROPERTY, 1925. This is a map of school district buildings located around Higgins Street in 1925. The primary school was for students in first grade and low second grade. The Humble Grammar School was for high second grade through seventh grade. Humble High School was for grades eight through eleven. The district was also operating the Singleton School (grades one through seven), the Woodward School (grades one through seven), and the Colored School (grades one through eleven).

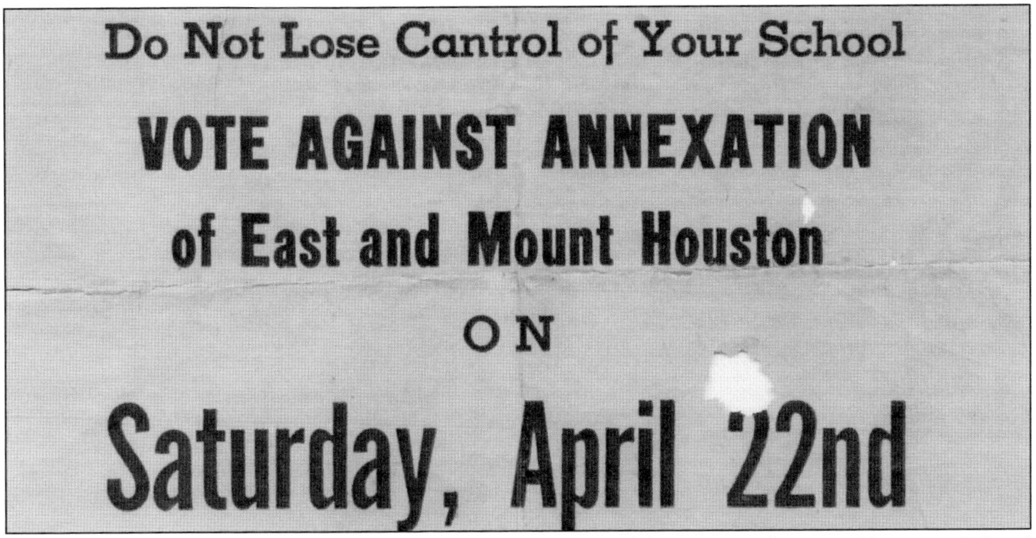

EAST AND MOUNT HOUSTON DISTRICT. In 1950, citizens of the East and Mount Houston School District, just south of Humble, asked to be annexed by Humble ISD. Students from this district were already being allowed to attend high school in Humble. The Humble School Board was in favor of annexation. However, area citizens ran ads like this one and voted against annexation. That district went on to become the North Forest Independent School District.

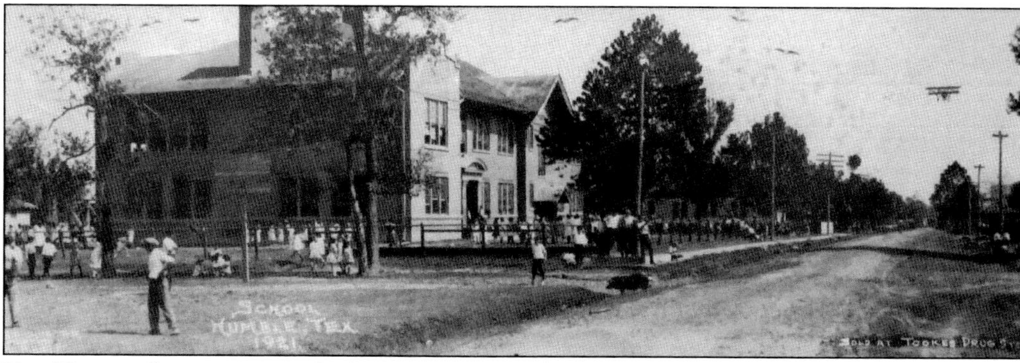

The Humble School, 1921. On January 26, 1929, the Humble School was destroyed in a predawn fire. The school board immediately authorized work to begin on a new building. During that time, the children attended school at the Humble High School building. High school students attended classes in the mornings, and grammar school students attended in the afternoons.

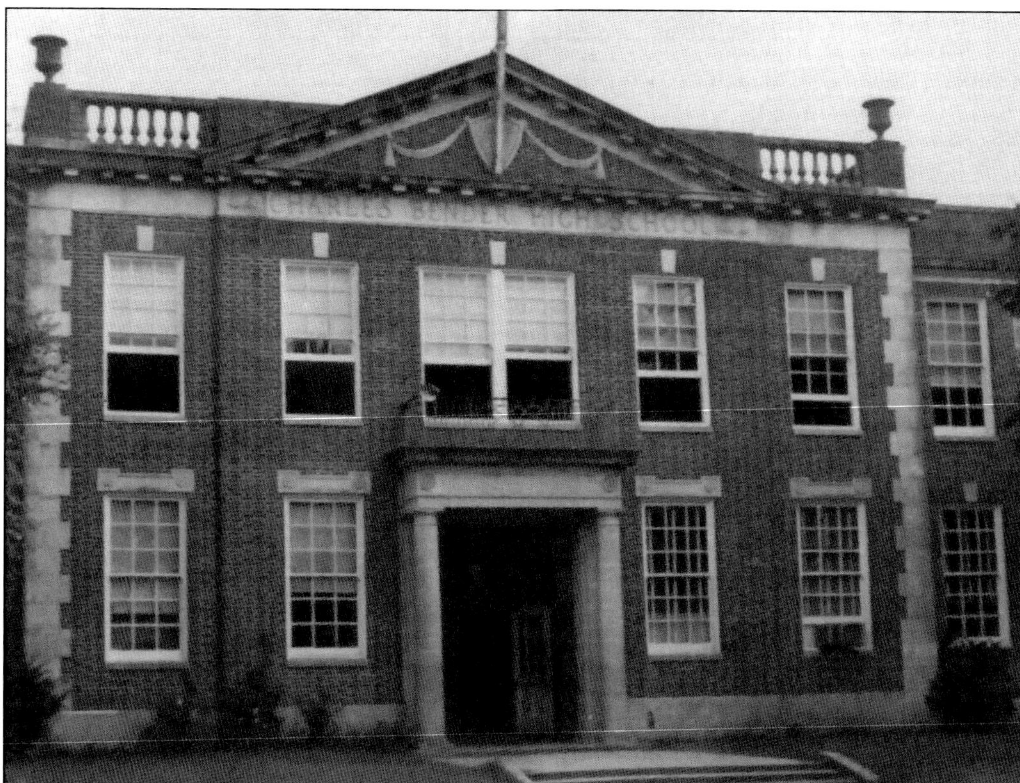

Charles Bender High School. To replace the Humble School, the school board wanted a building similar to the new Robert E. Lee High School in Baytown. Its architect, Harry D. Payne, was hired to design a similar, but smaller, version of it for Humble. The school was named Charles Bender High School in honor of the contributions that Charles Bender and his family had made to Humble over many years.

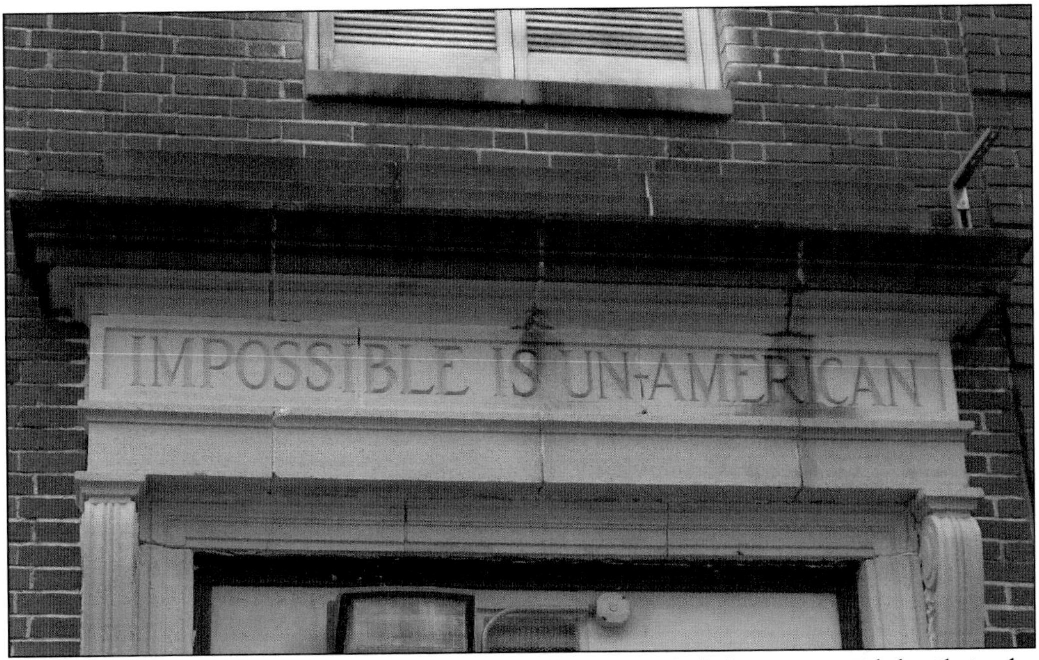

Impossible is Un-American. Architect Harry D. Payne included many special details in the construction of Charles Bender High School in 1929. "Impossible is Un-American," the motto from Humble High School, was engraved over one of the back doors. The phrase "Ever Onward" was engraved over another back door. "Impossible is Un-American" became the rallying cry of students and alumni dedicated to preserving the building in 2010.

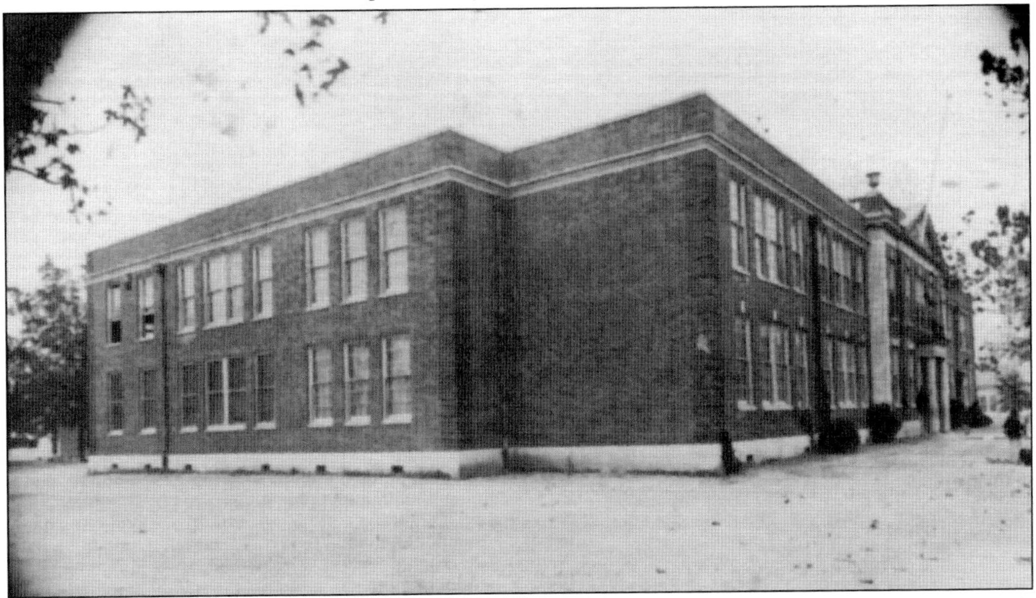

Charles Bender High School, 1940. When it was erected in 1929, Charles Bender High School was one of the most advanced high school buildings in Harris County. It was one of the few schools that had a cafeteria and kitchen. A $140,000 schoolhouse bond was passed in 1929 to pay for its construction. Harry Payne's next project was building the high school in Huntsville. (Courtesy of Sue Baker.)

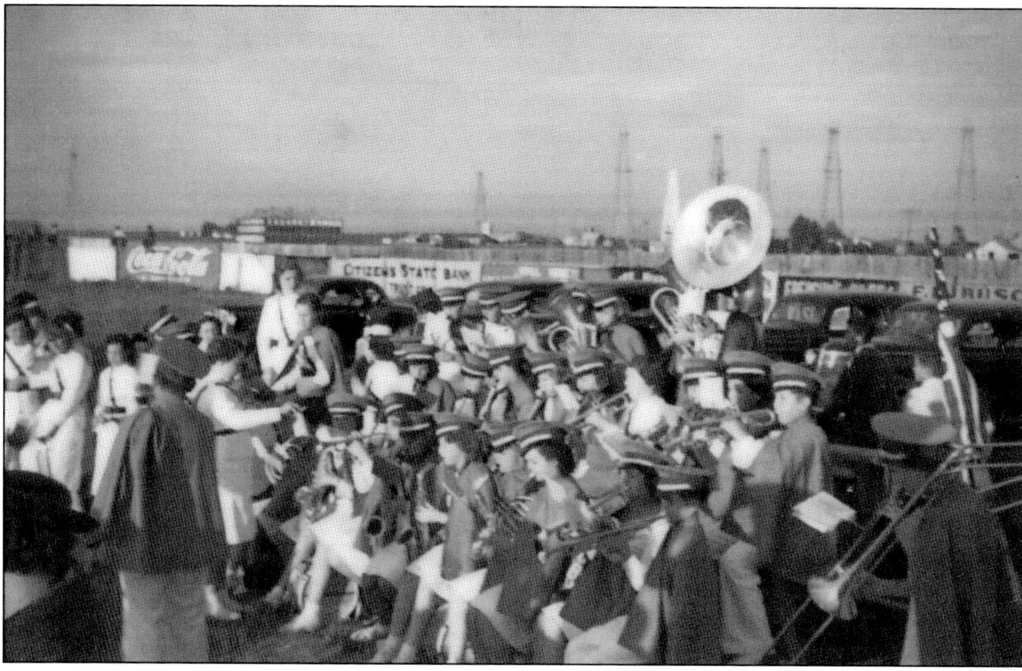

BENDER HIGH SCHOOL BAND, 1938. Music has been a part of the Humble schools since the early years. May Betting is the earliest recorded music teacher, during the 1916–1917 school year. The first mention of a band at Bender High School was in 1929, under the direction of band director Roy O'Briend. In this photograph, the band is playing at a Bender High football game in 1938.

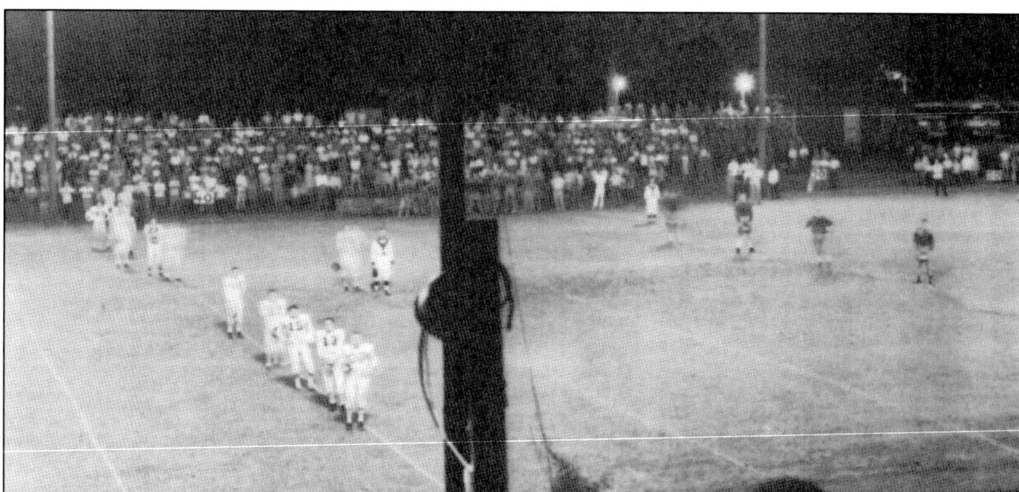

CHARLES STREET STADIUM. In 1938, the district purchased a large tract of land, north of present-day First Street and adjacent to the railroad tracks, from Bender Brothers for $2,500. A football stadium was erected on the property in 1946. Bender High School football games were played at this stadium prior to the opening of Humble High School on Wilson Road. Shown here is a 1959 game between Humble and LaMarque.

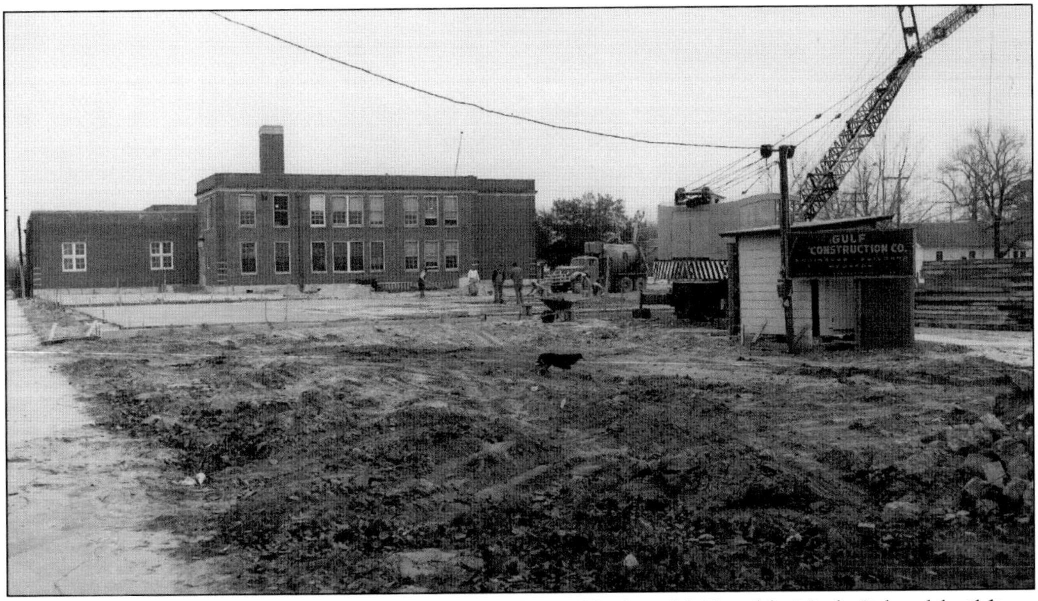

Bender High School Construction, 1956. In 1955, the old Humble High School building, erected in 1917, was demolished and the ground razed (above) to make way for additions to Charles Bender High School. A cafeteria, band hall, and gymnasium were built. The below photograph shows the foundation of the gymnasium being laid in 1956. In 2011, the vacant Charles Bender High School building was transferred to the City of Humble. The city demolished the gymnasium because of its poor structural condition. During the demolition, remains of the basement of the old 1917 Humble High School were discovered and reburied.

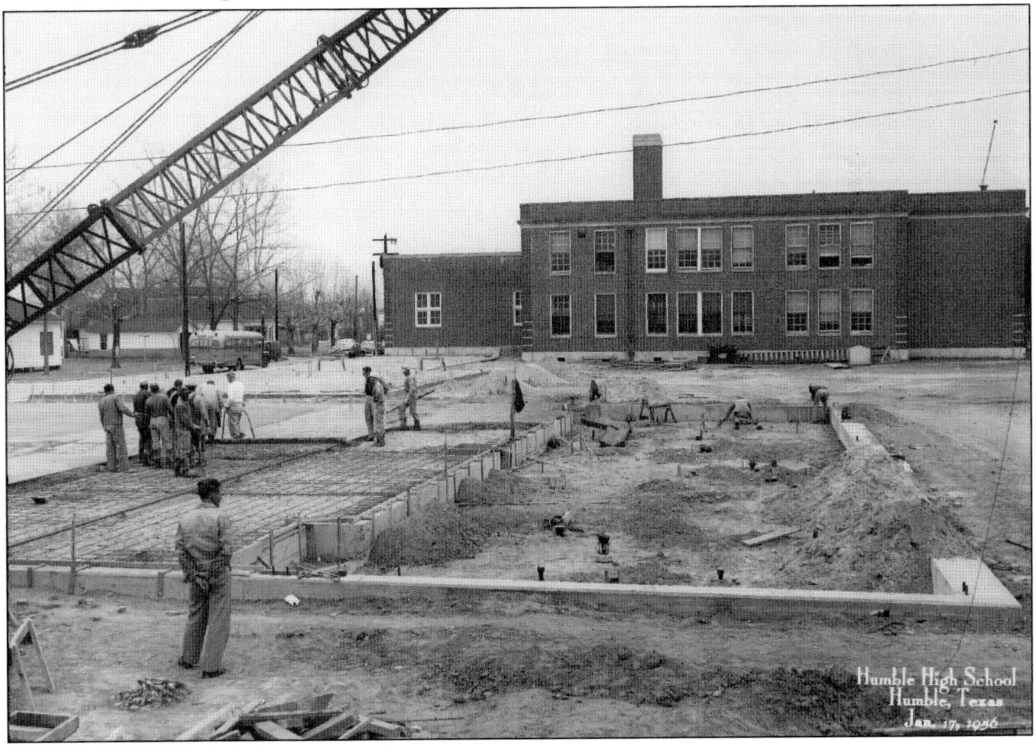

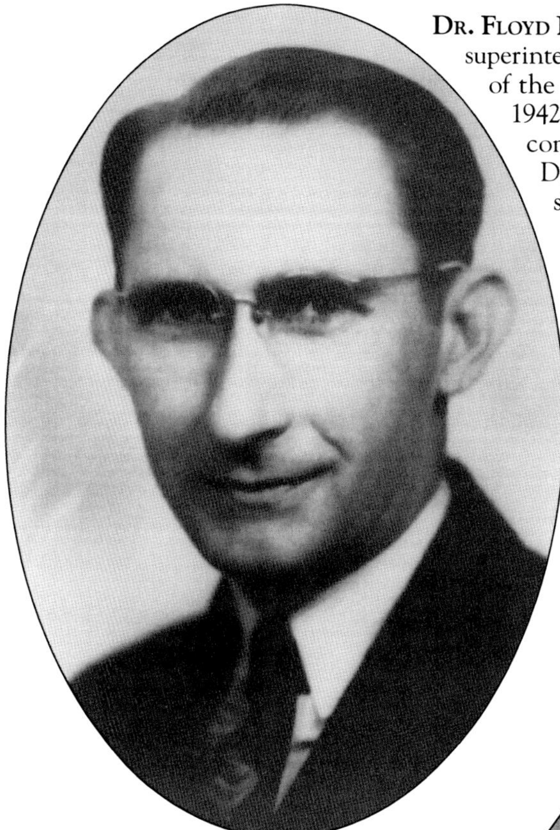

Dr. Floyd H. Burton. One of the most beloved school superintendents of Humble, Dr. Burton served as head of the Humble Independent School District from 1942 to 1961. He was active in all aspects of the community, including as a volunteer firefighter. Dr. Burton was critically injured when his car skidded off the road during Hurricane Carla on September 10, 1961. He died of his injuries two days later.

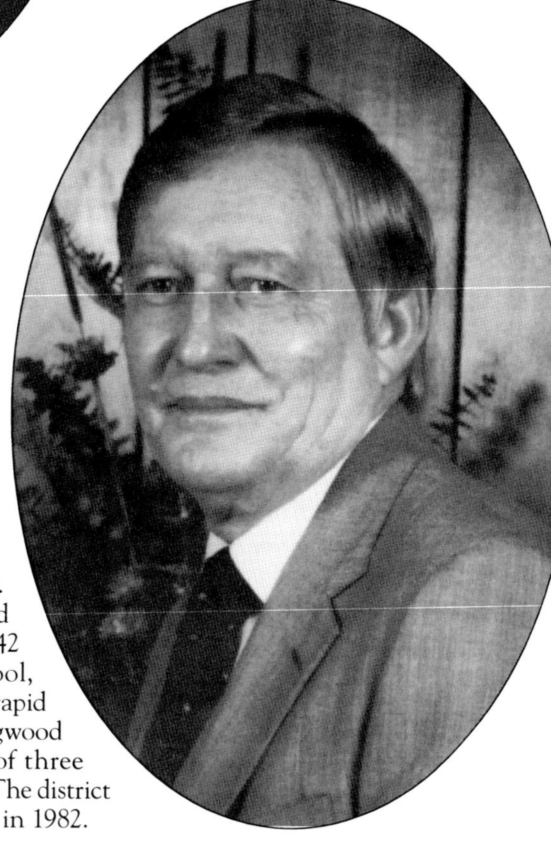

George E. Turner. After the death of Dr. Burton, George E. Turner was appointed to the position of superintendent. A 1942 graduate of Charles Bender High School, Turner led the district through a period of rapid growth, including building schools in Kingwood and Atascocita. Humble ISD consisted of three schools when Turner took over the district. The district comprised 13 schools when Turner retired in 1982.

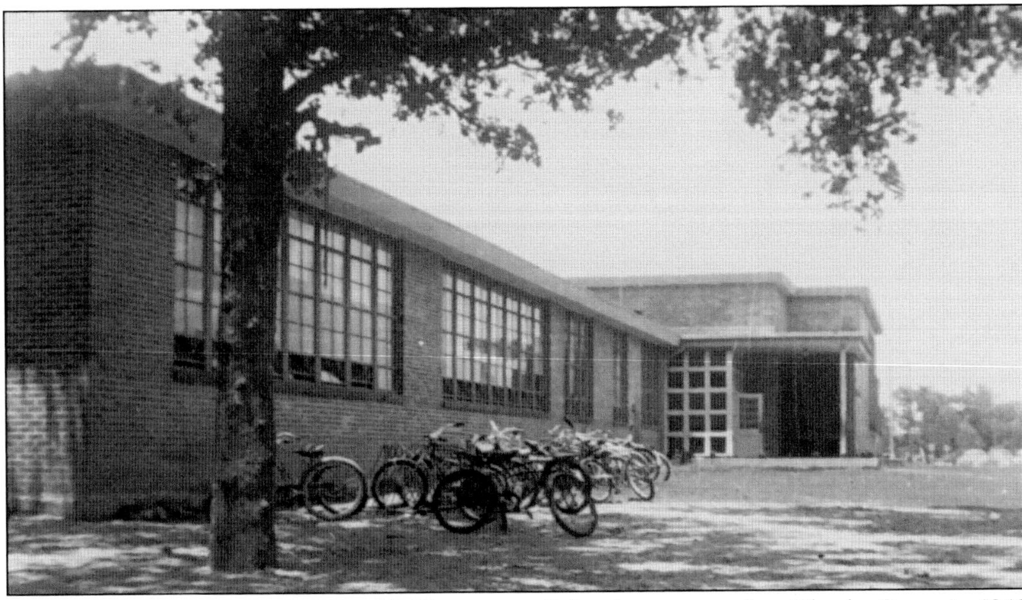

Humble Elementary, 1950. Humble Elementary School was opened on Charles Street in 1948, next to the Humble football stadium. Due to a pricing dispute with the landowner, the district ended up acquiring the land through eminent domain. This school was expanded in 1955. A new Humble Elementary School building was constructed behind Deerbrook Mall in 1999, and the 1948 building was sold.

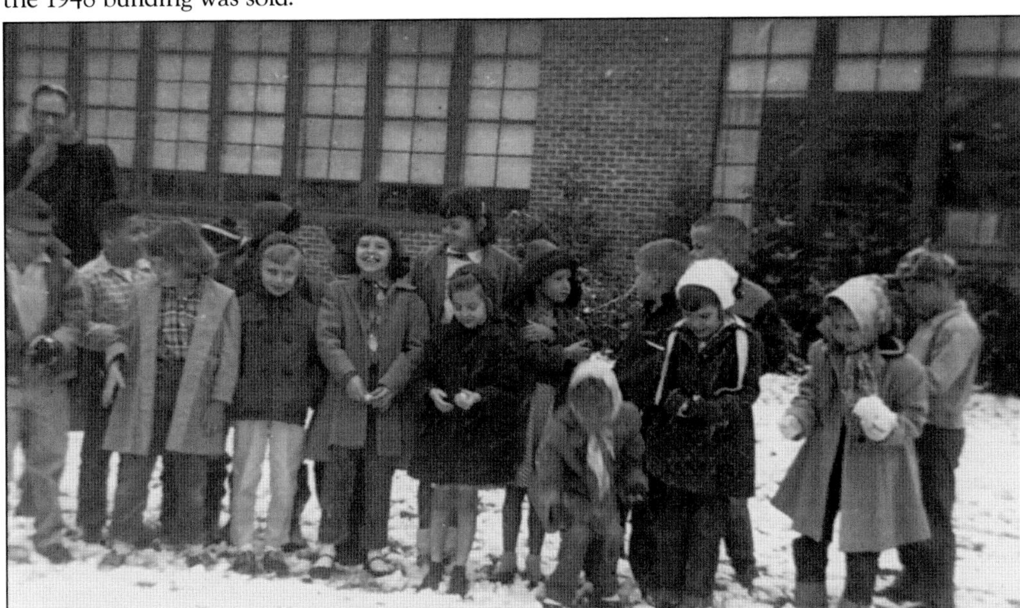

Snow at Humble Elementary, 1957. Snow is a rare occurrence in Humble. When snow does fall, it typically looks more like a light frost. The town does not experience the thick, blanketing snow that residents in the North are accustomed to. Here, children play at Humble Elementary in 1957 after enough snow fell to allow them to make snowballs.

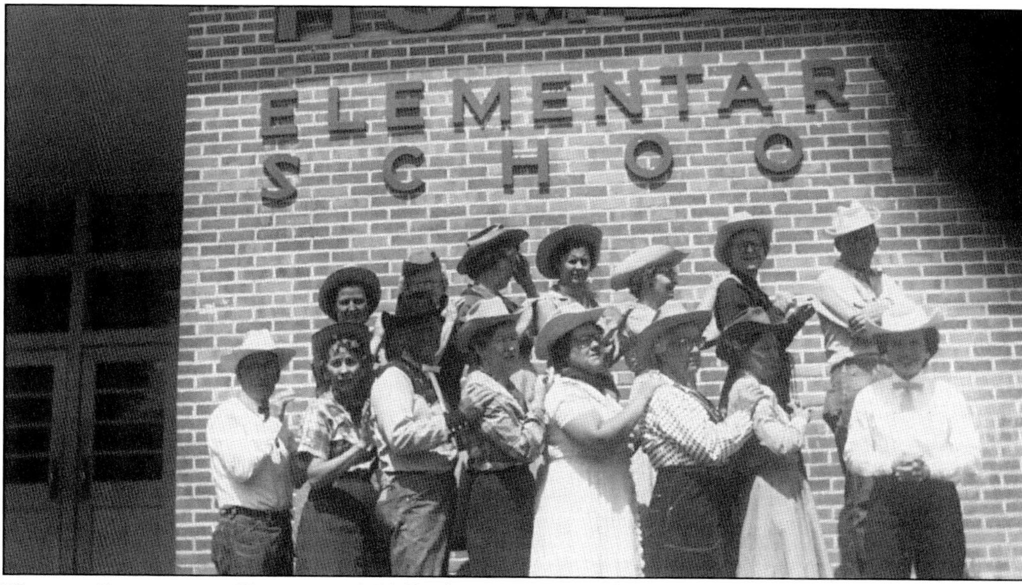

HUMBLE ELEMENTARY FACULTY, 1955. Rodeo Day in Humble was a time for students and teachers to dress up in their best Western attire and celebrate rodeo days. The Humble Rodeo, which started in 1947, was held in May during the 1950s. Students in the Humble chapter of the Future Farmers of America held their annual fair at the same time.

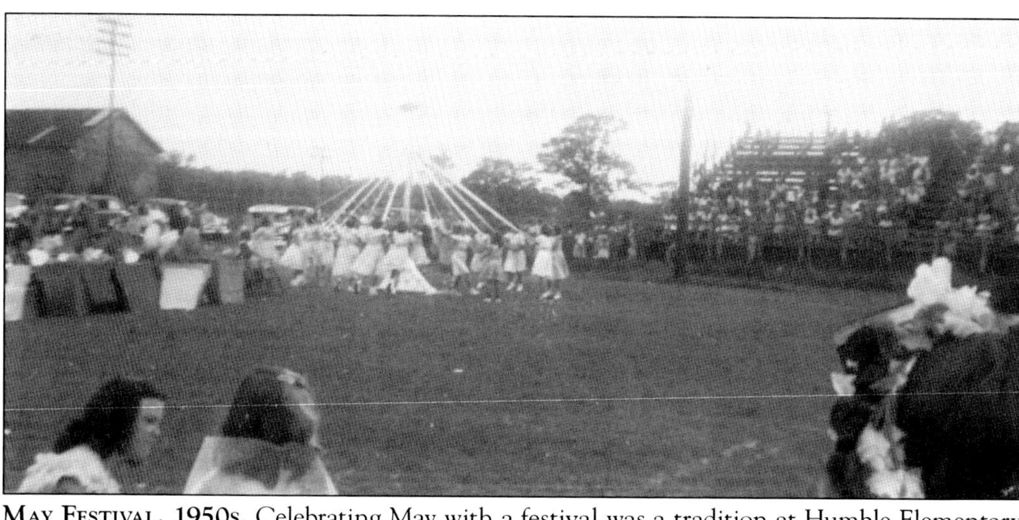

MAY FESTIVAL, 1950S. Celebrating May with a festival was a tradition at Humble Elementary. The celebration was held at the Charles Street Football Stadium, which was next door to the elementary school. The students and faculty participated in Maypole dances and other events. Field Day eventually replaced this tradition.

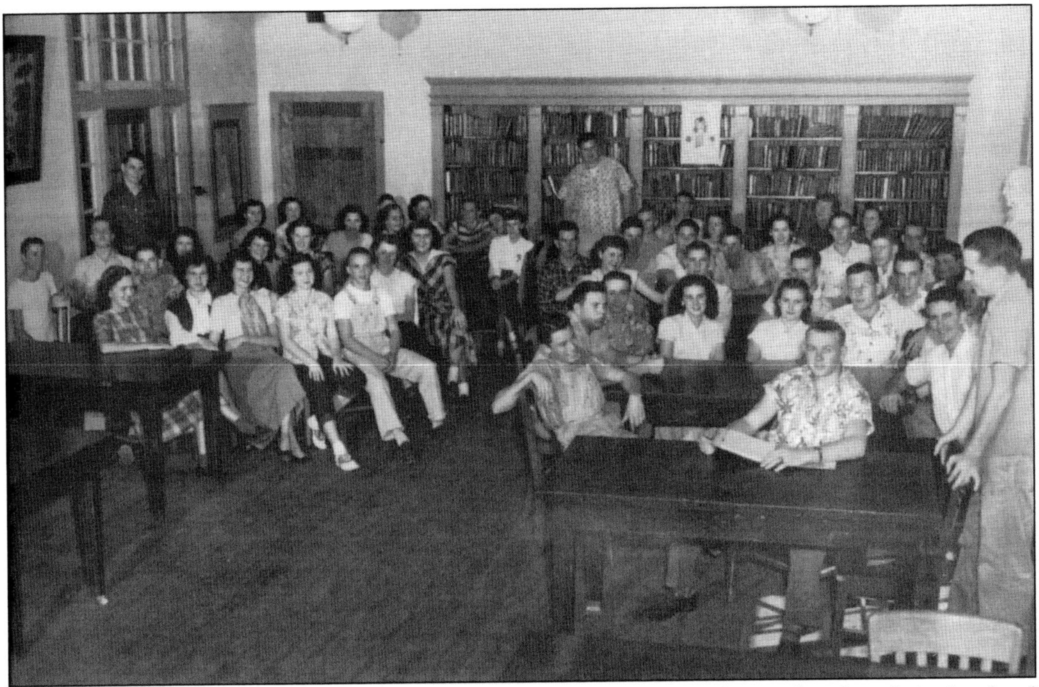

BENDER HIGH SCHOOL LIBRARY, 1950s. Charles Bender High School served as the sole high school in Humble for more than three decades. By the end of the 1950s, the many renovations to the school were not able to keep pace with technology and with the growing student population. In the early 1960s, plans were drawn up to build a new high school to replace Charles Bender High.

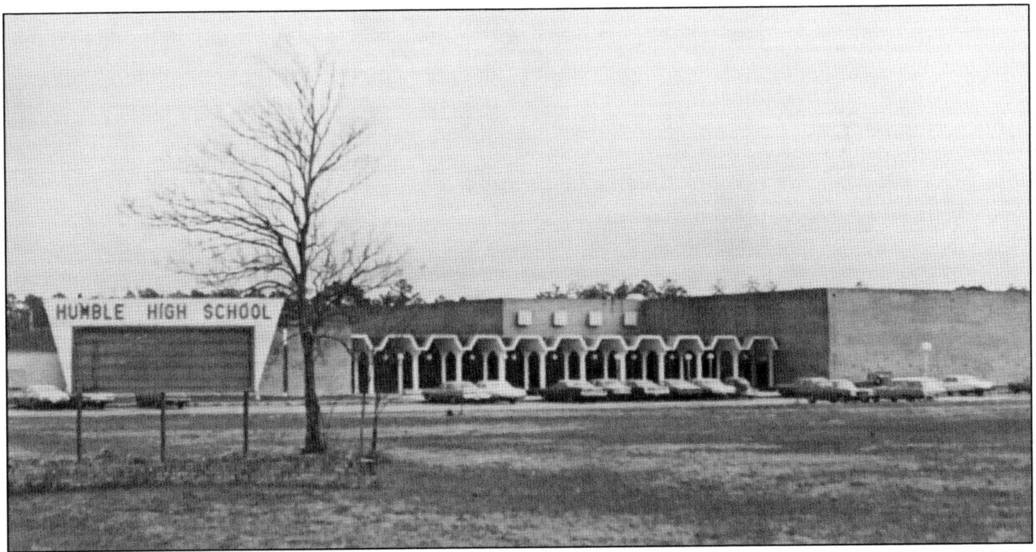

HUMBLE HIGH SCHOOL, 1971. A new Humble High School building was constructed on Wilson Road in 1965. Unlike the small, confined campus grounds on Higgins Street, the Wilson Road property had plenty of room for specialized buildings (such as a football stadium) and for future growth. This building is still being used as Humble High School, although it has been renovated many times.

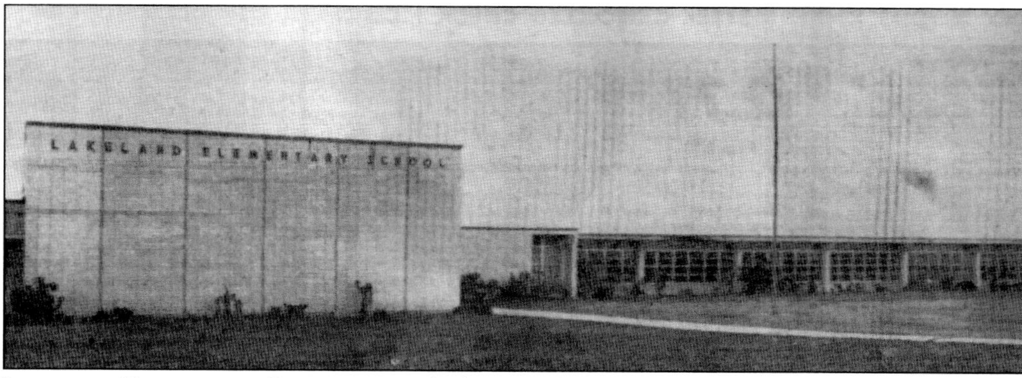

Lakeland Elementary. Due to a period of tremendous growth, another elementary school was needed. Lakeland Elementary was built in the new Lakeland subdivision off of Isaacks Road. Donald Cook was the first principal of the school. When it opened for the 1959–1960 school year, it was called the Lakeland School and only served grades four through seven. Students in grades one through three attended Humble Elementary.

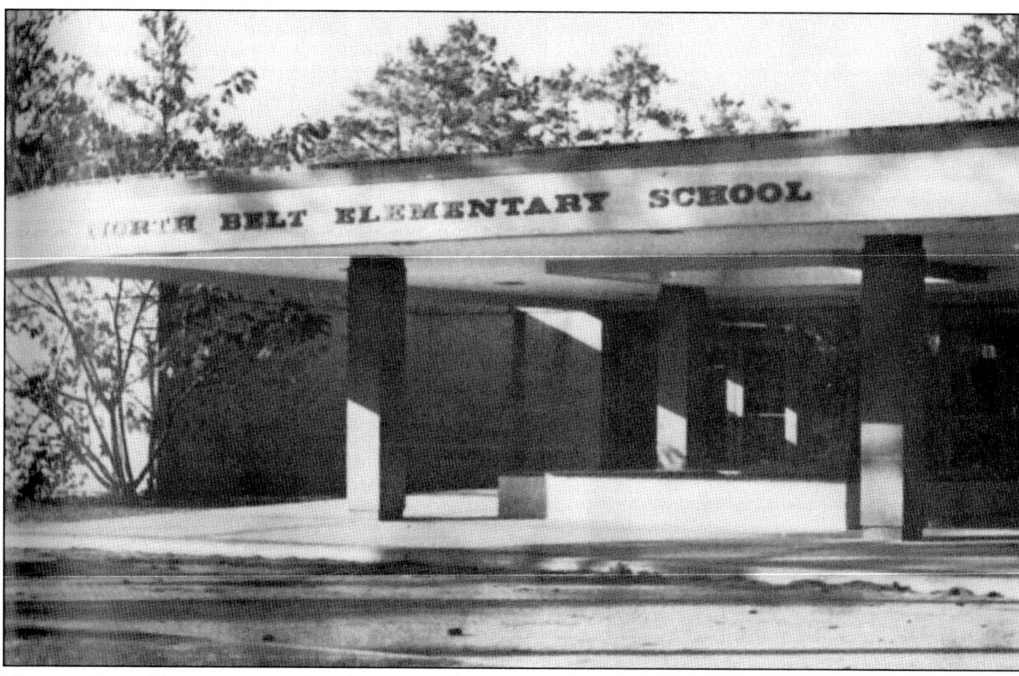

North Belt Elementary. Student enrollment in the Humble schools continued to increase throughout the 1960s. By the end of the decade, another elementary school was needed to alleviate overcrowding at Humble Elementary and Lakeland Elementary. North Belt Elementary, built on the south side of the district, was opened in 1968.

Five

EARLY CHURCHES

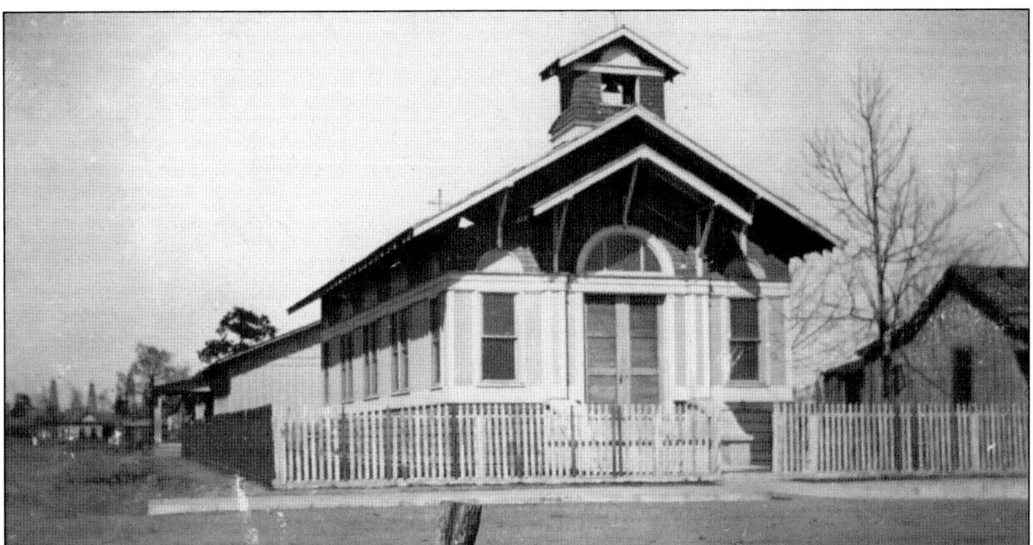

ST. MARY CATHOLIC CHURCH, 1923. St. Mary started as a mission church of the Immaculate Conception Church in 1911. A church building was erected in 1915 at the corner of Higgins Street and Avenue A, across from the Humble School. This building was moved to South Houston Avenue, across from the Humble Cemetery, between 1949 and 1953.

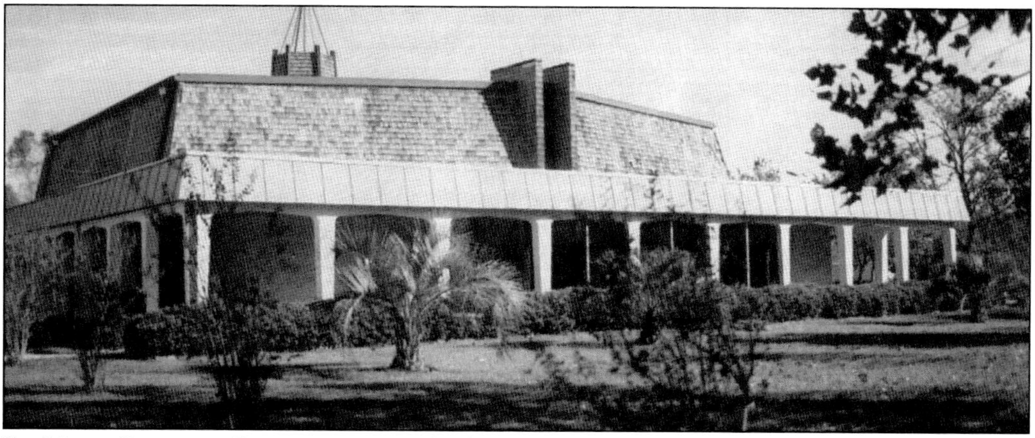

St. Mary Catholic Church, 1976. The first resident pastor assigned to St. Mary church was Father George Swilley in 1965. A new church building (shown here) was dedicated in February 1969. St. Mary was the name of the original mission church in 1911. In 1978, the name of the church officially became St. Mary Magdalene Catholic Church. (Courtesy of St. Mary Magdalene Catholic Church.)

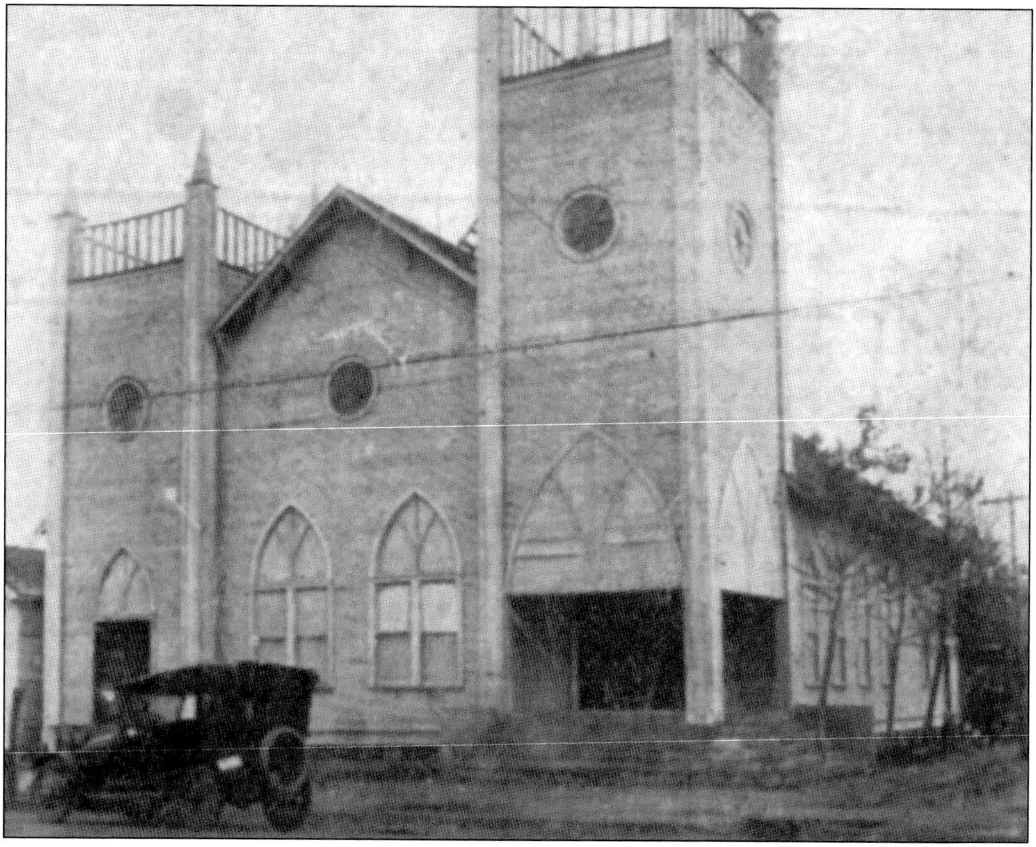

First Baptist Church of Humble, 1918. First organized in 1906, the congregation of the First Baptist Church of Humble held services in a remodeled food store on the corner of Main Street and Avenue C. After 1912, it erected its first church building on the same site. In 1955, a brick sanctuary was built to replace this wooden structure.

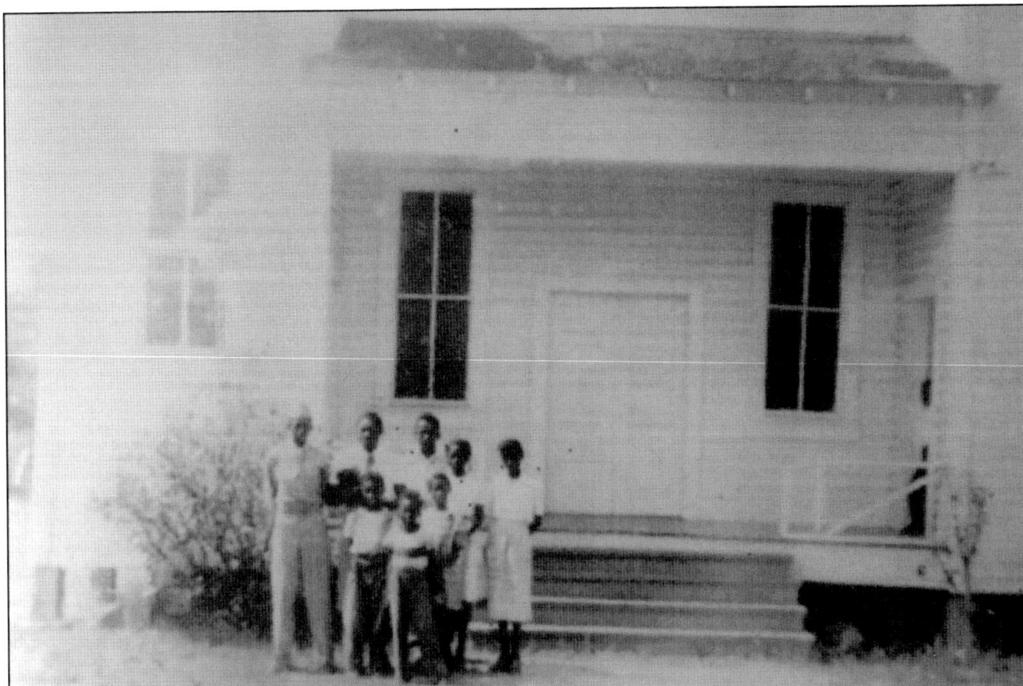

St. Luke Missionary Baptist Church. St. Luke, founded on September 12, 1900, was originally located in Humble, behind the Lindley Lumber Company. The church was moved to an unincorporated area known as Bordersville in the 1930s. The building, pulled by a mule team, was moved to land donated by a local grocery store owner and his wife, Arthur and Hattie Holland.

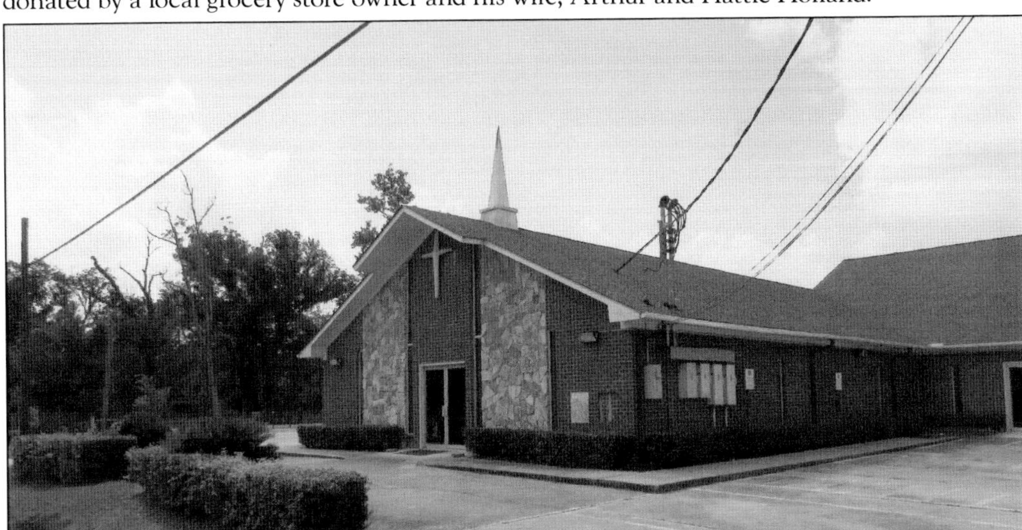

St. Luke Missionary Baptist Church, 2000. The original wooden St. Luke church building was destroyed by a fire on November 7, 1990. A new brick sanctuary (shown here), built at the same location, opened in September 1992. A new facility was opened in October 2011 on South Houston Avenue in Humble.

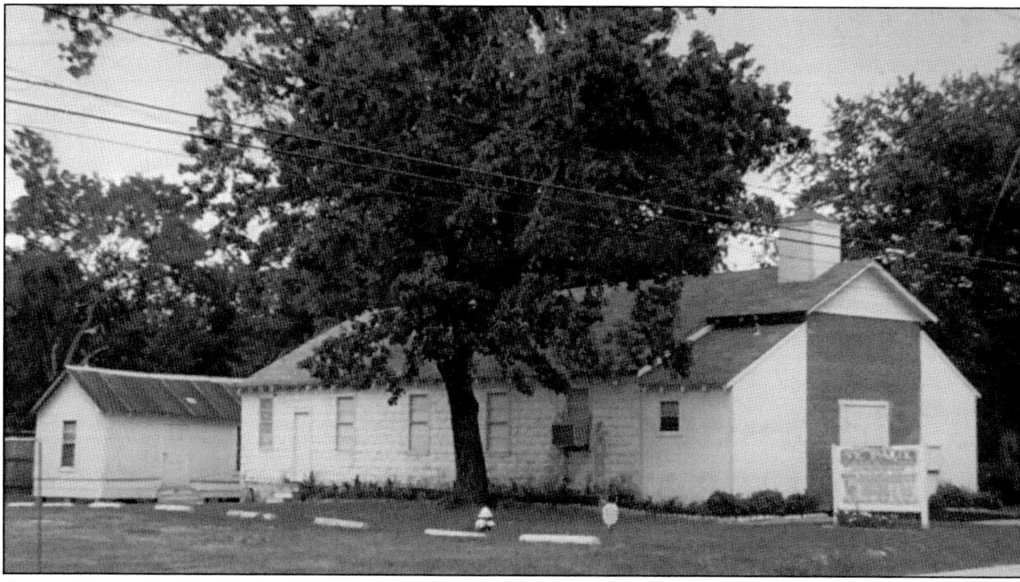

SAINT PAUL BAPTIST CHURCH, 2000. Originally called Pleasant Hill Baptist Church, the congregation was organized in 1869 on the north side of Humble. The building was moved several times, and the name was changed to Saint Paul Baptist Church over the years. The church was moved to its current location in June 1937. The concrete walls were added in 1947.

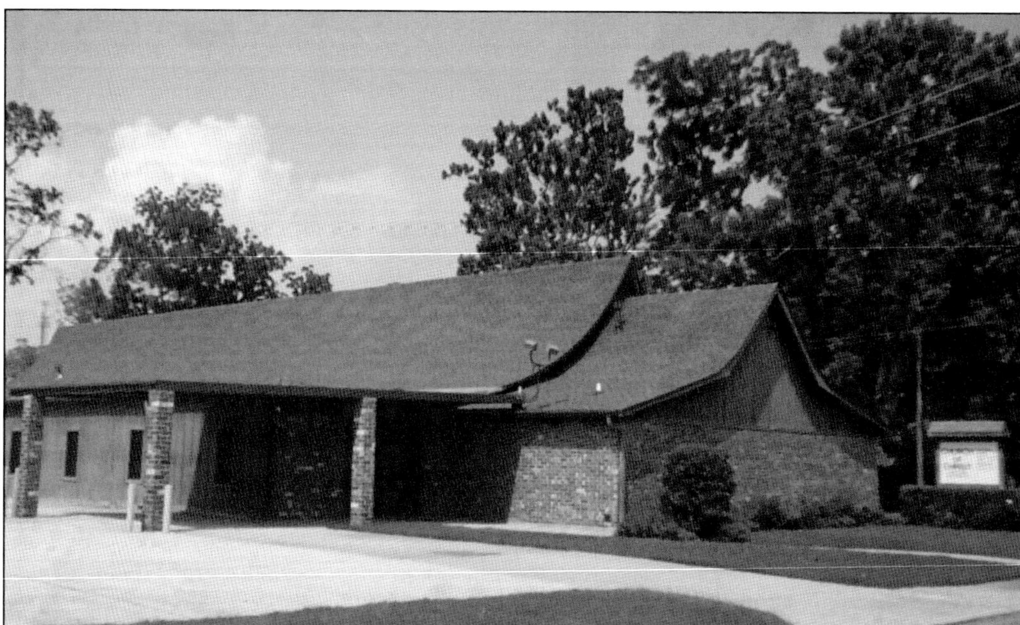

HUMBLE CHURCH OF CHRIST. In February 1925, church members met in the upper room over Sandlin Drug Store. They purchased lots at the corner of Avenue F and Hermann Street, where they erected a frame building in 1928–1929. Needing a larger facility, the church building was sold and construction started on a new edifice at the same location. The present building was erected in 1962.

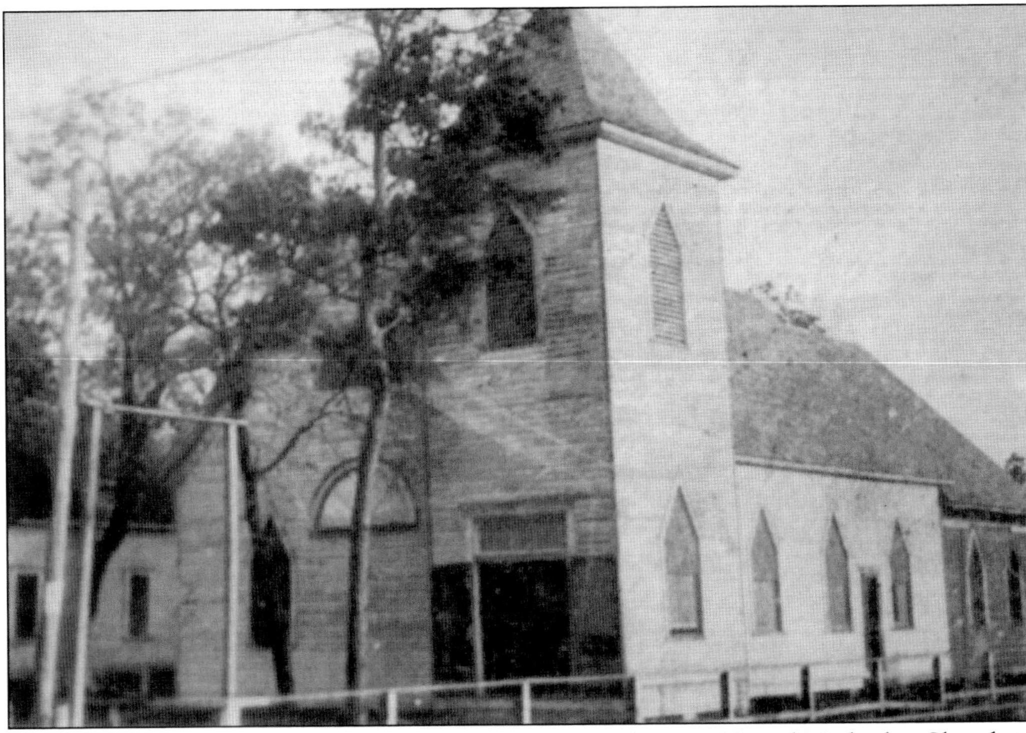

First United Methodist Church, 1918. Services for the First United Methodist Church in Humble began in 1907, led by the Reverend J.T. Browning. The congregation originally met in the old F.A. Peters Bottling Plant on Higgins Street. The first church building was erected in 1909 at 800 Main Street. It was destroyed by fire in 1931.

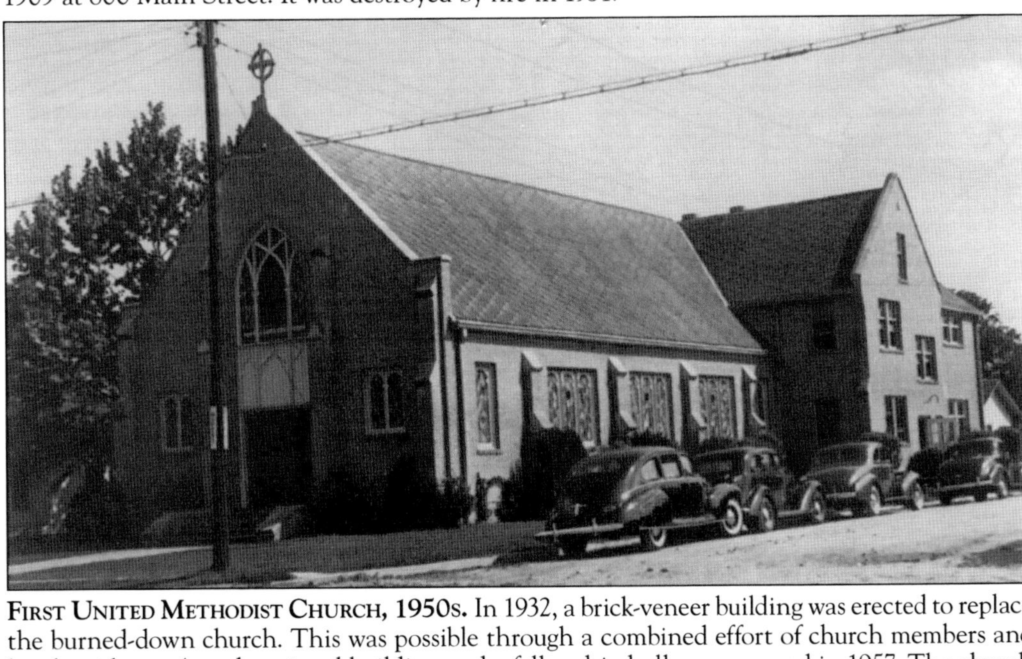

First United Methodist Church, 1950s. In 1932, a brick-veneer building was erected to replace the burned-down church. This was possible through a combined effort of church members and local residents. An educational building and a fellowship hall were opened in 1957. The church received a historical marker from the Texas Historical Commission in 1986.

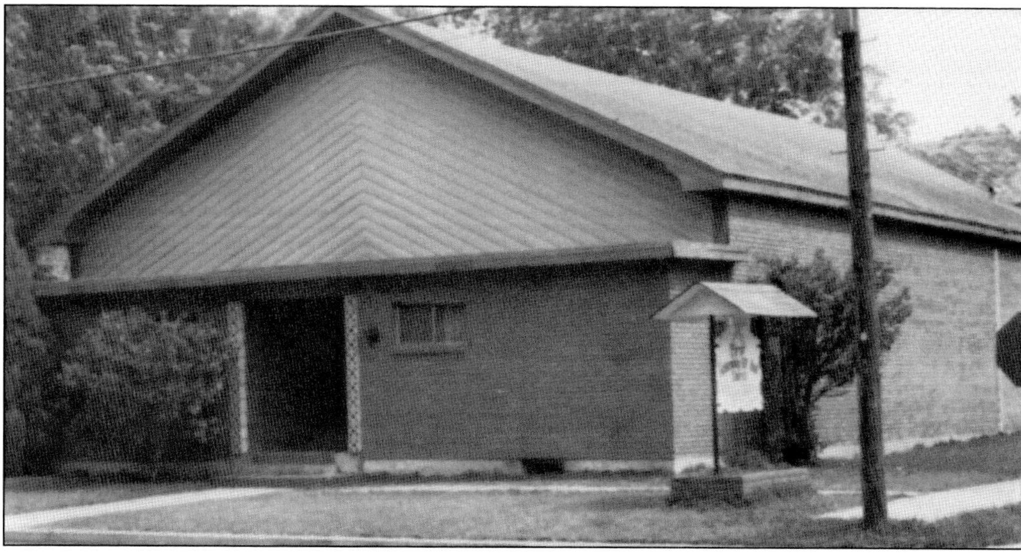

First Assembly of God Church. Organized in 1919, the First Assembly of God congregation erected a church at the corner of Granberry Street and Avenue D in 1923. In the early 1960s, the church building was enlarged at the front, the exterior was completely bricked, and the interior was modernized. The sanctuary was moved to South Houston Avenue in 1976, and then to FM 1960 Bypass in 1995.

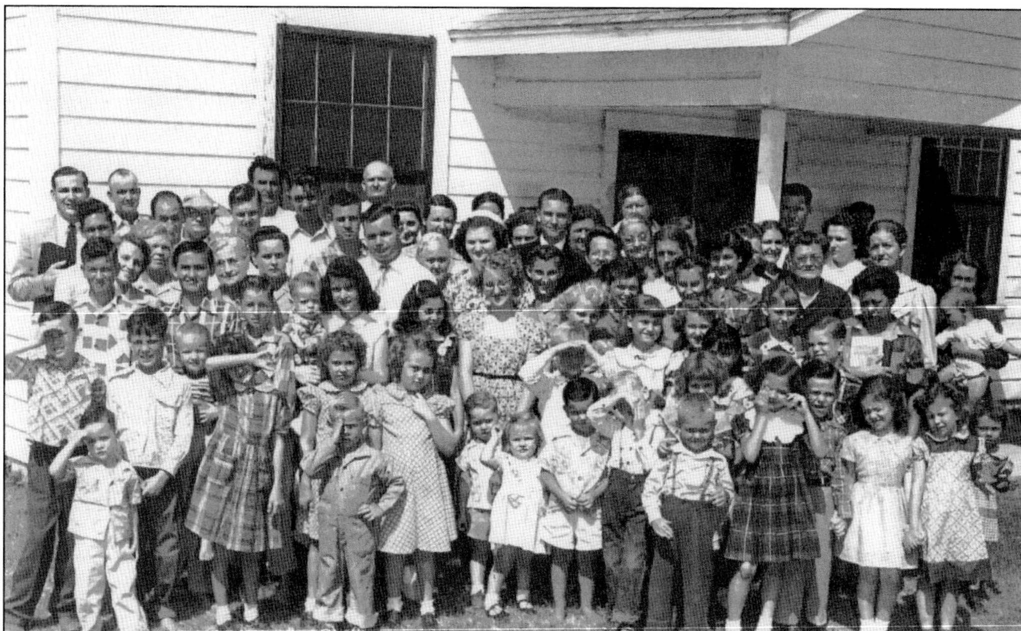

Pentecostal Church, 1948. A Pentecostal church was established in 1920 on Avenue D, between Sixth and Seventh Streets. At the time, it was called the Apostolic Church. In 1940, it became the First Pentecostal Church. Some members left the congregation and established the United Pentecostal Church in the late 1940s. This group is pictured in 1948 in front of the United Pentecostal Church, at the corner of Staiti Street and Avenue G. (Courtesy of the Young family.)

Six

AROUND TOWN

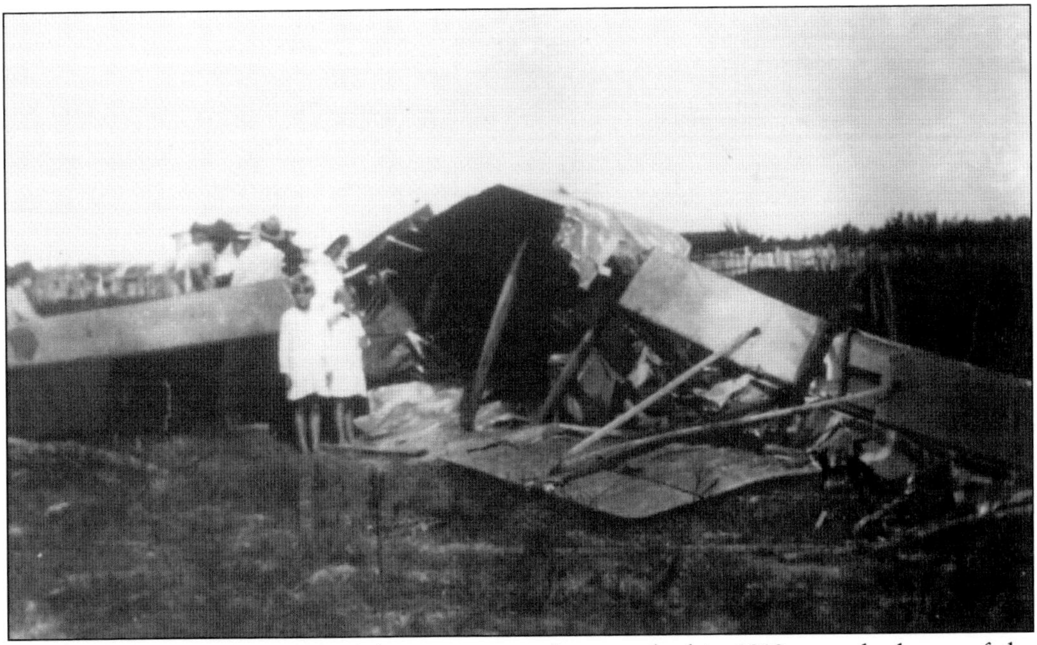

BARNSTORMER CRASH, 1919. A barnstorming plane crashed in 1919 near the home of the Redman family, southeast of the Humble Cemetery. The pilot (with the mechanic as a passenger) was performing a stunt when the plane went into a tailspin and crashed. The pilot was killed instantly. The mechanic died several days later. Posing with the wreckage are Violet Redman (left) and Thelma Redman.

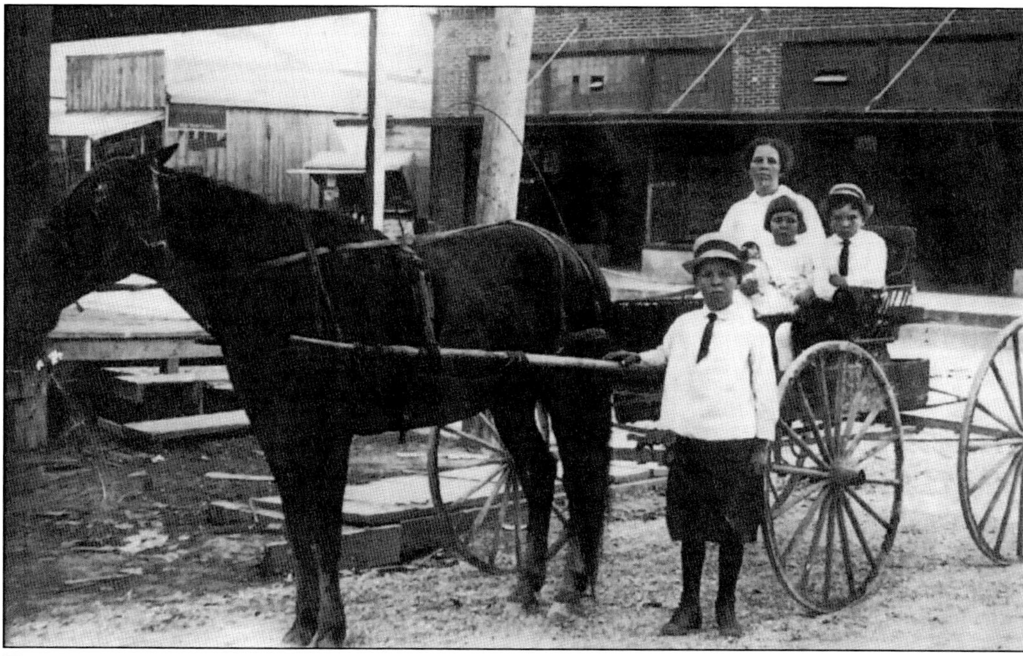

Thompson Family, 1919. The Thompson family poses for a photograph on the dirt road of Avenue B, at the corner of Barrett Street. Joseph Thompson is standing in front. Seated in the wagon are his mother, Mary, his sister, Mabel, and his brother, Ernest. The building behind them is still standing at 300 East Main Street.

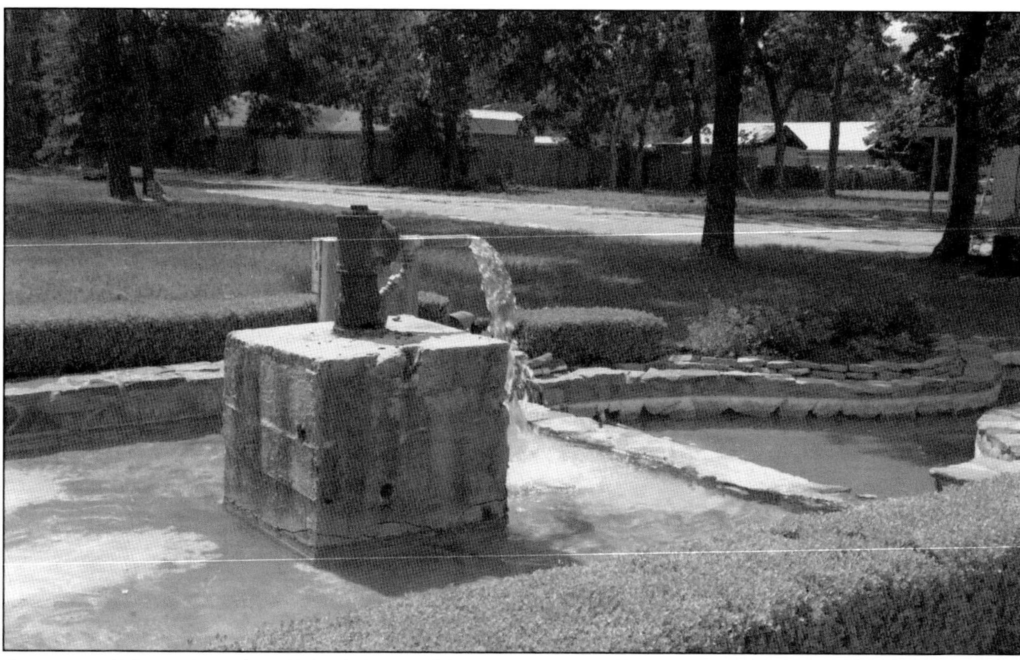

Artesian Well. An oil well drilled in 1912 at the corner of Business FM 1960 and North Houston Avenue resulted in an artesian well that flowed for many years. Numerous bathhouses were built on the property to provide bathing opportunities for oil-field workers and town residents. No longer free-flowing, water is now circulated with a pump. (Courtesy of Scott Meaux.)

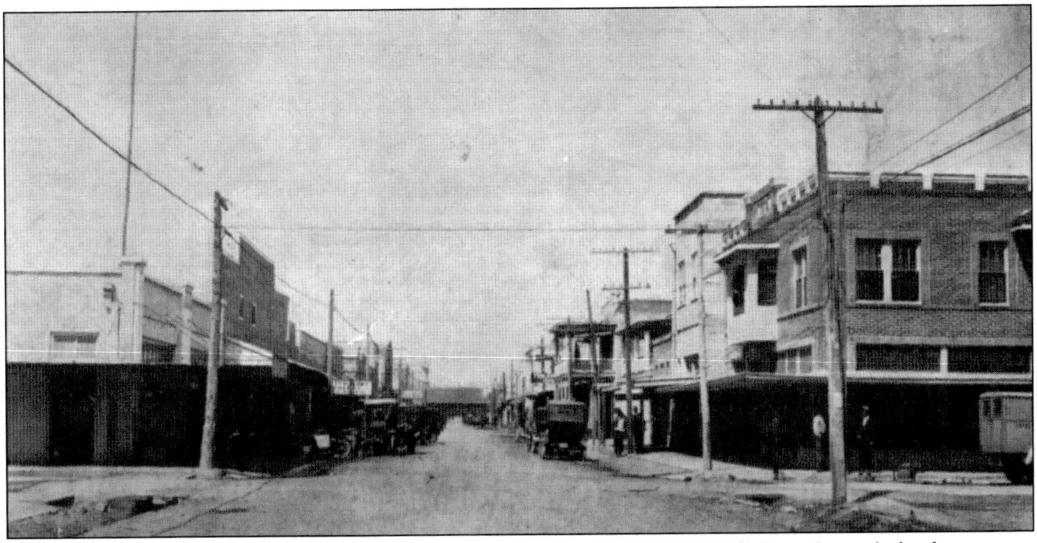

Barrett Street, c. 1919. This photograph shows Barrett Street (Main Street), looking west around 1919. Avenue C crosses in the foreground. The Guaranty State Bank building is on the right, and Rodger's Dixie Theatre is the closest tall structure on the left. The train depot is at the end of the street. Barrett Street did not continue across the tracks at that time.

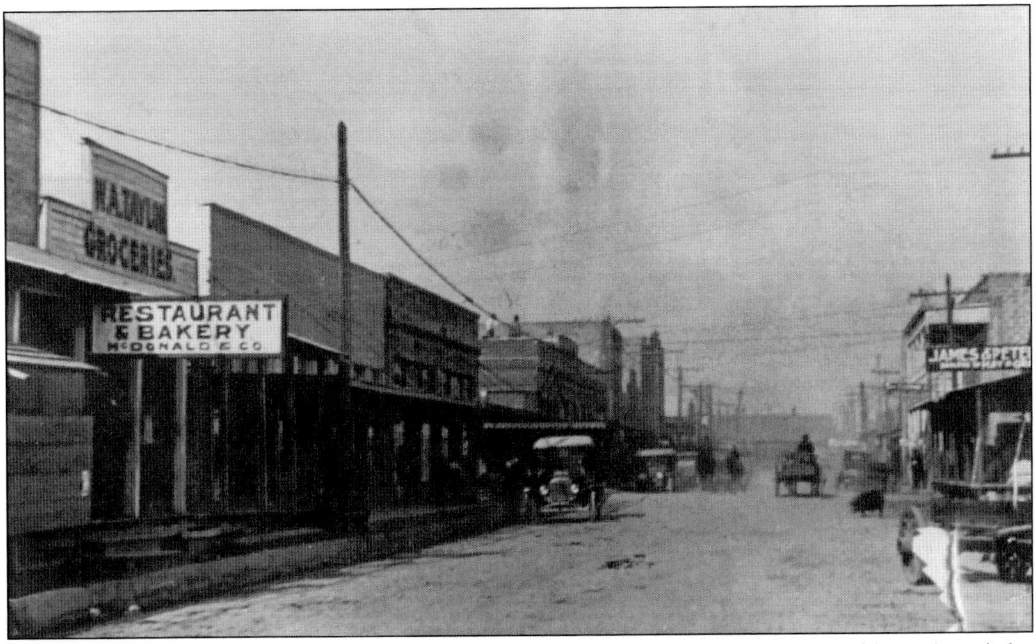

Overlapping Eras, 1919. The end of one era of transportation (the horse and buggy) and the beginning of another (the automobile) can be seen in this photograph of Barrett Street (Main Street) in 1919. W.A Taylor's grocery store and McDonald's Restaurant are on the left. The James & Peters feed store is on the right. A pig roams the street on the right.

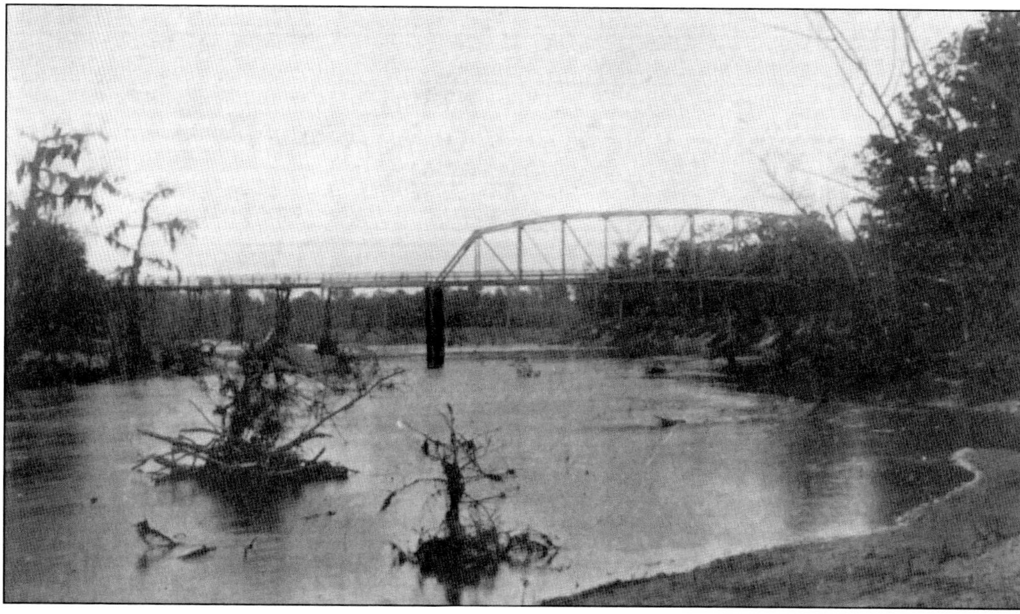

OLD HUMBLE ROAD BRIDGE, 1919. A two-ton steel bridge was built across the San Jacinto River on Old Humble Road, north of town, in 1918. The bridge was located on the east side of the Houston East & West Texas Railway tracks. This was the first large bridge built in the area, and the Humble residents were fascinated by it. It was common for people to park on or near the bridge to take photographs, like the one below. This span was abandoned when a new bridge was built for State Highway 35 on the west side of the railroad tracks. (Below, courtesy of Margaret Byron.)

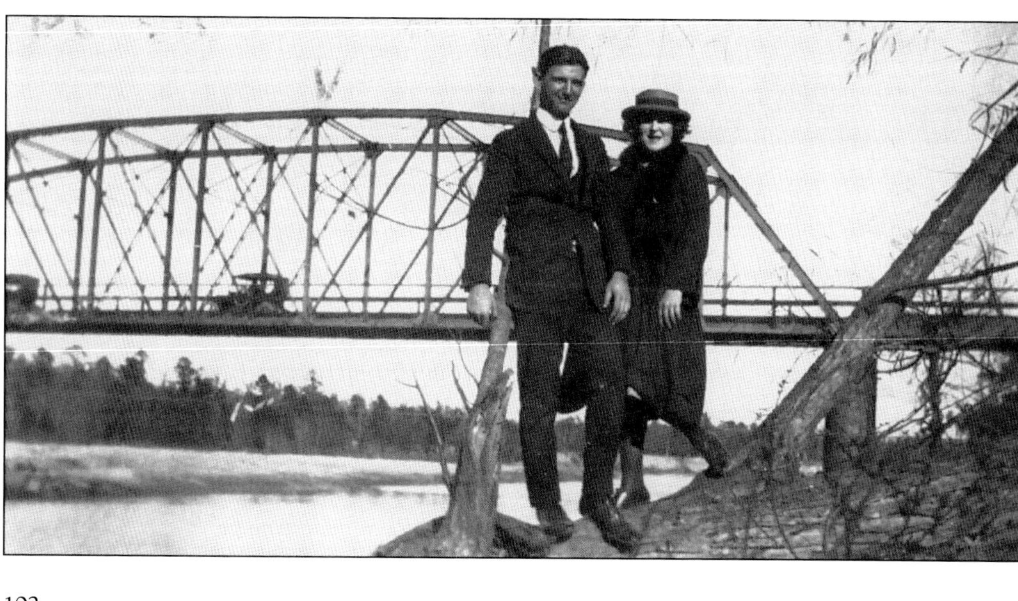

ABANDONED BRIDGE, 1934. The abandoned bridge on Old Humble Road at the San Jacinto River was purchased by L.D. Beago from Harris County for $10.50. The bridge, built in 1918, yielded 110 tons of steel when the dismantling process was completed in July 1934. The Beago Welding Company took three weeks to dismantle the bridge.

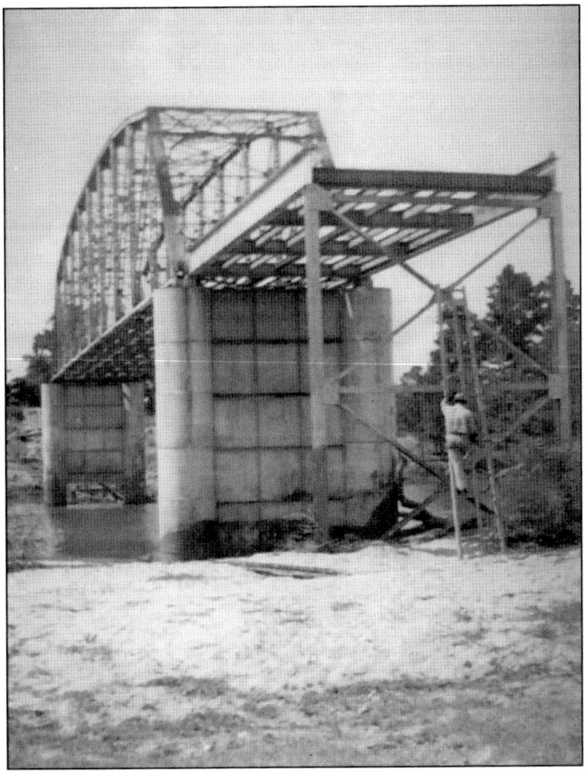

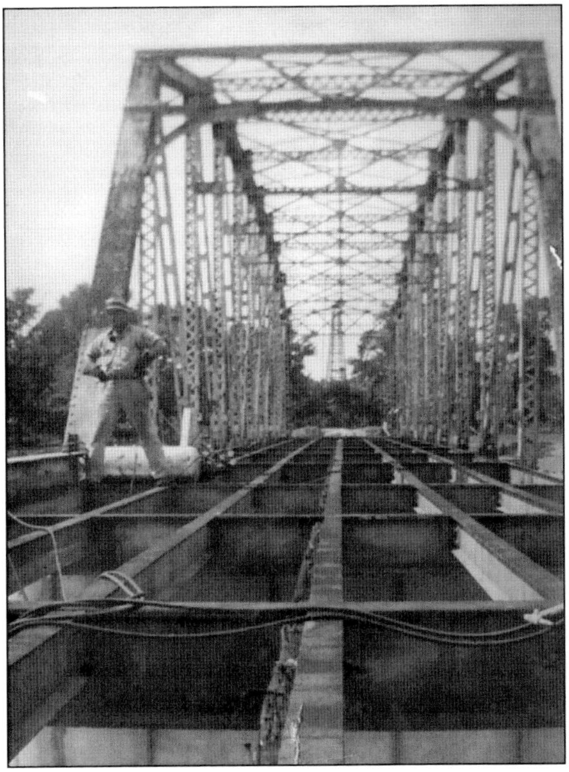

DISMANTLING THE RIVER ROAD BRIDGE, 1934. The wooden approaches to the 1918 steel structure were reclaimed by county workers and used for construction and maintenance work in the precinct. Parts of the reclaimed steel were used to enlarge the Beago Welding Company, while other parts were disposed of as junk. The rest of the steel was sold.

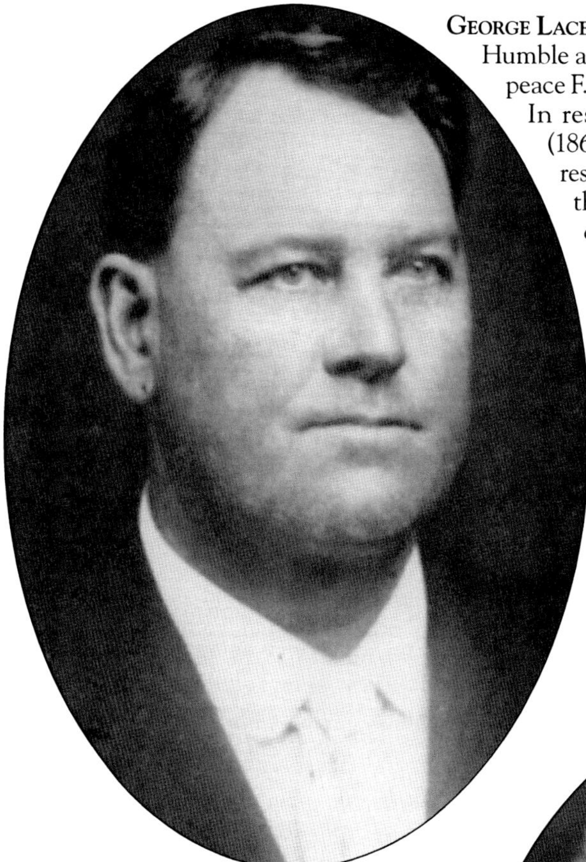

George Lacewell. Crime was spiraling out of control in Humble and in Moonshine Hill when justice of the peace F.K. Wise sent a plea for assistance to Austin. In response, Texas Ranger George Lacewell (1868–1936) was assigned to Humble to help restore law and order. Lacewell eventually quit the Texas Rangers and was elected constable of the local Harris County precinct for one term.

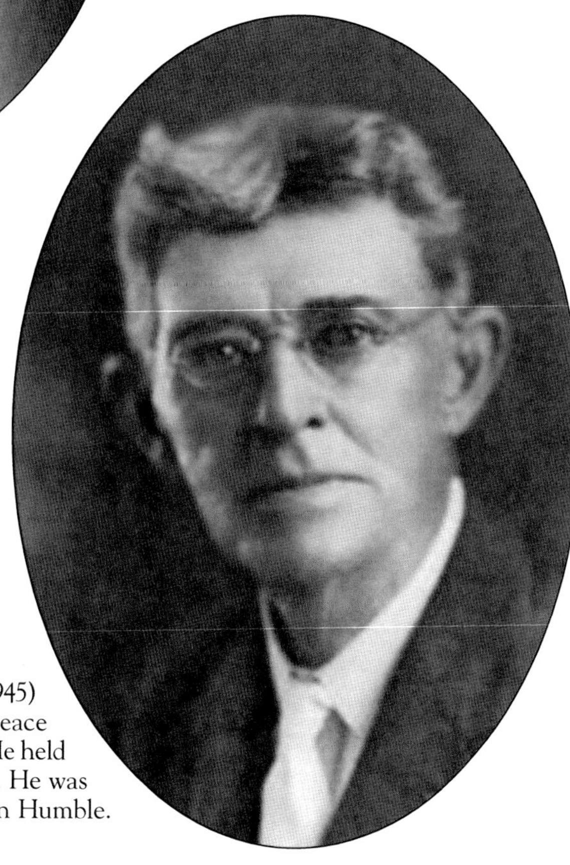

Judge Frost Keel Wise. F.K. Wise (1857–1945) was elected to serve as the justice of the peace for Harris County Precinct No. 4 in 1910. He held that position for over 30 years, until 1944. He was a charter member of the Masonic lodge in Humble. (Courtesy Humble Masonic Lodge.)

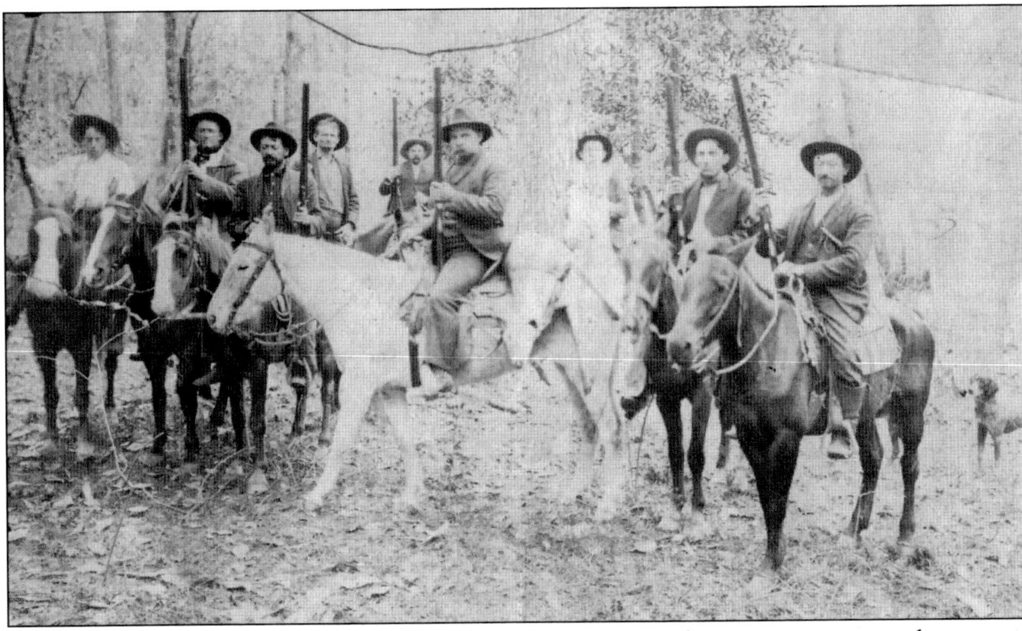

Old West Cowboys. A horse and a gun were necessary items for men to survive and prosper in the early years of Humble. The most common food on the tables of early residents was either wild game shot during the hunt, or livestock that was raised at the homestead. In this photograph, a group of men are hunting through the woods around Humble. (Courtesy of Margaret Byron.)

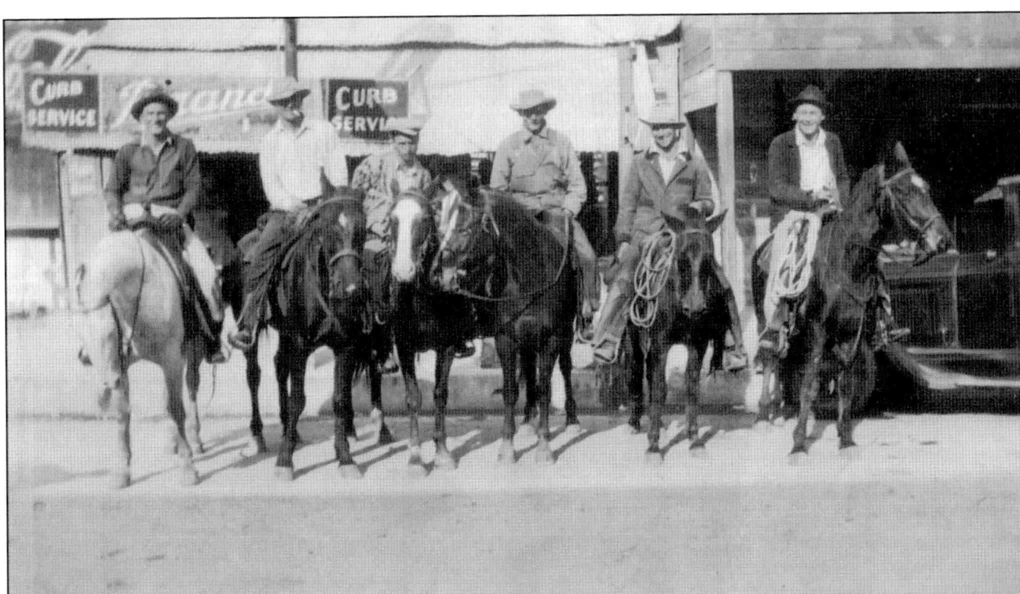

Cowboys on Main Street. Cattle ranching was common in the area, due to the large open ranges with plenty of grass. Many local families raised cattle, including the Lees, Longs, Benders, Schlobohns, Koinms, and Trahans. Cattle ranchers riding through town was a common sight in Humble. Pictured here from left to right are Harvey Bender, Laten Payne, Aubrey Teel, Buddy Johnson, Buddy Sammons, and Sterling Fields.

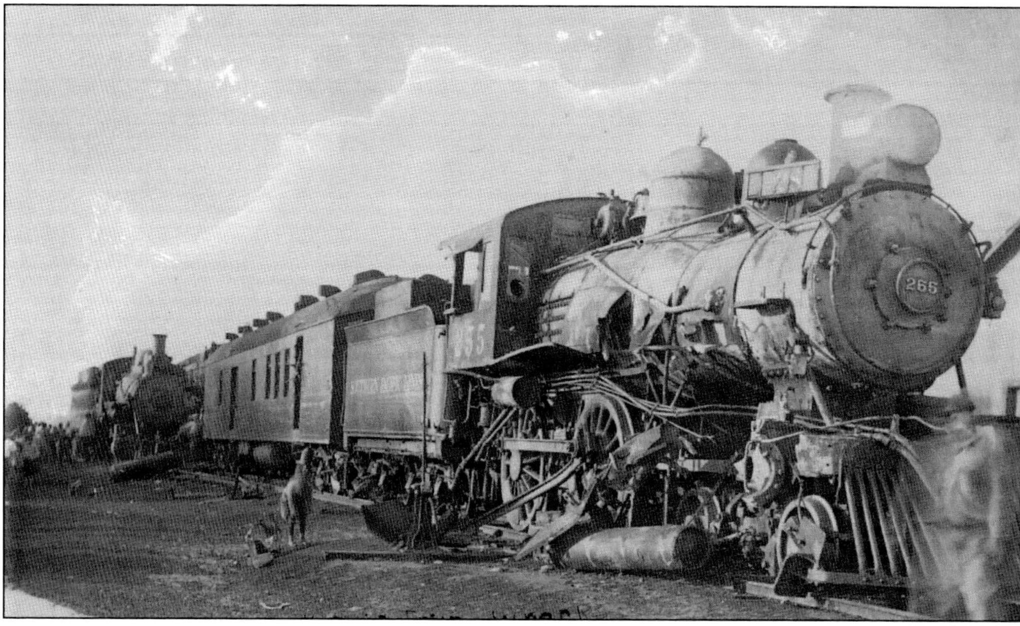

Train Accident, 1922. A Houston East & West Texas passenger train moving through Humble sideswiped a switch engine parked on an adjoining track. A steam pipe was torn loose from the switch engine; in an instant, a rush of high-pressure, superheated steam poured through the windows of a passenger car. In the end, seven people were scalded to death. Few passengers in the car succeeded escaping unhurt, and 35 passengers who fell or threw themselves on the floor of the car suffered terrible burns. Those killed included the train conductor, a news dealer, two African American men, and three African American women.

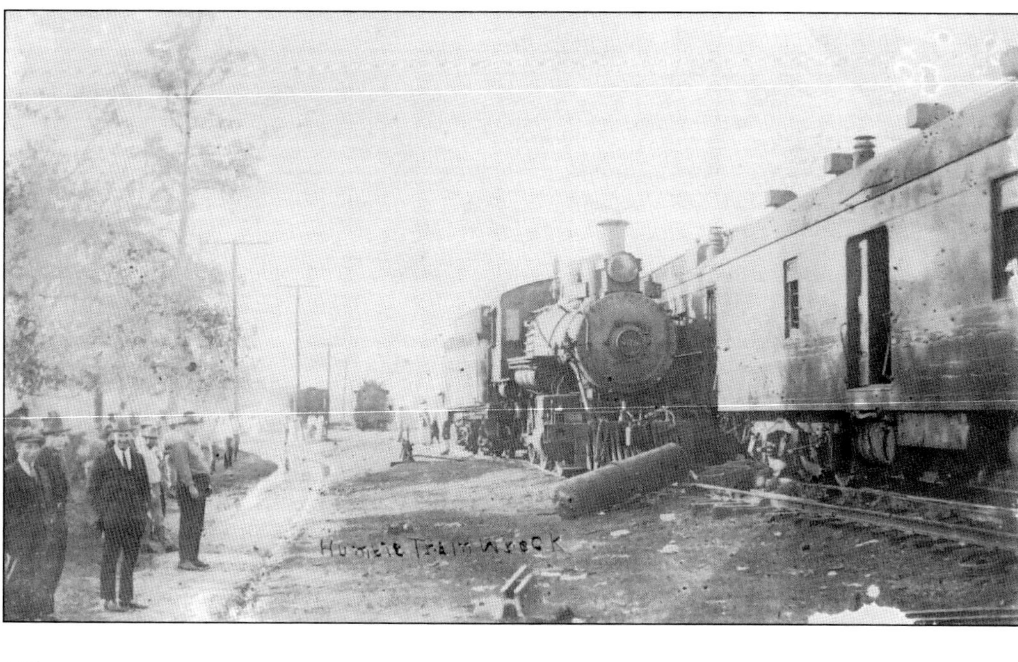

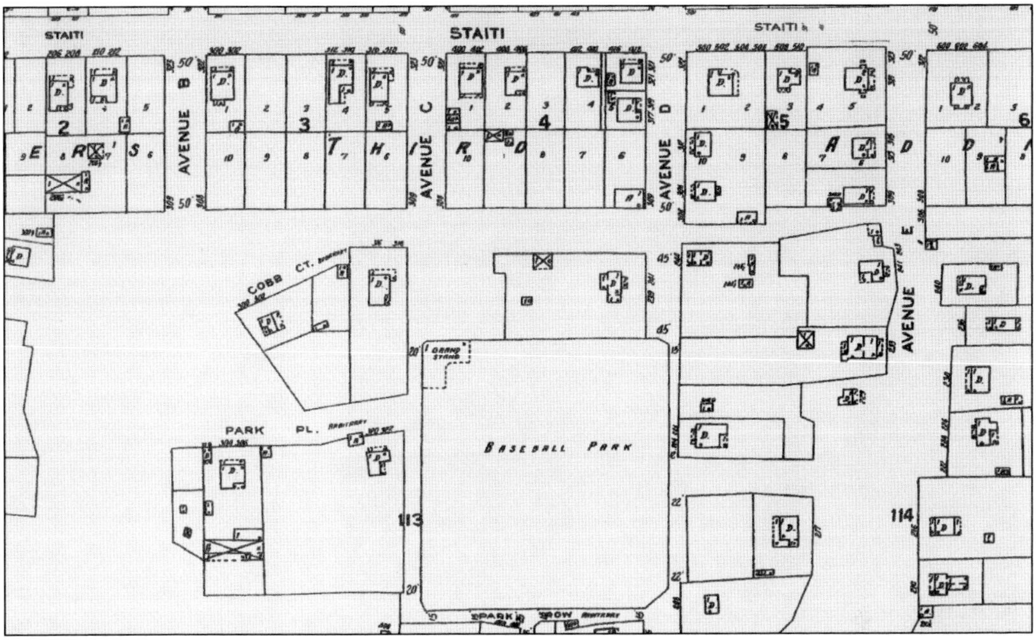

Humble Baseball Field, 1926. The 1926 map above shows the location of the old Humble baseball field, just south of Staiti Street. The field was used by baseball teams sponsored by the oil companies and by the Humble High School team. In the Humble area, the Texas Company and the Producers Oil Company fielded baseball teams. The Humble Oil Company also had a team, called the Humble Odds, who played in several venues across the state. This field was torn down during the 1930s after the county built a set of sports fields off of the old Humble Road (now South Houston Avenue), where Hirsch Park is now located. (Above, reprinted/used with permission from The Sanborn Library, LLC).

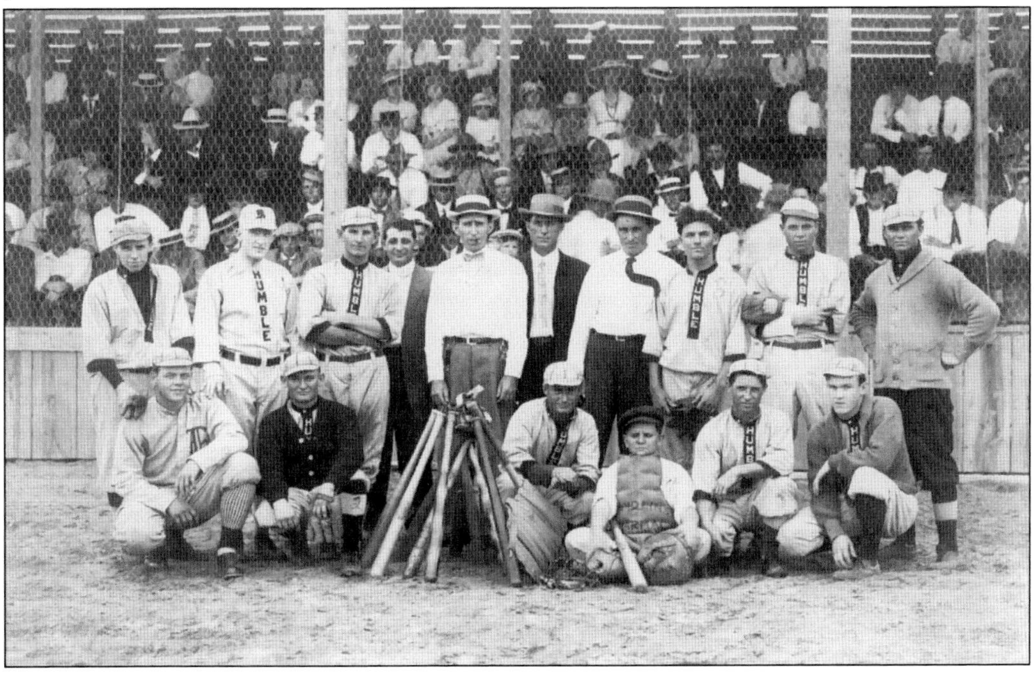

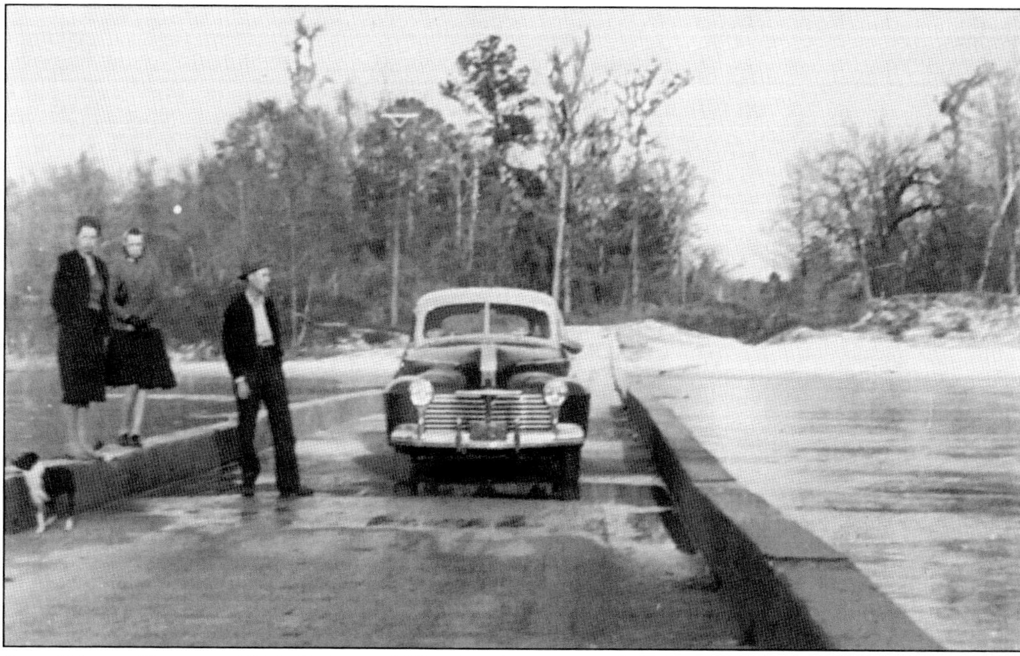

Low-Water Bridge, 1937. Prior to 1953, the Atascocita Road crossed the San Jacinto River on the east side of Humble, where Lake Houston is now located. A ferry was in use for river crossings during the 1920s. It was replaced by this low-water bridge in the 1930s.

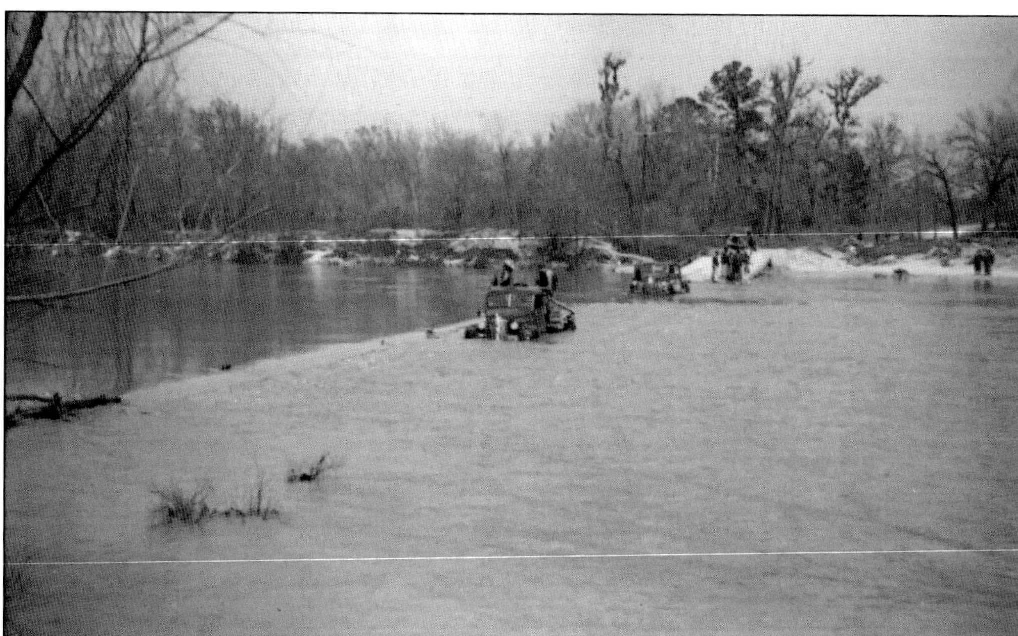

Flooded Bridge, 1937. The Atascocita Road follows the path of a road built by the Spanish in 1756. The old road started in present-day El Paso, then went through San Antonio, Houston, Liberty, and Beaumont, terminating in Opelousas, Louisiana. The low-water bridge, prone to flooding, was built in the 1930s.

ELISHA MADISON "BOOGE" ISAACKS. Isaacks (1852–1941) arrived in Humble around 1879. He first worked for the sawmill companies in Lord, and then became a farmer. As a resident of Humble, he operated a butcher shop for many years and ran a general store from time to time. He performed various duties for the West River School, including building furniture, supplying wood for fuel, and taking the scholastic census.

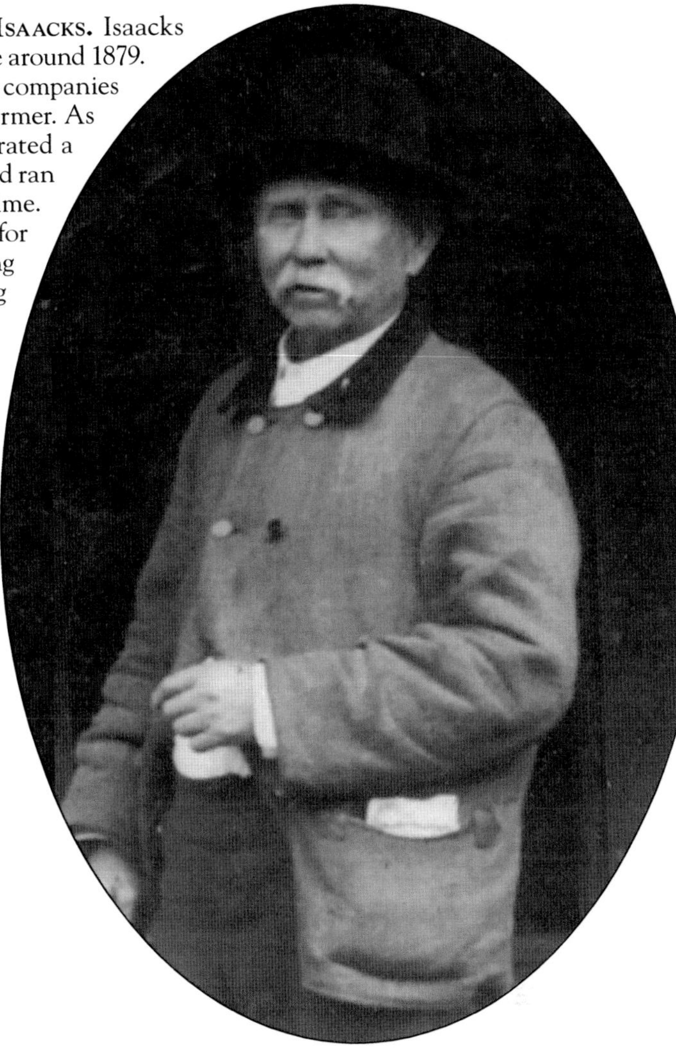

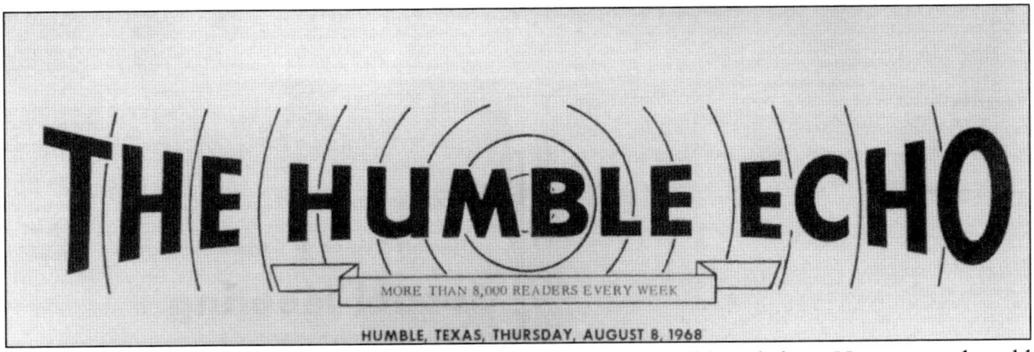

THE HUMBLE ECHO

MORE THAN 8,000 READERS EVERY WEEK

HUMBLE, TEXAS, THURSDAY, AUGUST 8, 1968

THE *HUMBLE ECHO*. Living close to Houston, Humble citizens could read about Houston and world news via the *Houston Post* or the *Houston Chronicle*. However, news specific to the Humble area could be found in the local newspaper, the *Humble Echo*, which began publication on June 19, 1942. Wedding announcements, sports scores, news from city hall, and other local information could be found within its pages.

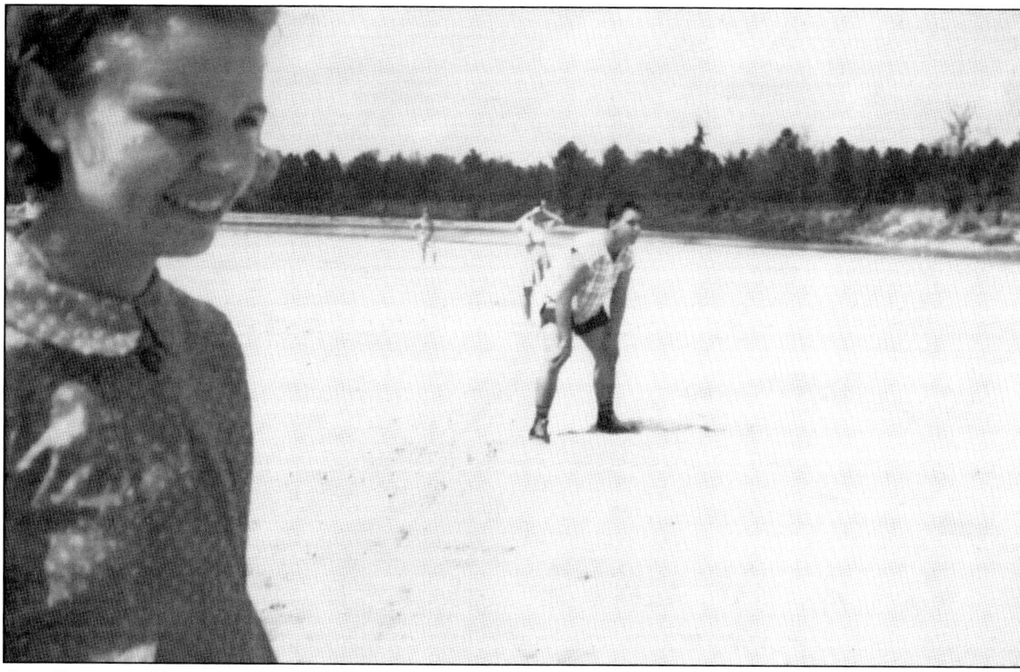

SAN JACINTO RIVER, 1939. The San Jacinto River, just north of town, was the ideal place for families to spend time together. A huge sandbar (shown here) was a popular setting for baseball and volleyball games. Many school outings and picnics were held at this sandbar. Good places to fish were also nearby.

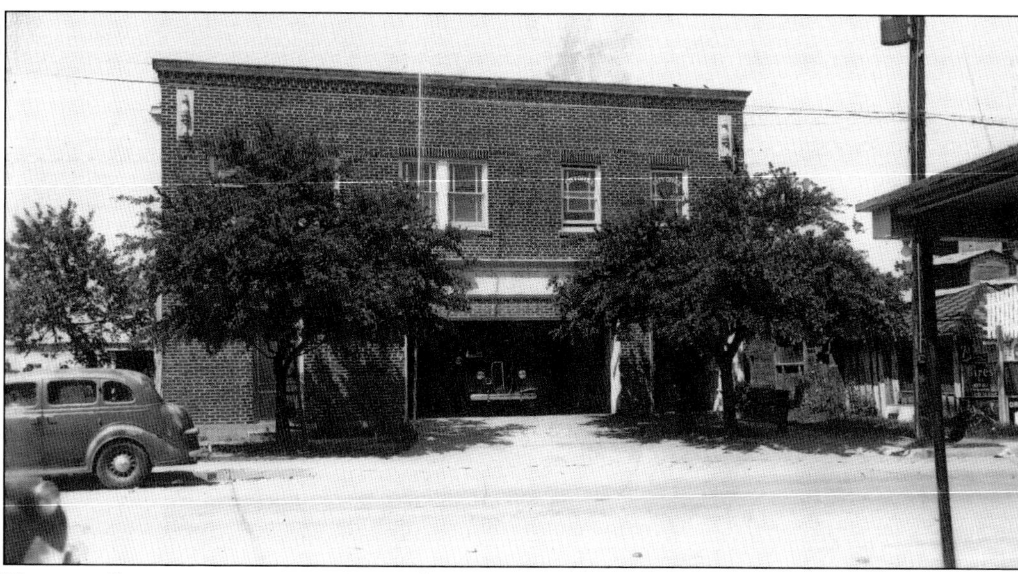

HUMBLE COURTHOUSE, 1940S. Erected on Barrett Street (Main Street) in 1928, this building originally housed the jail, the fire station, a courtroom, and the local library. The trees in front are called the "Trees of Knowledge," because longtime residents Dr. Bennett, Constable Busch, and others would sit on benches under the tree for hours every day, talking and philosophizing about life in general.

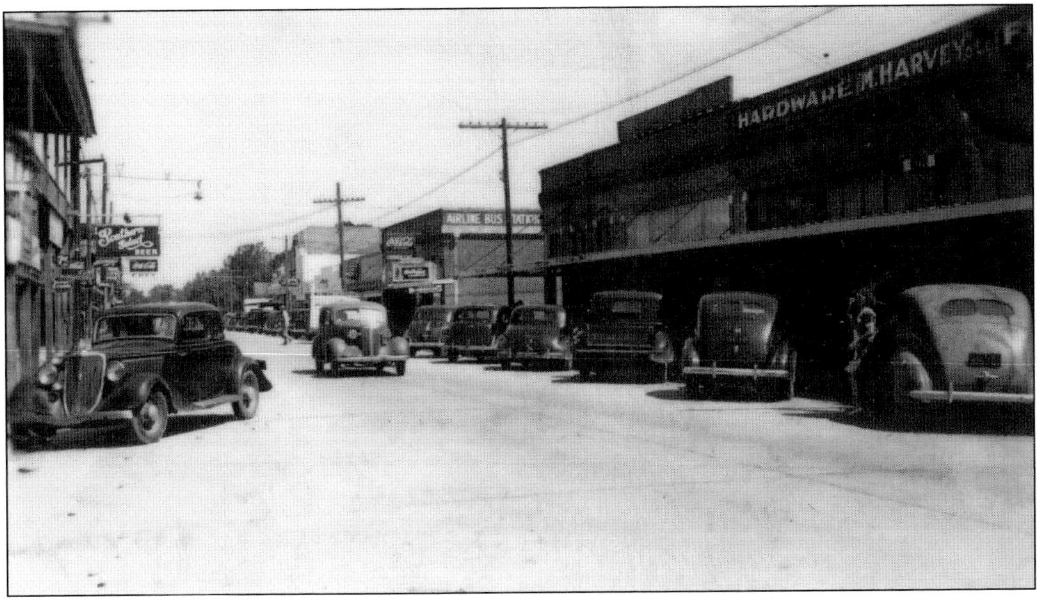

Main Street, 1940s. Cars are parked along Humble's Barrett Street (Main Street) in the 1940s. The above photograph shows the Harvey Hardware store and the Humble State Bank on the south side of Main Street. The brick Harvey Hardware store was originally the J.W. Hall Hardware Store when it opened after the fire of 1912. The building seen at left in the below photograph was demolished, and the location is where the Humble Museum now stands. Note the telephone and electricity poles along Main Street. While some are still there, the majority of these poles were moved to the backside of the buildings in the early 1970s.

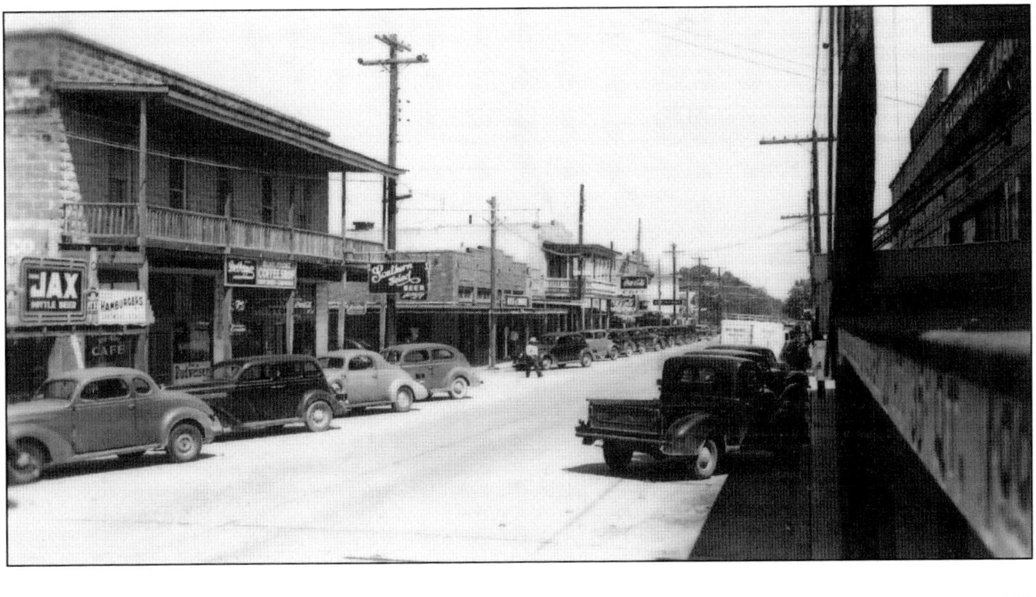

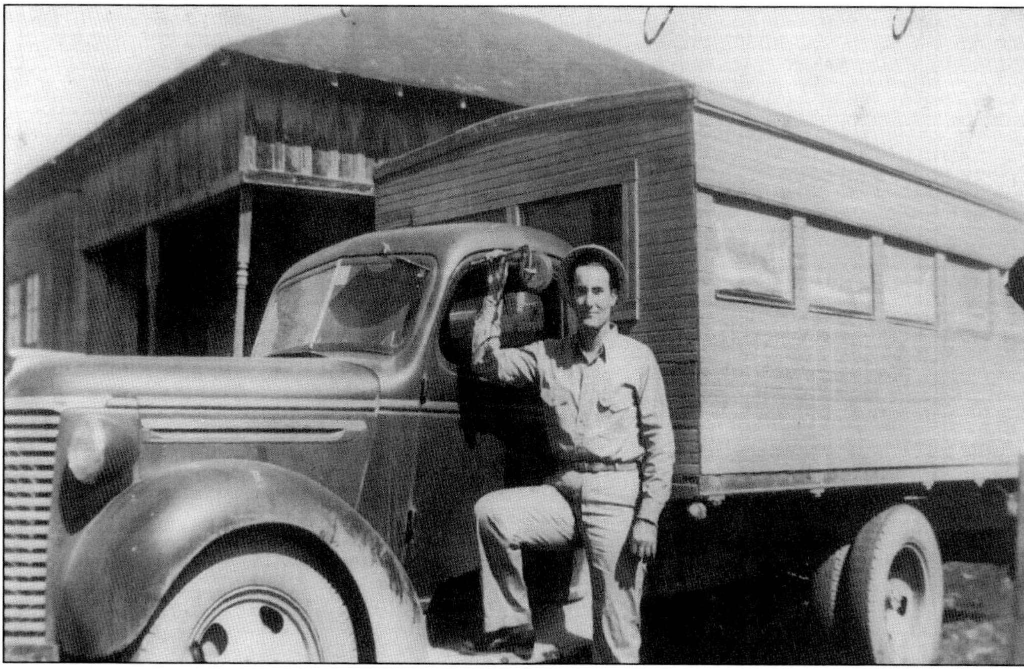

Boncy Young's Passenger Bus, 1944. During World War II, many men from the Humble area went to work in the Houston shipyards. The men were compelled to this work due to the overall war effort and the higher wages they could earn at the shipyards. Some men traveled to Houston in their own cars, and others made use of local transportation. Boncy Young was an enterprising gentleman who had multiple businesses over the years. During the war, he used his bus to transport men from Humble to the shipyards, and then back home again. (Courtesy of the Young family.)

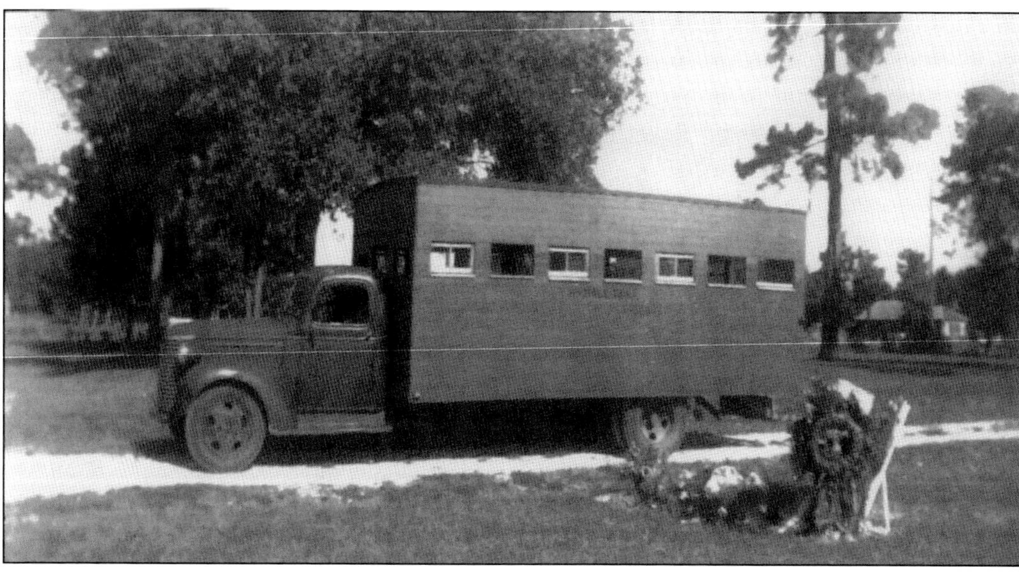

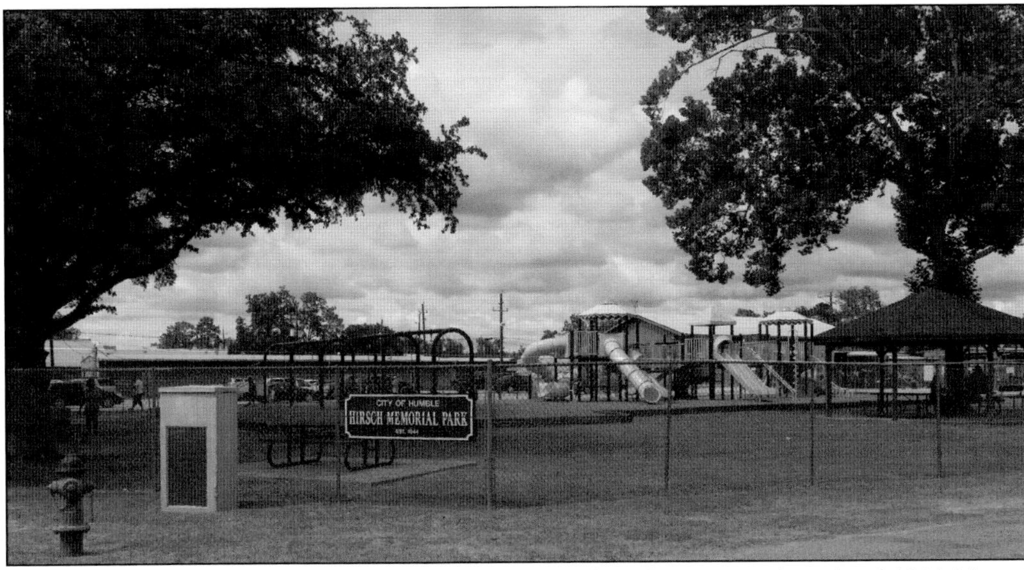

Hirsch Memorial Park. The Humble PTA started plans for a city park in April 1944. Named for Jules Hirsch, who donated the land, the park was built at the corner of Old Humble Road and Barrett Street (Main Street). The park was built with swings, merry-go-rounds, seesaws, tennis courts, and barbecue pits. A wading pool was added later. (Courtesy of Scott Meaux.)

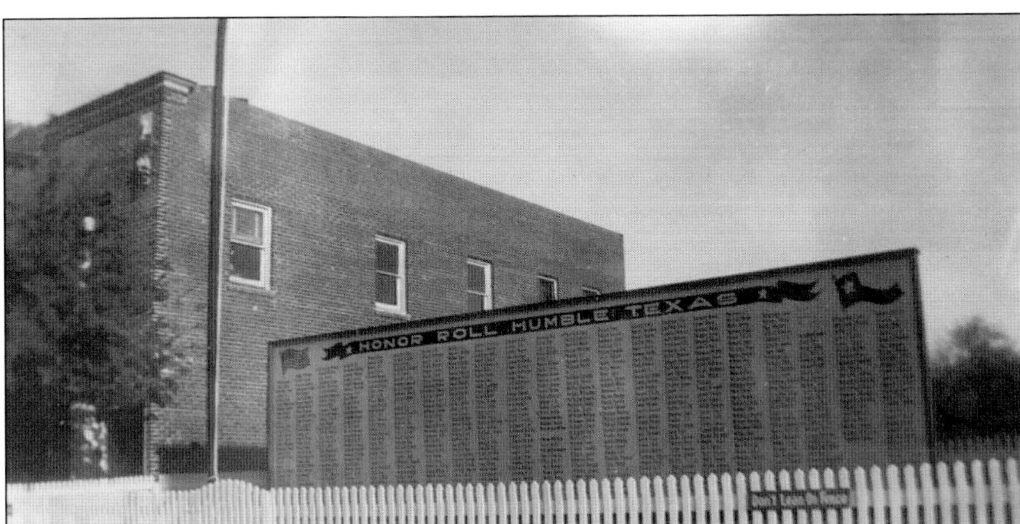

Honor Roll. During World War II, the citizens of Humble erected a large billboard that displayed the names of all Humble residents who were serving their country in the war. The billboard was posted next to the courthouse on Barrett Street (where the Humble Museum now stands). The Humble residents obtained mailing addresses for those serving overseas to send them letters and packages from home.

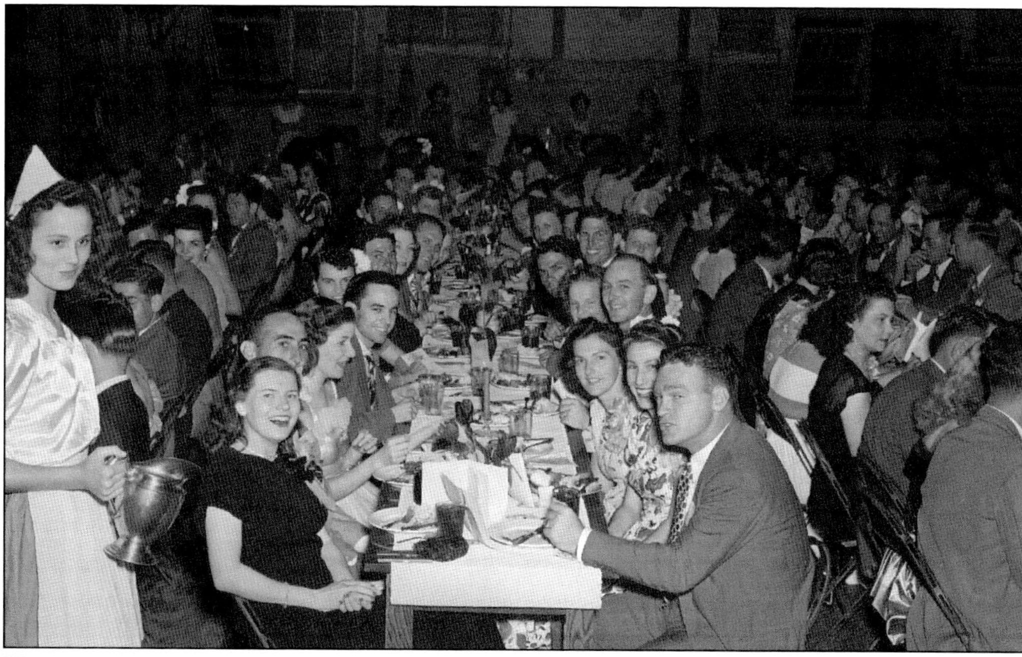

Humble Alumni Banquet, 1947. The tradition of holding an alumni banquet began with graduates of Bender High School in the 1930s. These banquets were open only to persons who graduated from the school. In the 1960s, when Bender High School closed and Humble High School opened, the Bender graduates carried on the tradition with the graduates of Humble High.

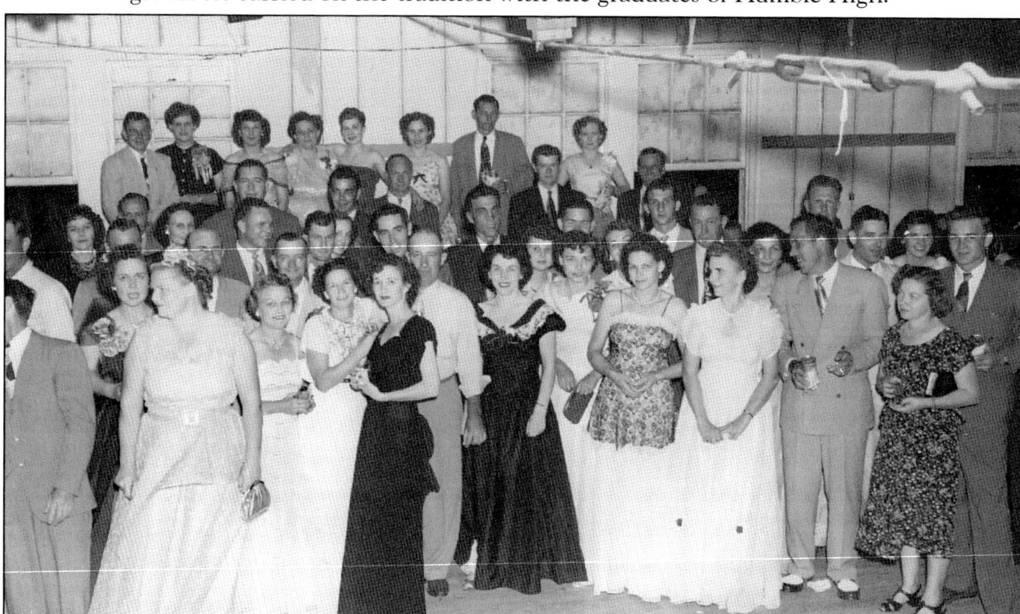

Illiterate Club, 1947. Humble High School alumni banquets were open to Humble graduates only. Spouses that did not graduate from Humble were not allowed. Jokingly calling themselves the "Illiterate Club," the spouses held their own party at Recreation Hall. They would join their spouses at the high school for the dance that was held after the banquet. Spouses were finally allowed to attend the banquets in 2001.

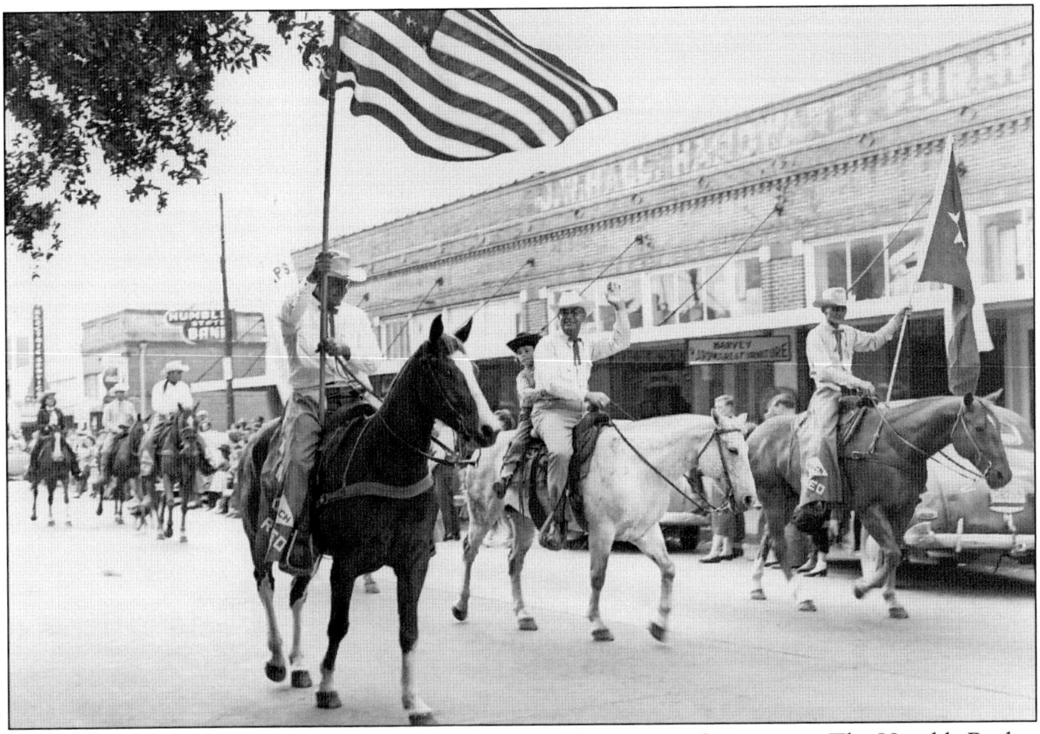

DOWNTOWN PARADE. Parades were common in Humble on special occasions. The Humble Rodeo was frequently initiated with a parade through downtown. This photograph was taken as the parade passed in front of the courthouse on Main Street. Shown here are Bennie Weid (left), W.E. Gray (center), and Buddy Johnson, Humble's professional cowboy.

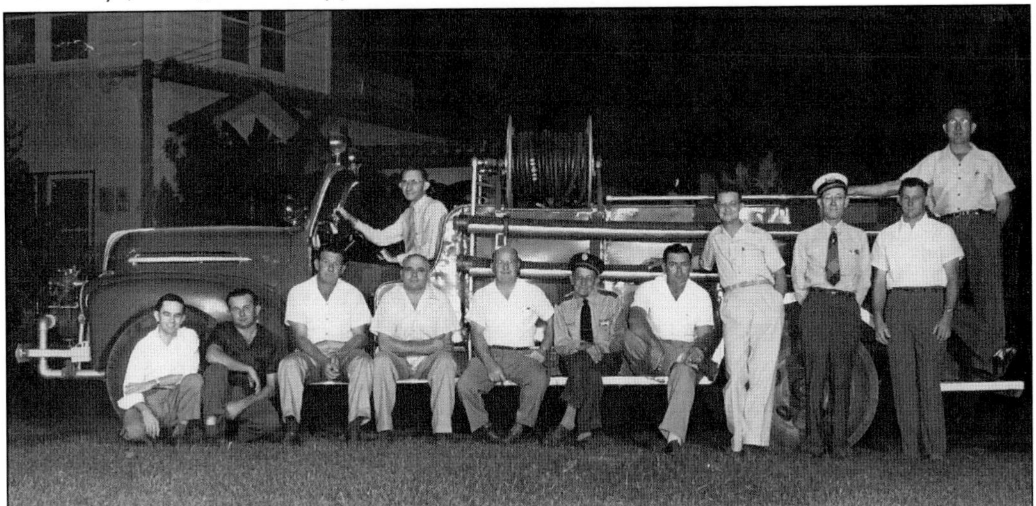

VOLUNTEER FIRE DEPARTMENT, 1958. The City of Humble Volunteer Fire Department was formed in December 1935. They were assisted by the Women's Auxiliary Club of Humble from 1939 to 1950. Volunteer fireman and Humble school superintendent, Dr. Floyd Burton, is at the wheel. Posing in front of the truck are, from left to right, Nate Martel, Melvin Randow, Phil Cezeaux, J. Borders, W. Treadwell, unidentified, W.E. Gray, Don Williams, A.C. Whitney, Raymond Isaacks, and Gus Cezeaux.

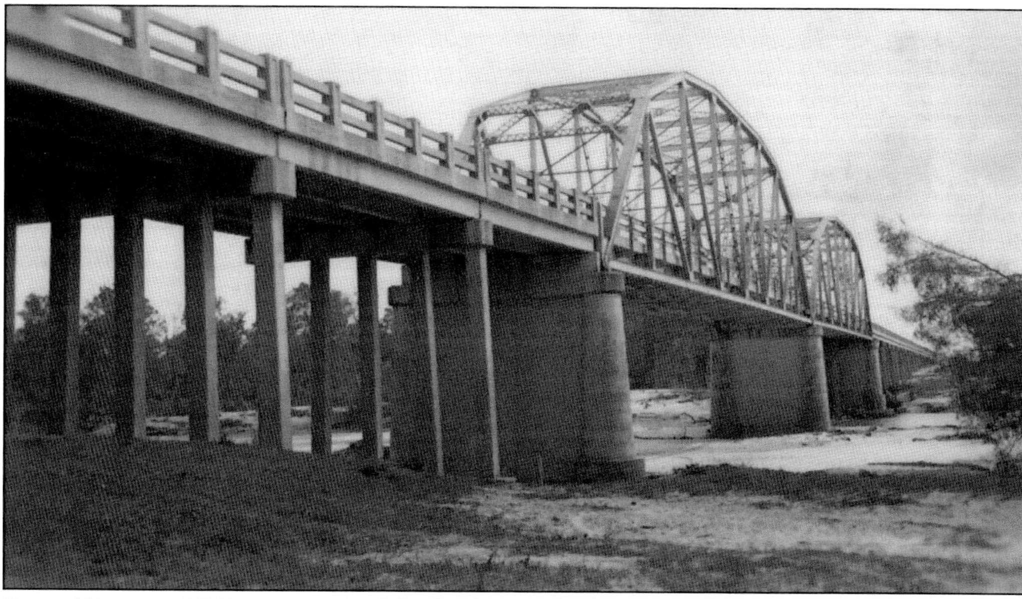

State Highway 35 Bridge, 1949. This bridge was built as part of the new State Highway 35 on the west side of Humble, running parallel to the HE&WT Railway tracks. Construction started on the bridge on October 14, 1930, and was completed on September 17, 1931. The narrow lanes on this bridge were used for all traffic going north and south, until a bridge for southbound traffic was completed in 1961.

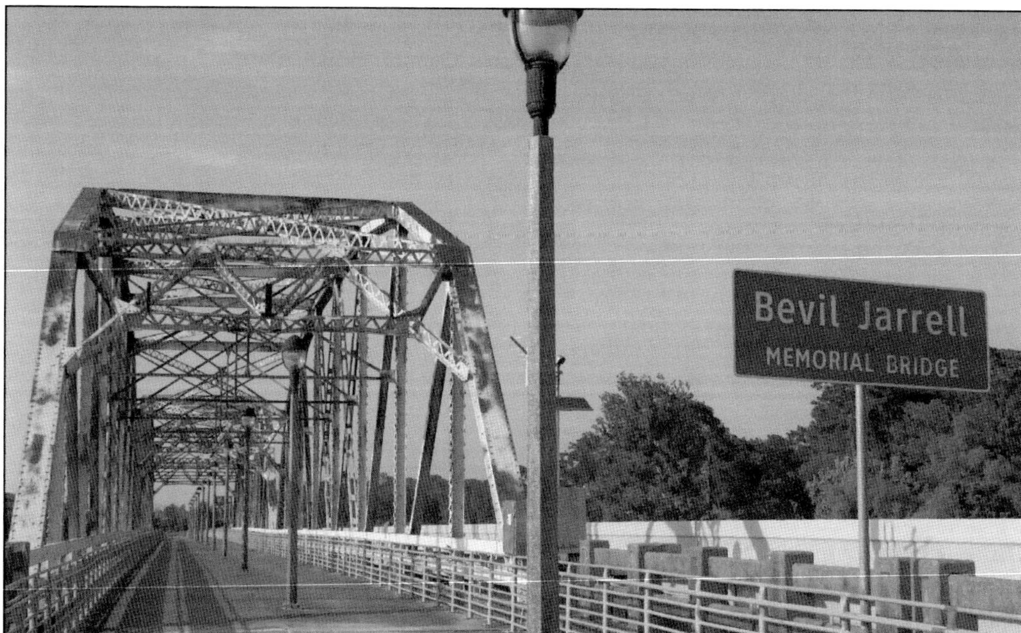

Bevil Jarrell Memorial Bridge, 2013. The old State Highway 35 bridge (now US 59) was converted to a pedestrian bridge. The project began in 1997, and work was completed in 2007. Thanks to the efforts of Harris County Precinct 4 commissioner Jerry Eversole and the Humble City Council, the bridge was renamed the Bevil Jarrell Memorial Bridge in 2011. Bevil Jarrell, a longtime Humble educator, died in 2003. (Courtesy of Scott Meaux.)

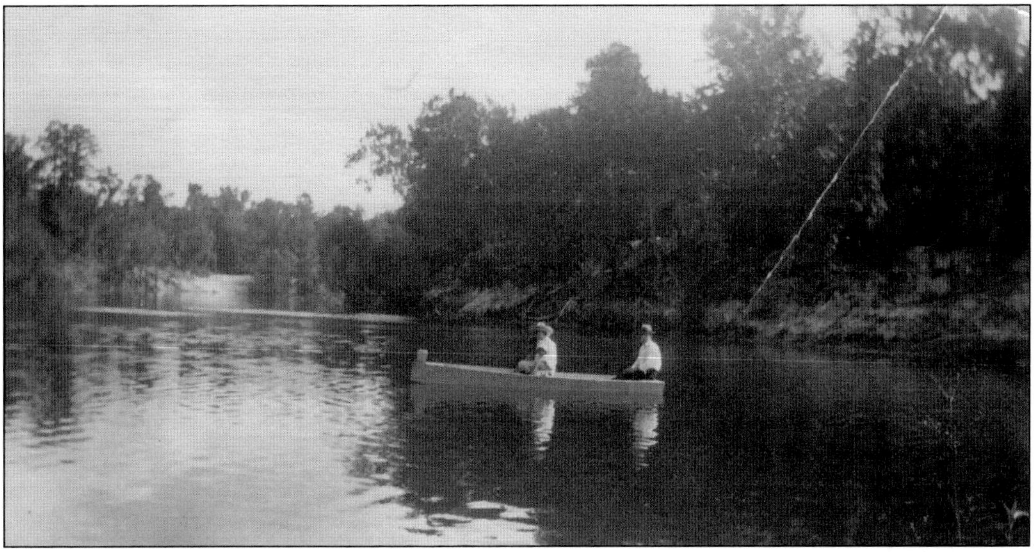

Silver Lake, 1925. There existed several small lakes east of Humble near the San Jacinto River, south of the Atascocito Crossing. The largest of these lakes was Silver Lake, situated on land owned by the Charpiot family. These lakes were consumed by Lake Houston when it was completed in 1953. (Courtesy of Margaret Byron.)

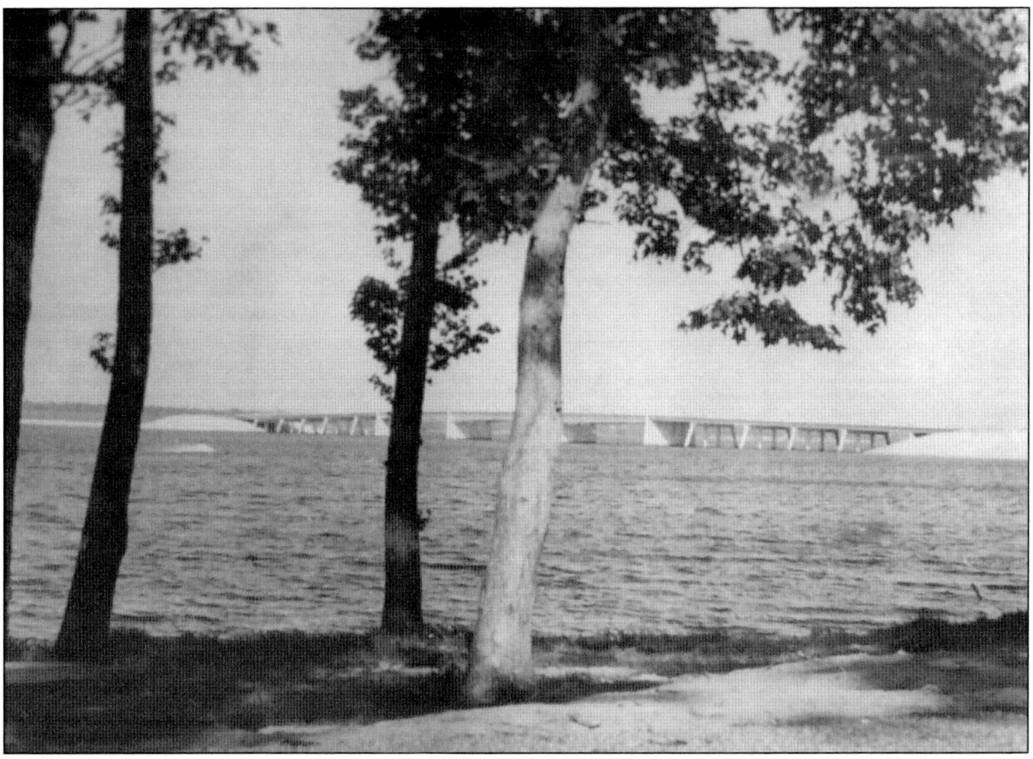

McKay Bridge, 1953. When Lake Houston was being created in 1951, a temporary wooden bridge was built across the lake. When the lake was completed in 1953, a new concrete bridge was erected. The bridge was named in honor of Dr. Haden McKay Sr., a local doctor who spent many years traversing the low-water bridge at the Atascocito Crossing to make house calls.

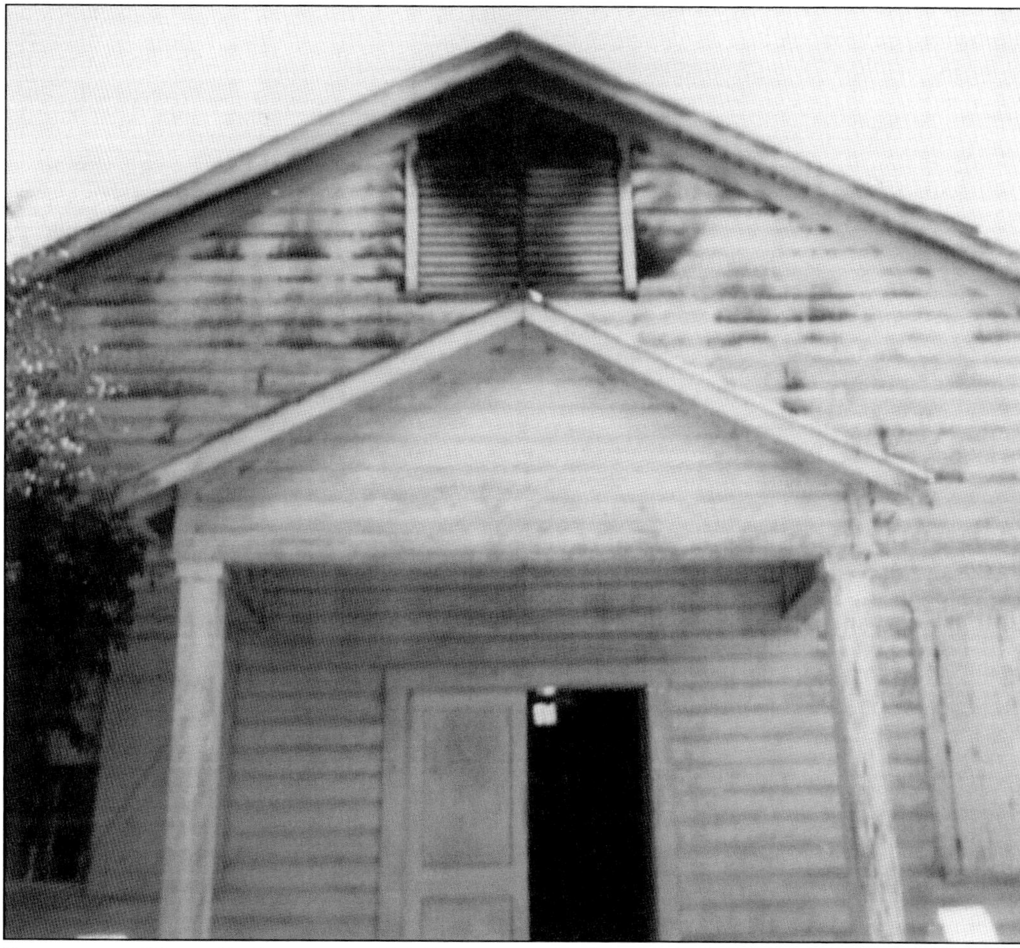

Recreation Hall. Built prior to 1940, Recreation Hall was located on Old Humble Road (now South Houston Avenue), between Barrett Street (Main Street) and Higgins Street. Hirsch Memorial Park was built next to Recreation Hall in 1944. The hall had a large banquet room for dinner and dancing, a small stage, and kitchen facilities. It was used for dances, town meetings, and recitals. The Illiterate Club used the hall for its annual party for many years. The Recreation Hall was demolished after being damaged by a fire in March 1960. (Above, courtesy of the Young family.)

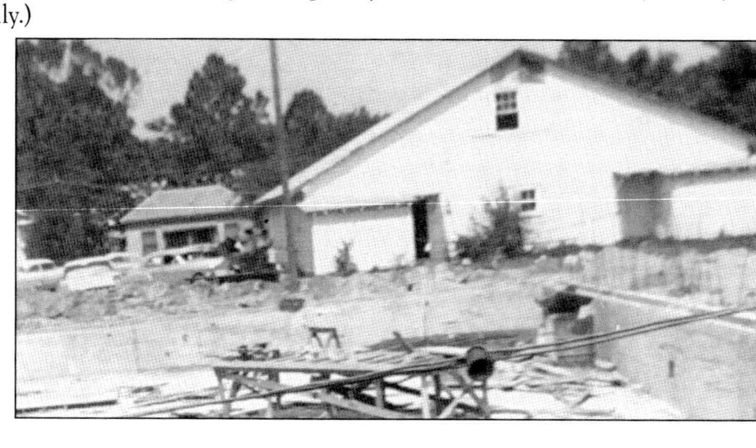

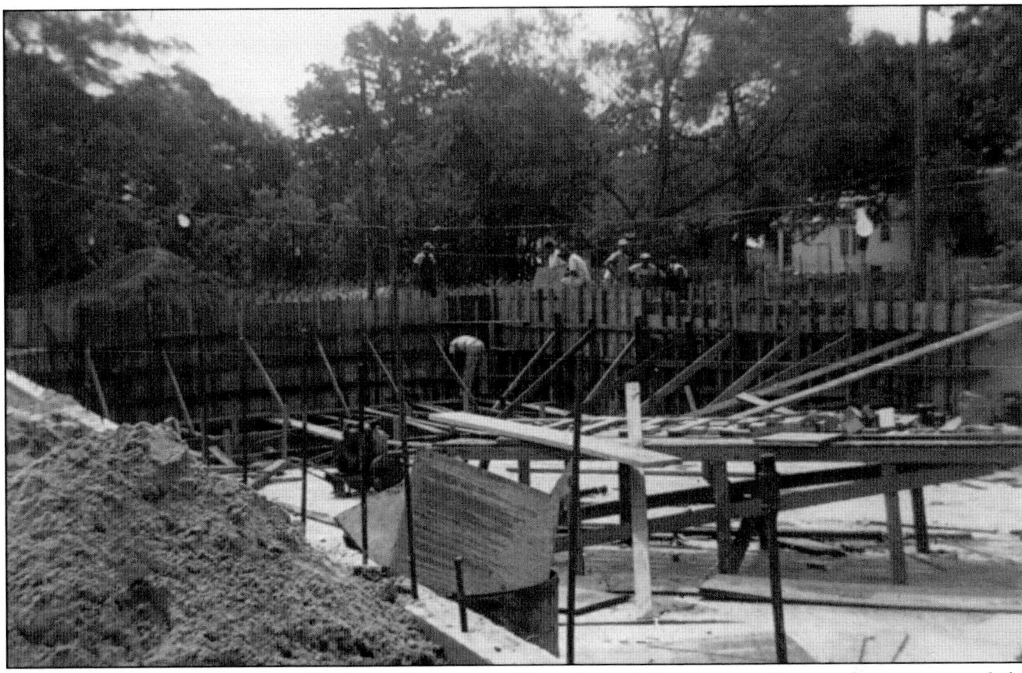

Humble Swimming Pool. The Humble Junior Chamber of Commerce (Jaycees) constructed the swimming pool in 1956 (above), at the northeast corner of Main Street and Old Humble Road. The pool was 92 feet long, 35 feet wide at the deep end, and 50 feet wide at the shallow end. Underwater lights were installed to allow for night swimming. For months, volunteers worked every night until 10:00 to build the pool. Most of the materials were donated, including pipe, sand, and gravel. The Jayce-Ettes paid for the fence around the pool and the two diving boards (below). The volunteers managed to build a $70,000 pool for only $5,330. Both groups helped to continue the development of Hirsch Park, located in front of the pool.

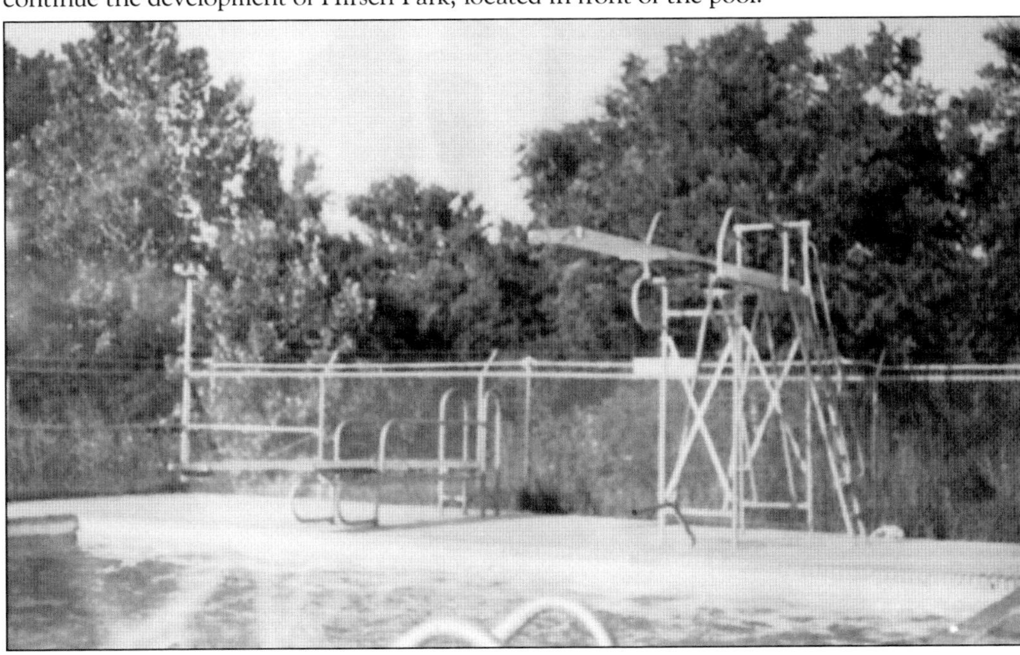

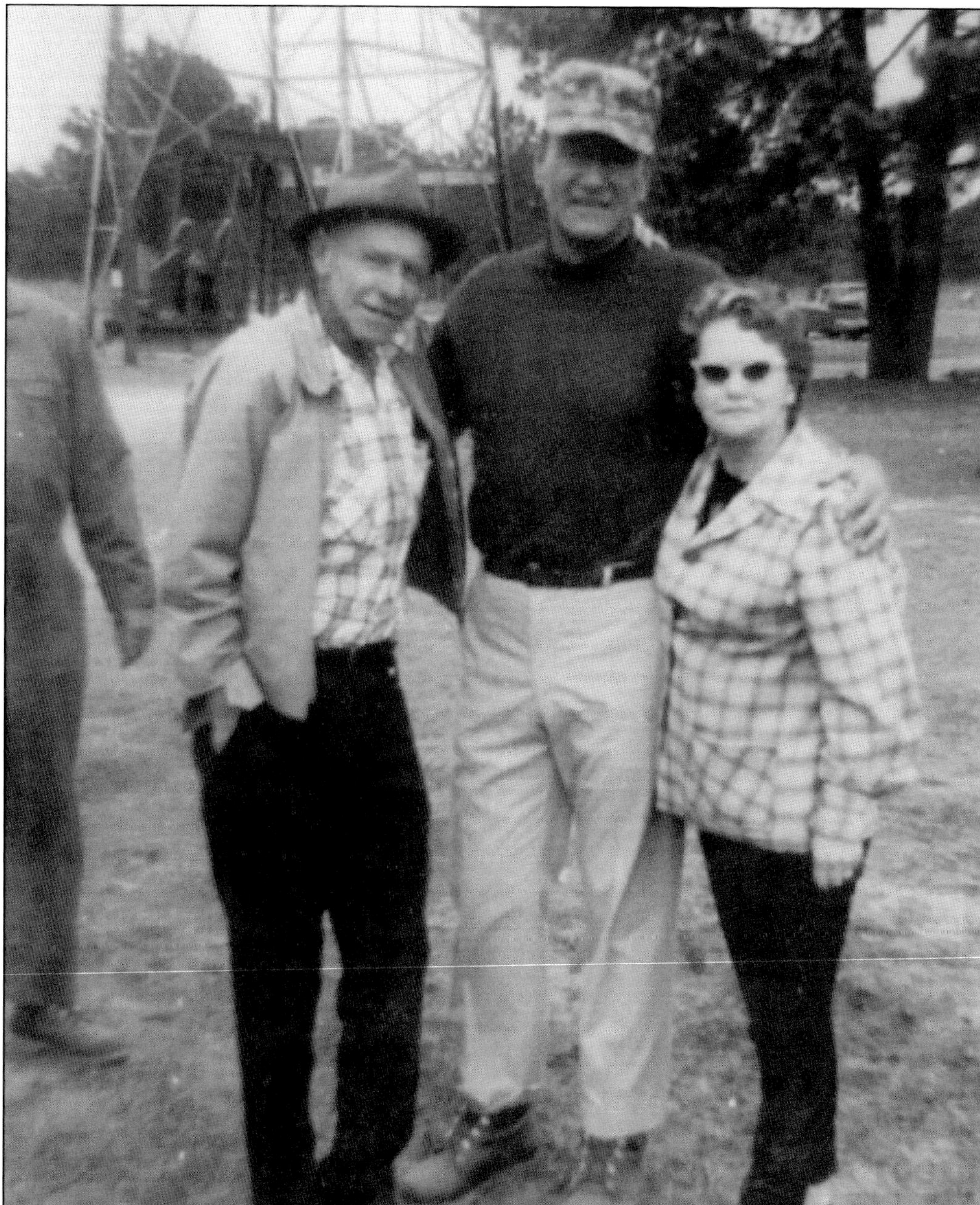

HELLFIGHTERS, 1968. H.V. Street (left), John Wayne (center), and Brookie Mooring posed for this photograph in 1968. Wayne was in the Humble area filming *Hellfighters*. The movie was loosely based on the life of Houston native Paul Neal "Red" Adair, famous for extinguishing and capping oil-well blowouts. H.V. Street provided electrical service for local scenes.

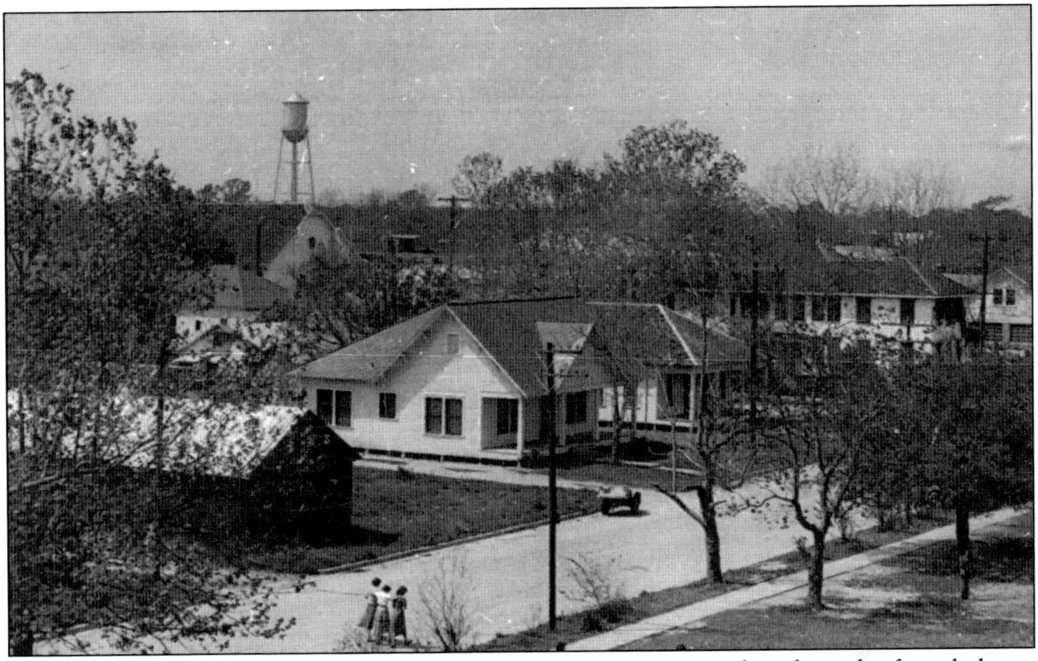

HIGGINS STREET, 1940s. This photograph of Higgins Street was taken from the front balcony of Charles Bender High School. The two-story Falvey Hospital can be seen on the right, and the Humble water tower is visible in the distance. Many of the houses seen here have remained relatively unchanged over the years.

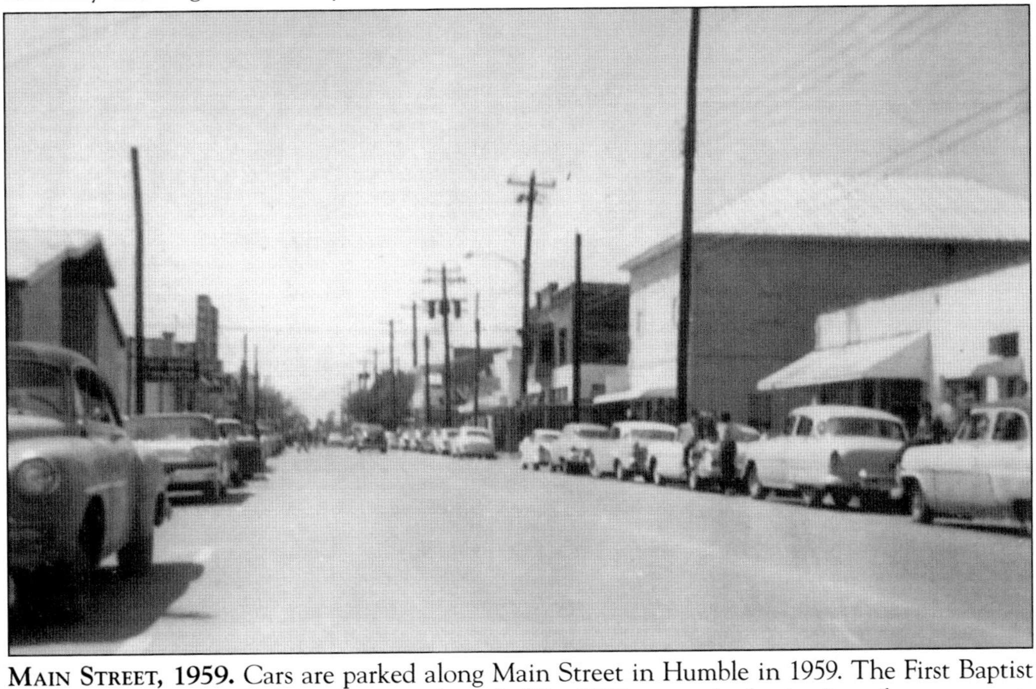

MAIN STREET, 1959. Cars are parked along Main Street in Humble in 1959. The First Baptist Church and the Jewel Theatre are on the left. The 1950s were the beginning of an economic boom in Humble, when many families fled to the suburbs to escape life in the city of Houston. Humble's population increased dramatically during this time.

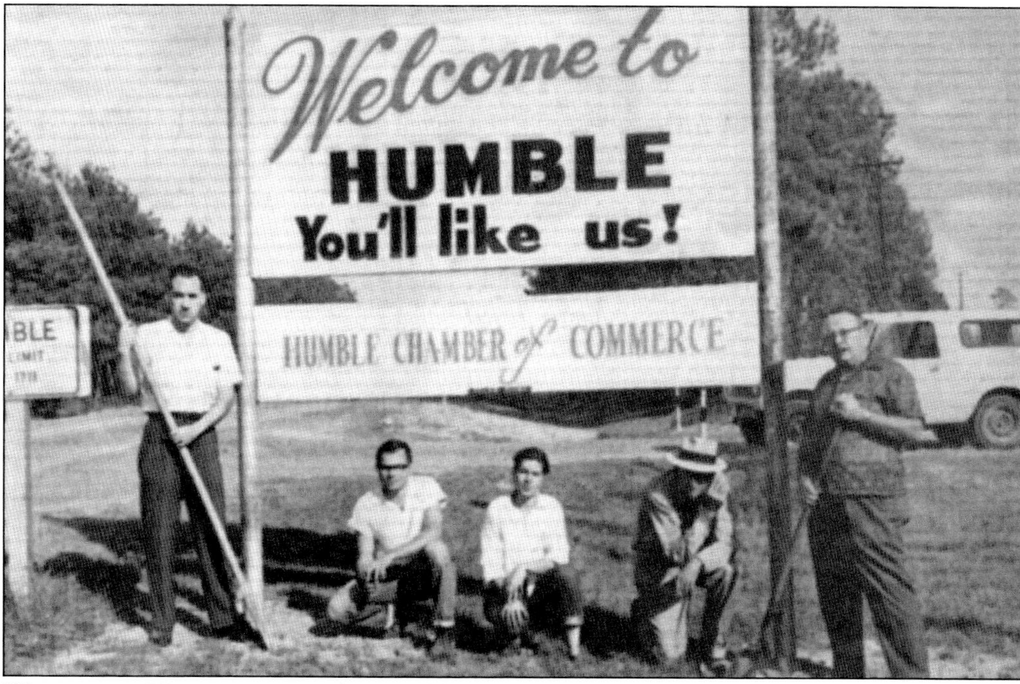

Welcome to Humble, 1963. The Humble Chamber of Commerce erected welcome signs along roads leading into town. This one was placed at the west city limits on FM 1960. Pictured from left to right are chamber manager Jack Taylor, J.D. Kersh, Jennie Beth Kersh, E.L. Seale, and chamber president J. Printous Smith II.

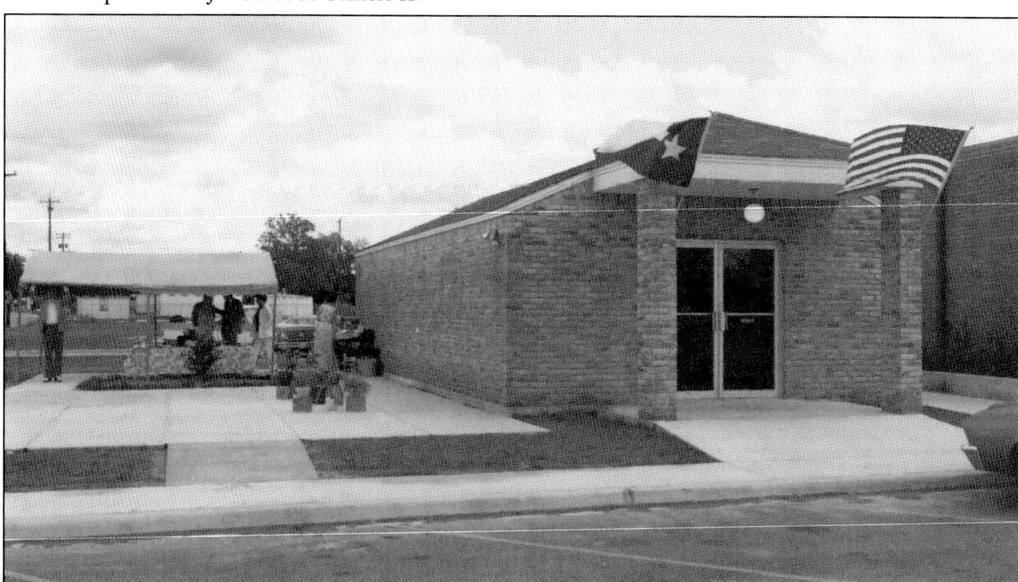

Humble Museum, 1976. Organized as a bicentennial project, the Humble Museum was dedicated on July 4, 1976. The original building, a replica of a one-room schoolhouse, stood next to the library, in the city hall complex on Higgins Street. Artifacts from the surrounding community were gathered and placed on display. In 1988, the museum was moved to the downtown area, on Main Street at Avenue B.

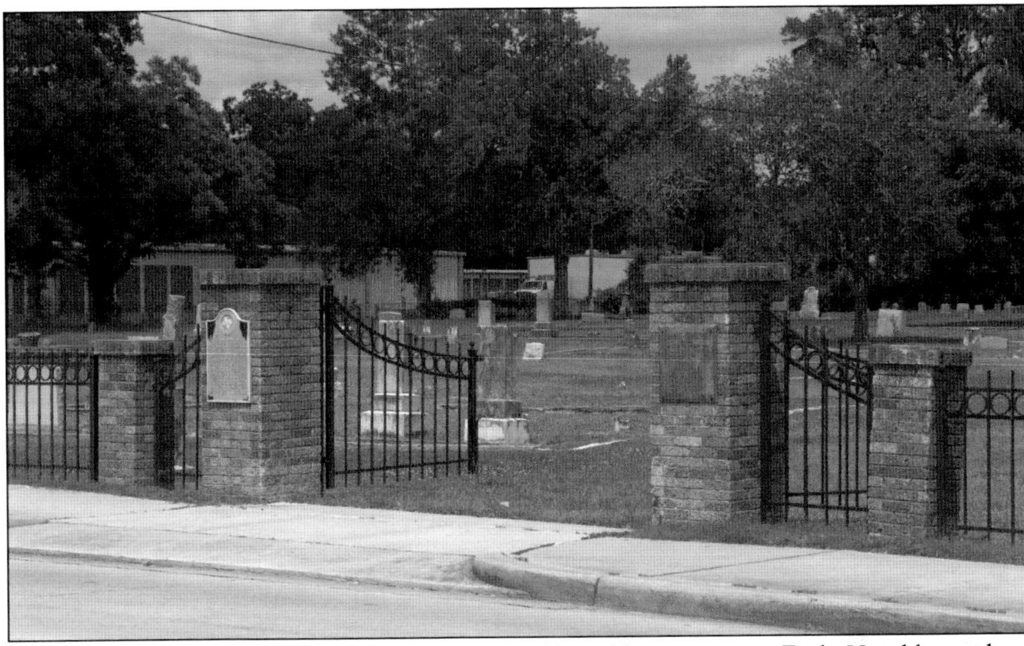

Humble Cemetery. This is believed to be Humble's oldest cemetery. Early Humble residents buried here include Joseph Dunman and Jane Humble, wife of town founder Pleasant Humble. The southern part of the cemetery was the location of the West River School from 1888 to 1909. The school land was purchased from W.E. DeFee in 1920 and was used to expand the cemetery to its current configuration. (Courtesy of Scott Meaux.)

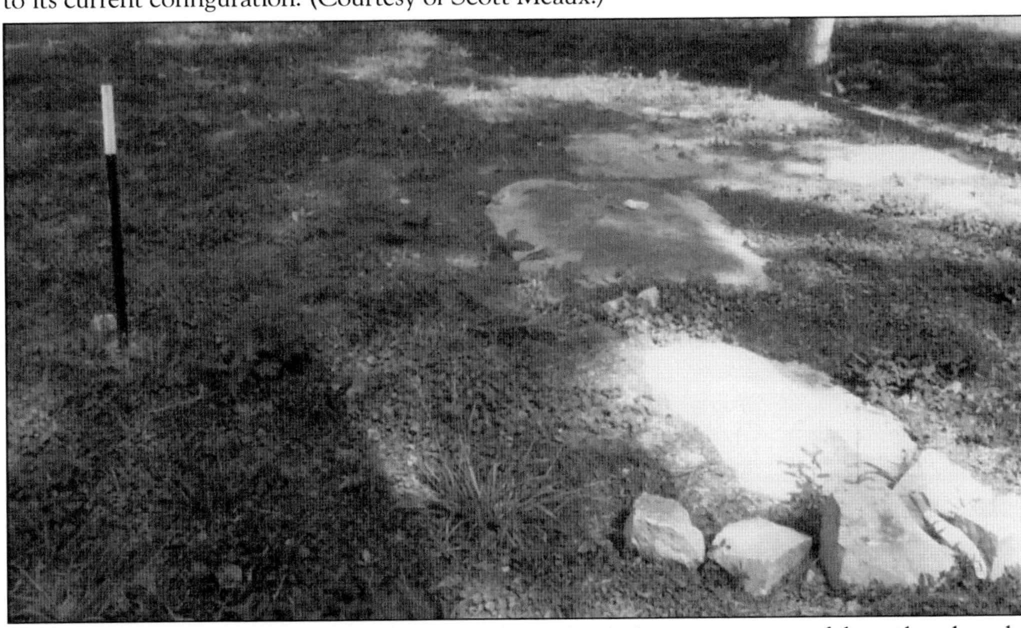

Humble Negro Cemetery. Located north of the FM 1960 bypass, just east of the railroad tracks, this cemetery dates from an era when Humble was racially segregated, as were most Southern towns at the time. The graves were not set up in rows or plots, and they remained overgrown and forgotten for many years. Recent efforts have been made to restore the cemetery. (Courtesy of Nancy Coker.)

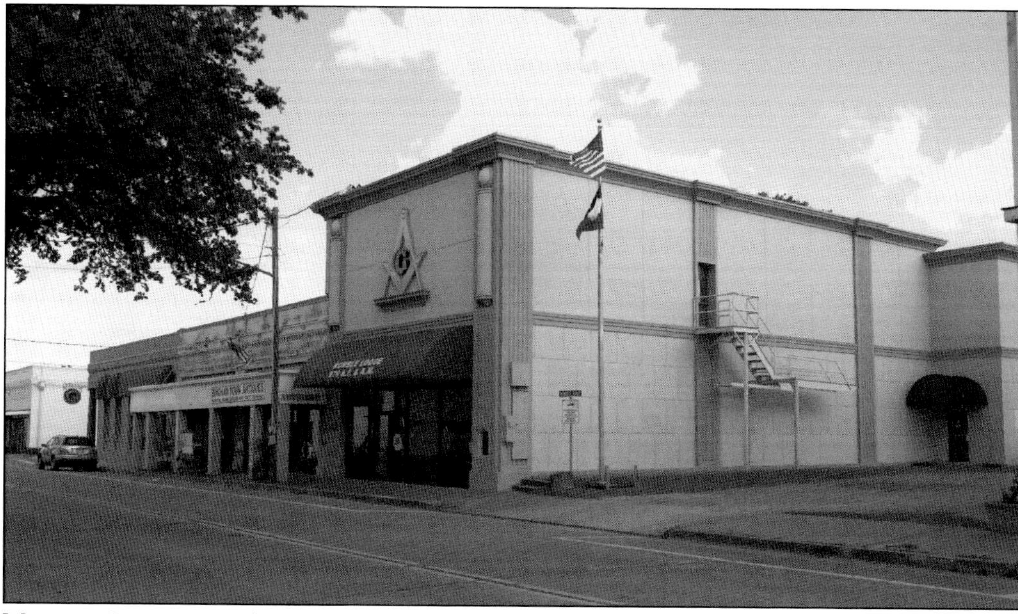

Masonic Lodge. Members of the Humble Masonic Lodge originally met on the second floor of the Humble State Bank building. When that building burned down in the 1912 downtown fire, the Masons purchased the land from Ross Sterling and built a new lodge in the same location. The Humble State Bank was rebuilt on the corner of Barrett Street (Main Street) and Avenue B. (Courtesy of Scott Meaux.)

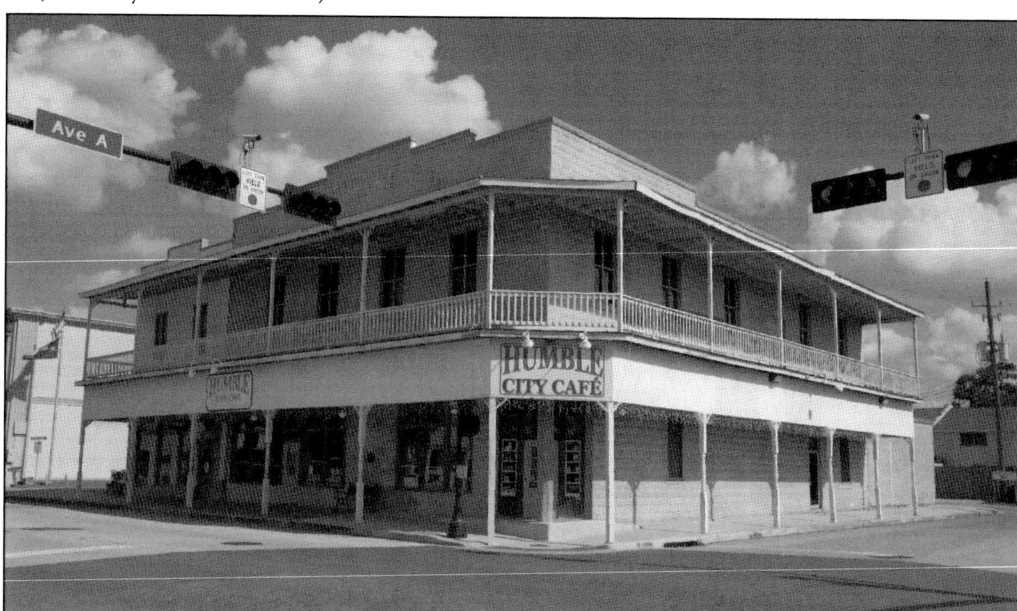

Pangburn Building. This building was erected in 1914 by Bill Pangburn, who made his own cement bricks for the structure using sand hauled from the San Jacinto River. Bill's wife ran a boardinghouse at Moonshine Hill (see page 26). A dry-goods store and a drugstore occupied the first floor. The second floor was the location of the original W.O.W. hall, where many dances were held. (Courtesy of Scott Meaux.)

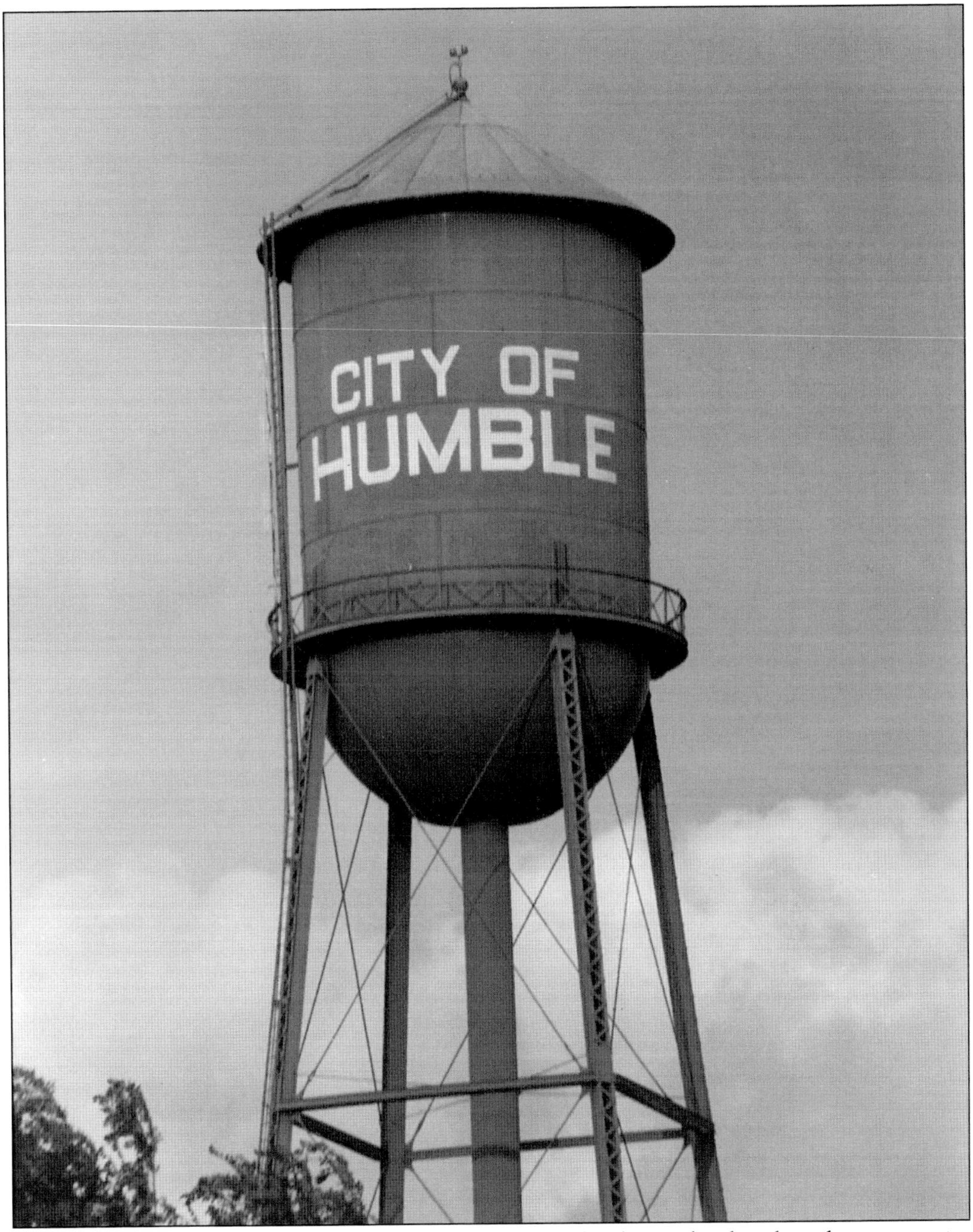

Humble Water Tower, 1983. The Humble water tower has been a landmark in the community since the early days. Located near downtown, by the railroad tracks, the tower can be seen by motorists driving on US Highway 59. The tower has been painted different colors over the years, and various slogans have been displayed on its side. For years, the Humble Fire Department had a siren located on the water tower. When a fire was called in to the station, the siren was turned on to alert local firefighters to report to the station.

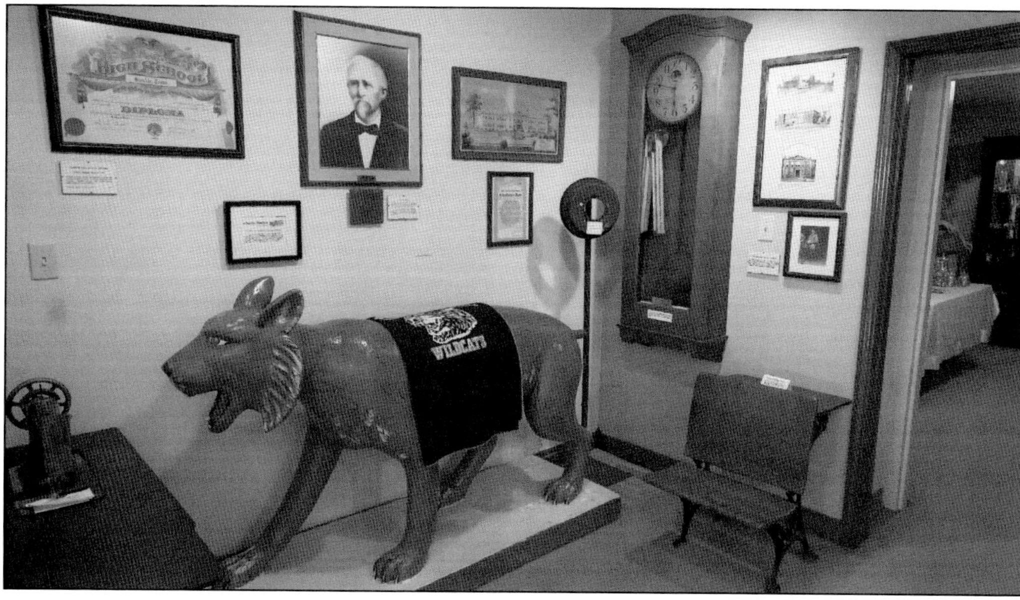

HUMBLE MUSEUM

The Humble Museum has been preserving the history of the Humble area since 1976. Pictures and artifacts donated by generous citizens fill the museum, telling the story of the little sawmill town that thrived and grew into a large community. The collection includes artifacts from oil fields and schools, vintage cameras, dinnerware and other household items from the early 1900s, and much more.

The museum also operates the McKay Clinic Medical Museum, where Dr. Haden E. McKay Sr. and Dr. Haden E. McKay Jr. treated patients starting in 1938. Dr. McKay Jr. worked at the clinic until his death in 1996. The clinic collection includes medical instruments used by the McKay doctors, a microscope purchased in 1908, and a 1938 EKG machine.

On the museum's board of directors are Martha Jo Bell, Marian Burrows, Nancy Coker, Roberta Francis, Bettie McCaa, Dr. Robert Meaux, Amelia Shrader, Juanita Steagall, and Mary Lea Taylor. The museum's docents are Jerri Christian, Bertie Hammonds, and Sheila Thornton.

Humble Museum
219 Main Street
Humble, Texas 77338
(281) 446-2130

HUMBLE MUSEUM
SAVING THE PAST FOR THE FUTURE

Bibliography

Commissioners' Court Minutes, 1866–1954. Harris County Clerk's Office, Houston.

County School Superintendent Records, 1884–1919. Harris County Department of Education, Houston.

Goodwin, Charles R. *Main Street and the Back Sides of Main Street.* Gloria O. McGettigan Promotional Writing Services, 1988.

Huffman, Peggy. "Be it ever so Humble." The *Humble Echo* (1988–1989).

Maxwell, Robert S. *Whistle in the Piney Woods: Paul Bremond and the Houston, East and West Texas Railway.* Denton: University of North Texas Press, 1998.

McDaniel, Robert W. and Henry C. Dethloff. *Pattillo Higgins and the Search for Texas Oil.* College Station: Texas A&M University Press, 1989.

Moore, Jerry. *A History of the Greatest City on the Planet!: Humble, Texas.* Baltimore: Independence Books, 2010.

Olien, Diana Davids and Roger M. Olien. *Oil in Texas: The Gusher Age, 1895–1945.* Austin: University of Texas Press, 2002.

Smith, Nina, ed. *A History of the Humble, Texas Area.* Humble, TX: James Tull Chapter, Daughters of the American Revolution, 1976.

Texas Education Agency. Annual Report of County Superintendent of Public Instruction, 1884–1919. Austin: Archives and Information Services Division. Texas State Library and Archives Commission.

Wilkins, Donald, ed. *80 Years of Humble "Wildcat" Football.* Humble, TX: D. Wikins, 1999.

Woodyard, Estelle. *Pioneer and Sundry Times.* Houston: The House of Fine Printing, 1980.